DEBATING PORNOGRAPHY

DEBATING ETHICS

General Editor
Christopher Heath Wellman
Washington University of St. Louis

Debating Ethics is a series of volumes in which leading scholars defend opposing views on timely ethical questions and core theoretical issues in contemporary moral, political, and legal philosophy.

Debating Pornography

ANDREW ALTMAN

LORI WATSON

OXFORD
UNIVERSITY PRESS

OXFORD

UNIVERSITY PRESS

Oxford University Press is a department of the University of Oxford. It furthers
the University's objective of excellence in research, scholarship, and education
by publishing worldwide. Oxford is a registered trade mark of Oxford University
Press in the UK and certain other countries.

Published in the United States of America by Oxford University Press
198 Madison Avenue, New York, NY 10016, United States of America.

© Oxford University Press 2019

CIP data is on file at the Library of Congress
ISBN 978–0–19–935871–7 (pbk.)
ISBN 978–0–19–935870–0 (hbk.)

9 8 7 6 5 4 3 2 1

Paperback printed by Sheridan Books, Inc., United States of America
Hardback printed by Bridgeport National Bindery, Inc., United States of America

CONTENTS

PART II A DEFENSE OF A SEX EQUALITY APPROACH TO PORNOGRAPHY

Lori Watson

ACKNOWLEDGMENTS

Sex is not a topic that I am comfortable discussing in public, or in private. So I was very hesitant when Kit Wellman first suggested, more than a decade ago, that I write a piece on pornography for an anthology that he was editing. But Kit is a persuasive personality, and he was very encouraging when I floated some tentative ideas about what I might say on the topic. I ended up writing the piece.

Some years later, Kit encouraged me to expand my piece on pornography and to write, in collaboration with a suitable philosophical opponent, a book on the topic in a debate format. I was a bit less hesitant this time around. "In for a penny, in for a pound." My contribution to the current volume greatly expands and, in some respects, revises what I wrote for the anthology. Had Kit not originally undertaken to nudge me out of my comfort zone, there might well have been a book on pornography by two philosophers writing in a debate format, but I would not have been one of them.

I would also like to thank my co-author, Lori Watson, for coming on board with the project and working so efficiently and assiduously on it.

Andrew Altman

March 26, 2018

I would like to thank Kit Wellman and Andy Altman, who together conceived of this book, and asked me to join the project after the fact. Both of them convinced me to write the "against" portion of the book, on the grounds that I was an ideal person to represent this view. I appreciate their confidence in me. I would also like to thank Christie Hartley, my long-time co-author in many other projects. She generously read this manuscript and gave helpful feedback. Turner Nevitt read the entire manuscript as well and helped to improve it. I would also like to thank Dan Steinberg and John Christman for their feedback as well. Pornography is not an easy subject to write about. Reading first-person accounts of their experience of violation through pornography is necessary for the work, but also difficult to do. The support of my wife, Michelle Watson, throughout this project provided much needed respite. Finally, I would like to dedicate my contribution to this volume to Catharine A. MacKinnon, for her inspiration.

Lori Watson

March 17, 2018

DEBATING PORNOGRAPHY

Introduction

FOR THE PAST HALF CENTURY and more, the citizens of free and democratic societies have debated questions concerning the production, sale, and consumption of pornography. The debates have addressed such issues as whether there is a fundamental right to access pornography and whether such materials are sufficiently harmful to justify their legal regulation. This volume is a contribution to those debates. It proceeds from the premise that considerations of equality between women and men are foundational to any defensible view concerning whether and how to legally regulate pornography.

Other perspectives have played an influential role in the debates and have even helped to shape the legal standards that apply to pornography. From these other perspectives, pornography is judged in terms of whether it is obscene or, more specifically, involves an excessive or inappropriate interest in sex (a so-called "prurient" interest). The present volume does not ignore such approaches, but its authors are highly critical of them for resting on the misguided idea that there is something inherently offensive and morally suspect about sexually explicit material as such. By contrast, the principle of equal citizenship, understood to apply substantively to both women and men, is essential for any reasonable understanding of justice, and it is the implications of that principle for issues of pornography that lie at the heart of the disagreements between the authors of this volume. The authors are in agreement that any reasonable case for legally restricting pornography in some way hinges on the idea that it threatens and undermines women's equal standing as citizens.

Andrew Altman argues that there is a moral right of sexual autonomy, held equally by all adults, and that it includes their right to buy, sell, and use pornography made with consenting adults. His argument fits within the broader framework of philosophical liberalism insofar as it maintains that individuals have moral rights that place limits on how the law legitimately treats them, even when the law rests on a principle as important as one that demands equality between women and men. At the same time, the argument departs from the conventional way of framing questions about pornography in terms of freedom of expression. Although Altman regards some forms of pornography as sensibly treated under the umbrella of free expression, he thinks that much of the pornography currently in circulation, especially on the Internet, cannot be plausibly treated in that way and should instead be seen in terms of the control that individuals have over their own sex lives. In his view, such control is rightfully located in each individual adult and not in the political community or those authorized by the community to make its laws. He thinks that legal restrictions on the access of adults to pornography whose production involves consenting adults violate that rightful control.

In Altman's view, the current controversies over pornography have developed out of social and intellectual transformations wrought by the sexual revolution of the 1960s. His argument is linked to key ideas that animated the revolution, including its affirmation of the right of individual sexual autonomy and its corresponding rejection of the traditional view that human sexuality posed a special danger to society and needed to be strictly disciplined and policed by law and informal social norms.

Under the constraints of the traditional view, premarital sex and sexual relations outside of marriage were categorically forbidden, as were same-sex relations. In addition, sexually explicit language and images were excluded from the media and the public sphere more generally. The sexual revolution was pursued in the name of individual autonomy and in opposition to social restrictions unduly circumscribing that autonomy. Altman's line of thinking is an extension of this rebellion against the traditional view of sexuality.

At the same time, Altman recognizes that the feminist movements of the 1960s and subsequent decades have rightly had a decisive impact on the debates over whether adult access to pornography is justifiably subject to legal restriction. Taking women's equality seriously means that those debates cannot be settled with the simple assertion of the individual's right of sexual autonomy. Reasonable advocates of legal restrictions will not claim that pornography is obscene or appeals to a prurient interest, but they can and do contend that pornography harms women and contributes to the perpetuation of a social and political system in which women are second-class citizens. And so Altman examines the evidence on which such contentions are made. He finds the evidence to be lacking.

Altman does not deny that, in some instances in which women are maltreated, pornography plays a causal role. However, he thinks that there is scant evidence that, at the macro-level of society as a whole, increased accessibility to pornography means, other things held equal, increased maltreatment of women. Nor does he think that there is any evidence of what the social scale might be of the harm that pornography causes. In contrast, there is abundant evidence of the existence and scale of the harm caused by alcohol consumption, including the considerable harm done to women. Yet, Altman points out, in free societies, adults have a right to buy, sell, and consume alcohol, even though such a right cannot be sensibly counted as carrying the moral importance of the right of sexual autonomy. He thinks that sexual autonomy carries such importance that any harmed-based argument for its restriction needs to rest on much firmer empirical grounds than do arguments for restricting alcohol consumption. In the case of pornography, Altman finds the grounds much weaker.

Additionally, Altman finds no evidence that the past several decades have seen a substantial increase in harms to women, despite the vast increase in access to pornography over that period. In fact, such evidence as we do have shows a decrease in such harms, contrary to what would have been predicted by the hypothesis that pornography causes harm at the macro-level.

Lori Watson advances a sex equality argument for restricting pornography under civil rights law. In this analysis, pornography is defined more narrowly than common usage, which simply emphasizes sexually explicit images or words as constitutive of "pornography." Drawing on the pioneering work of Catharine A. MacKinnon and Andrea

Dworkin, Watson adopts the legal definition of pornography advanced in the civil rights ordinances they authored in the 1980s. There pornography is defined as the graphic, sexually explicit subordination of women, which must contain one of a number of further elements, including for example, women being presented as enjoying sexual violence, including rape. Watson clarifies MacKinnon and Dworkin's view against a common misreading by emphasizing that the fact that some material meets the definition of pornography specified in the ordinances is not sufficient by itself to ground any legal claim. Rather, in addition to the definition of pornography captured in the ordinances, some harm as specified by the various causes of action as enumerated in the ordinances must be proven before an impartial adjudicator (judge, jury, or other legal administrative body). These causes of action include: coercion into a pornographic performance, forcing pornography on a person, assault or physical attack due to pornography, and discrimination by trafficking in pornography. Thus, for the ordinances to be used, two conditions must be met: first the material in question must meet the definition of pornography; and second, the complainant must allege, and then prove, an injury specified by the ordinances.

In addition to clarifying the scope and meaning of the ordinances, Watson carefully explains their legal and philosophical grounding representing a sex equality approach to pornography. Unlike obscenity-based approaches to pornography, which regard pornography as a threat to proper moral values and aim to regulate, through the criminal law, sexually explicit material deemed to violate such values, a sex equality approach to pornography does not rely on any controversial moralism about sexually explicit materials.

Rather, it advances the view that pornography is a social practice through which women's equal status as citizens is undermined and threatened, both particular women (when they are harmed by and through a particular piece of pornography) and women as a class. Given this analysis, the sex equality approach to pornography does not advocate for regulation of pornography under the criminal law; rather, it addresses pornography through the civil law, the area of law primarily concerned with equality. Clarifying and defending this view is Watson's concern in the first part of her contribution.

Following this presentation and defense of the sex equality approach to pornography, Watson presents the empirical evidence of the ways in which pornography (as defined by the ordinances) harms women. Decades of empirical research establish that pornography is both correlated and causally implicated in a range of sex-based harms, including encouraging rape, trivialization of rape and other forms of sex-based violence, encouraging (increasing) attitudes supporting violence against women, minimization of the harms of sexual violence, as well as impairing users' abilities to identify sexual violence as sexual violence. Watson directly engages with Altman's opposing views on this point, addressing his claims that such evidence is lacking, and arguing contrary to Altman's skepticism, the empirical evidence is quite overwhelming that pornography harms women and undermines principles of sex equality.

In the second half of her contribution, Watson evaluates and responds to three common defenses of pornography: the free speech defense, the feminist pro-porn position, and the argument from sexual autonomy. Although

Watson rejects the free speech defense of pornography, it is the most popular and common defense and thus deserves careful analysis. Watson argues that free speech defenses fail to recognize that expressive acts are one powerful mechanism through which dominant groups are able to enact the social inequality of subordinate groups.

Perhaps it will be surprising to some readers that some of the fiercest advocates for both the protection and promotion of pornography, including unfettered rights to access pornography, are self-declared "feminists." The "feminist pro-porn position" may well be the most common "feminist" position on pornography in the 21st century, as opposed to early decades in which feminism was often considered synonymous with an anti-pornography position. In brief, such defenders of pornography claim it has either liberatory effects or potential for women and sexually marginalized groups, including gays and lesbians. Watson exposes their argument as resting on the false idea that liberation for women as a class can come from some women being in the dominant position. It may be hard to envision what true sexual liberation for women as a group amounts to, given that we have operated under the yoke of male-dominant sexuality for so long. But re-inscribing the norms of dominant male sexuality in the context of women's sexuality or LGBT sexuality, which is essentially what these pro-porn feminists advocate, doesn't have emancipatory potential for all.

Finally, Watson considers and rejects the argument from sexual autonomy as a basis for grounding "a right to pornography." Here she engages directly with Altman's substantive view that sexual autonomy entails a moral right to pornography. While Watson agrees that a right to sexual autonomy is an important right of persons, she argues that a right to pornography does not follow. Moreover, depending upon how one defines and characterizes the right to sexual autonomy, it may, in fact, require limiting pornography so that women's rights to sexual autonomy are secured on an equal basis.

PART I

PORNOGRAPHY AND

THE RIGHT OF SEXUAL

AUTONOMY

ANDREW ALTMAN

1

Sex, Speech, and Autonomy

1.1 OVERVIEW

Debates about pornography have raged across democratic societies since the 1960s. What is pornography? Should it be banned? Should it be subjected to legal restrictions that do not apply to non-pornographic material? Is it morally objectionable? Does its production and consumption cause serious harm to women? These are some of the questions around which the debates have swirled.

Perhaps it is not surprising that pornography should be at the center of so much controversy. Whatever else pornography might be or do, it is about sex. And there are few aspects of human life that can compete with sex for our attention, and few aspects of a person's self-conception are more central than those that involve sexual attraction and repulsion. Michel Foucault claimed that sex has not always been such a highly charged topic: the ancient Greeks, he asserted, "were not much interested in sex. It was not a great issue" (1984: 340). I am dubious of Foucault's suggestion and think that Mary Lefkowitz was much closer to the mark when she suggested that Foucault had focused too narrowly on the writings of the Greek philosophers and that a broader sampling from Greek culture would show that the ancient Greeks were "almost as preoccupied with sex as we are" (1985: 462).

In any case, current arguments about the legal and ethical issues surrounding pornography are almost always framed in a way that focuses on freedom of speech and expression and on whether pornography is encompassed by the principle that protects such freedom. This way of framing the issue is common to those who argue on opposing sides. On one side are those who argue that pornography is rightly regarded as a form of speech and should be protected from legal restriction in the same way as forms of speech that do not have any pornographic content. On the other side are those who argue that pornography is "low-value" speech, or a form of speech that is also a kind of conduct, and so can be legitimately restricted in more robust ways than can speech that is "high value" or is not a kind of conduct.

There are sensible historical reasons explaining why freedom of speech and expression has held such an important place in the arguments over pornography. As we will see, many great works of art and literature, such as the novels *Ulysses* and *Lady Chatterley's Lover* and the play *Lysistrata*, have been banned due to their sexual content. The freedom of authors and artists to create, and of the public to read and view, works dealing with sex was at the center of efforts to eliminate such censorship. And for some sorts of sexually explicit and suggestive materials, freedom of speech and expression remains quite important to an understanding of why individuals have a right to produce and to view them. However, cultural and technological changes over the past two decades have brought into focus a vast body of pornographic materials that are far more difficult than even bad works of art and literature to place under the umbrella of freedom of expression. Put simply, the Internet has created a vast world of sexually explicit representations that are without any significant literary, artistic, or political value. The value of these representations is to the consumer and lies in the function they play in the consumer's sexual activity: the material helps to induce sexual arousal and release and is an element of a certain way of engaging in sex, often but not always involving masturbation. Thus, such pornography is not like the sexually explicit novels or works of art that were subject to government censorship, even in free and democratic societies, until the 1960s. Those works clearly had value other than any role they might have played in the sexual activity of the reader or viewer. And even bad art and literature make at least some significant effort in the direction of having value other than their ability to produce sexual arousal. By contrast, the bulk of Internet pornography is for having sex, period.

In this latter respect, Internet pornography is also different from the classic feature-length pornographic movies of the 1970s, such as *Behind the Green Door* and *Debbie Does Dallas*, along with a number of other "adult" films of that time. Those movies have plots and characters, however crude, and often contain satire and other forms of humor. Their dominant purpose is unquestionably to produce sexual arousal, but they also seek to provide comedic interludes or other kinds of amusement between the sex scenes.

It might be a stretch to place *Debbie Does Dallas* under the same freedom-of-expression umbrella as D. H. Lawrence's *Lady Chatterley's Lover* (either the novel or the movie version), but it is not entirely implausible to do so as a way of providing a sufficiently broad zone of protection around material to which individuals clearly do have a right of access. Given the historical propensity of political authorities to vastly overreach when it comes to material involving sex, there is some *prima facie* cogency in arguing that *Debbie Does Dallas* should be protected by law for the sake of ensuring that material having substantial literary, artistic, or political value is protected. I do not claim that such an argument is ultimately convincing, but it is not entirely implausible. In contrast, it is completely unconvincing to make a parallel argument about the video clips or images available on *PornHub*. If individuals have a right to produce and consume the material on *PornHub*, then the reasons have little to do with protecting access to *Lady Chatterley's Lover* or anything with substantial literary, artistic, or political value.

Pornographic magazines consisting almost entirely of sexually explicit photographs are comparable to what one finds on *PornHub*. Such magazines have circulated for many decades, albeit with restricted access: they could not, and still cannot, be mailed, and the commercial outlets have been largely limited to adult bookstores located in certain seedy areas of some cities or along rural roads having considerable truck traffic. Arguing that the production and consumption of such magazines is a matter of free speech and expression misses the role that the material plays in the life of the individual: he has sex with it. The same goes for the images and videos on *PornHub*.

The idea that freedom of speech and expression does not plausibly extend to cover material used exclusively for sex does not mean that government is thereby given a free hand to regulate and restrict the material. To the contrary, any government efforts at restriction now face another important freedom that must be addressed in order for the restriction to be justified: the right of sexual autonomy. Accordingly, when it comes to the bulk of Internet pornography and similar sexually explicit material in printed form, the discussion and debate need to focus on a person's right to control his or her own sex life and the implications of that right.

I am not the first person to suggest that the issue of pornography is more about sexual autonomy than about freedom of speech and expression. In 1979 and then again in the early 1980s, the law professor Frederick Schauer proposed that very idea. He argued that "the prototypical pornographic item on closer analysis shares more of the characteristics of sexual activity than of the communicative process. . . . [The item] takes pictorial or linguistic form only because some individuals achieve sexual gratification by those means. . . . [T]he true issue in the regulation of hardcore pornography is not freedom of speech but personal liberty" (1979: 922 and 926 n. 169). Thus, Schauer writes, "At its most extreme, hard core pornography is a sex aid" (1982: 181).

It has been four decades since Schauer wrote about hard-core pornography "at its most extreme," and the main difference now is that what he spoke of is no longer the extreme but rather the typical. As I have said, some of the hard-core pornography of the 1970s made at least an effort at interspersing humor and other entertainment in between the sex scenes, even if the dominant purpose of the material was to sexually arouse the viewer. Perhaps the presence of such an effort was why Schauer's arguments did not gain much traction among his colleagues, who were First Amendment experts and might have thought that it would be impossible to draw a clean legal line between the pornographic movies of the time and works with more substantive artistic value. Also, for those colleagues who were philosophically inclined to oppose the regulation of pornography and who sought a solid legal argument against regulation, freedom of speech and expression might have seemed firmer ground on which to make their legal case than the personal liberty of sexual autonomy would have been.[1]

The deluge of pornography on the Internet over the past decade and a half makes it an auspicious time to revive Schauer's view. The arguments he gives are, I think, deficient in crucial ways that I examine later. To anticipate: he is well off the mark in his central claim that "the use of pornography may be treated conceptually as a purely physical rather than mental experience" (1979: 923). This claim is not just an "oversimplification," as he puts it. The claim is totally wrong and reveals a serious lack of understanding of the nature of the experience of using pornography. Nonetheless, Schauer's view of pornography as material used for sex is both right and important.

Schauer did not explore the implications of his view of pornography for the moral legitimacy of government regulations and restrictions with respect to pornography. As a law professor, he was more concerned with addressing the constitutional issues, which the American courts and lawyers have seen as revolving around the First Amendment and its Free Speech Clause. But my main concern is not primarily with issues of legality; rather, it is with whether government restrictions on pornography violate sexual autonomy understood as a moral right of adult individuals. I will argue that legal restrictions that block the access of adults to material that graphically depicts sex violate that right. Laws aiming to regulate how and where such material may be advertised or publicly displayed are consistent with the right. Laws that aim to prevent adults from gaining access to the material violate the right.

Some thinkers single out pornography depicting sexual violence, arguing that such material is legitimately prohibited by law (Brison 2014). Sexual violence is, indeed, an especially appalling form of violence, not the least because it violates a right so central to human dignity and to the equal moral status of every person, the right of sexual autonomy. Sexual assaults involve the imposition of the sexual will of one person on that of another person and so violate the autonomy of the victim. However, in my view, depictions of sexual violence should be treated by the law no differently than depictions of nonsexual torture and other egregious forms of nonsexual violence. The most defensible set of responses in a free and democratic society would not involve placing special legal restrictions on adult access to words or images that graphically represent the violence but rather would include making the criminal justice system more respectful of the victims and more effective in identifying and punishing the perpetrators. The responses would also include more vigorous efforts at inculcating cultural norms of respect for individual sexual autonomy, though such efforts would not take the form of the special legal restrictions just mentioned. Any plausible account of the right of sexual autonomy must include a condition of equality: every adult has an equal right to such autonomy. Sexual assaults violate that equality condition. And just as the assault is a wrong to the victim, the photographing or filming of the assault is an additional wrong to the victim, as is any distribution of such photographs or films. The rights of the victim against the photographing and the distribution of the pictures is part of her right of sexual autonomy.

Certain sorts of sexually explicit material, even when it does not involve actual violence, lie beyond the range of the right of sexual autonomy that I wish to defend. Material involving children is one example. The idea of sexual autonomy explains why such material is not covered. Children cannot exercise sexual autonomy due to their lack of intellectual and emotional development, and that same lack of development makes children vulnerable to serious harms from sexual activity.

Advocates of the broad right to sexually explicit materials that I defend often argue as though the establishment of any restrictions that violate such a right would be a terrible injustice and pose a danger to our free society, pushing it back to the bad old days when great works of art and literature were subject to censorship. I regard such arguments as hyperbolic. I do not think it plausible that the imposition of special legal restrictions on materials graphically representing sex would be a step down a slippery slope ending with censorship of great, or even mediocre, works of art and literature. Over the past sixty years, free and democratic societies have come to place extremely high value on sexual autonomy and the freedom of individuals to create and disseminate art and literature. Legal restrictions on sexually explicit materials would not weaken the intensity or breadth of society's affirmation of those liberties; rather, that intensity and breadth would make it politically impossible to go very far with such restrictions.

In the United Kingdom, a recent law bans the possession of "extreme pornography." The law defines an extreme pornographic image as one that is reasonably thought to have been produced "solely or principally for the purpose of sexual arousal," is "grossly offensive, disgusting or otherwise obscene," and depicts "in an explicit and realistic way, any of the following—(a) an act which threatens a person's life, (b) an act which results, or is likely to result, in serious injury to a person's anus, breasts or genitals, (c) an act which involves sexual interference with a human corpse, or (d) a person performing an act of intercourse or oral sex with an animal" (*Criminal Justice and Immigration Act*: sec. 63).

In my judgment, this law violates the right of sexual autonomy, and I will argue so below. The law is also prone to discriminatory application by the authorities against gays, making it doubly objectionable on grounds of sexual autonomy. However, the United Kingdom remains a robustly free society with no prospect that it will return to the days when it banned *Ulysses* and *Lady Chatterley's Lover*. The situation in the United States is no different. Indeed, it is difficult to see how any legislation similar to the United Kingdom's ban on extreme pornography would be upheld by the federal courts in the United States.

During the 1980s two prominent American feminists, Catharine MacKinnon and Andrea Dworkin, first proposed laws that would have made producing and distributing pornography, defined in part as the "graphic sexually explicit subordination of women, whether in pictures or in words," subject to civil lawsuits for sex discrimination (1997: 444).

A version of the proposal was adopted as law in Indianapolis but subsequently struck down in federal court as an unconstitutional incursion on freedom of speech. Yet, even if the law, or similar legislation, were to be upheld now, the nation's existence as a free society would not thereby be under threat nor would it face the risk of being propelled back into the 1950s, when sexually explicit works of literature were often legally prohibited and even Aristophanes's classic play *Lysistrata* was seized from the mails as obscene (De Grazia 1969: xvii). In my view, which will be elaborated later, several important elements of the MacKinnon-Dworkin ordinance[2] go much too far in restricting individual liberty, but making the case against the ordinance does not require arguing that it would constitute such a grave incursion on liberty as to send us back to the 1950s.

Proponents of a right to pornography have an unfortunate tendency to take the view that protections of our basic rights will come undone if any unjustified incursion on the right to sexually explicit materials takes place. Nadine Strossen writes, "The feminist pro-censorship movement is a far greater threat to women's rights than is the sexual expression that it condemns with the epithet 'pornography.' For women who cherish liberty and equality, Big Sister is as unwelcome in our lives as Big Brother" (1995: 15). In a similar vein, the head of the Minnesota Civil Liberties Union at the time a version of the MacKinnon-Dworkin ordinance was proposed in Minneapolis reacted to the proposal by saying, "It's thought control. . . . It's the worst form of government oppression" (Downs 1989: 96). And at the hearings in Boston on legislation based upon the MacKinnon-Dworkin proposals, the lobbyist for the Civil Liberties Union of Massachusetts opposed the law, saying,

"I speak from experience. When I was in college in the early 50's, you couldn't read *Lady Chatterley's Lover* in this country. . . . What happens is that things of artistic merit, things that are on the cutting edge of artistic expression, are the things that always get censored" (MacKinnon and Dworkin 1997: 383).

The claims that the MacKinnon-Dworkin ordinance would introduce "Big Sister" into our lives and would amount to thought control are implausible. And the invocation of the past censorship of *Lady Chatterley's Lover* and other works of artistic merit is misguided in this important respect: although it cannot be ruled out that such an ordinance would be applied in some cases against sexually explicit works that have genuine artistic merit, there are crucial differences between the 1950s and now that make such an application unlikely to stand for very long. The 1950s were prior to the sexual revolution and to the vast expansion of sexually suggestive and explicit images and words in everyday public life.

One might suggest that I am too optimistic about the advances society has made since the 1950s in its opposition to the censorship of work with sexual content, and one might point to the controversial 1990 decision in the United States of the chairman of the National Endowment of the Arts to deny grants to Karen Finley and several other performance artists due to the sexual content of their work. But the controversy actually helps to show how far society had actually come since the 1950s: the issue was not whether these artists should be fined or imprisoned for their work but whether they should receive federal grants for it. The forces that would like to see society pushed back to the days when *Lady Chatterley's Lover* and other sexually explicit works of art were banned were reduced to arguing that taxpayer funds should not support such works. Thus, even a quarter of a century ago, American society had moved well beyond the pro-censorship mentality of the 1950s and earlier. Warnings about the emergence of Big Brother and Big Sister, should feminist-based anti-pornography laws be adopted, are absurd exaggerations.

I do not mean to suggest that the arguments of the opponents of a right to pornography have been free from absurd exaggeration. The prominent feminist Susan Brownmiller has written that pornography poses as serious a threat to women as "storm troopers, concentration camps, and extermination" had once posed for Jews (1975: 395). Brownmiller's exaggeration is not only absurd, it is morally grotesque, given that two-thirds of all Jews in Europe were murdered in the Holocaust. So unfortunate hyperbole is not limited to one side of the pornography debate.

Even if nothing remotely like Big Sister or Big Brother is in the offing, a right is a right, and to make the case that adults have the broad right of access to sexually explicit materials that I defend, it is not necessary to show that dramatic injustices or calamitous consequences would flow from legal restrictions that infringe on that right. What is necessary is to make the case that adults are wronged when they are denied the broad access in question. How grievous the wrong happens to be is another matter. Some restrictions that deny access are more grievous wrongs than other such restrictions.

The UK law on extreme pornography is more problematic in certain respects than the MacKinnon-Dworkin ordinance, because, unlike the latter, the UK legislation imposes criminal penalties and targets simple possession of certain sexually explicit material, even though the material involves no children and all of the participating adults took part voluntarily. The criminal punishment of individuals who possess such material is a serious wrong against such persons, in my judgment. The civil penalties and requirement of restitution provided for by certain provisions of the MacKinnon-Dworkin ordinance would have been less serious wrongs, though still wrongs, in my view.

Moreover, the MacKinnon-Dworkin ordinance has the distinct advantage over the UK legislation and many other anti-pornography laws in that it seeks to delink its prohibitions from the idea that sexually explicit materials ought to be outlawed because they are "obscene." In this respect, the proposal represents the feminist approach to pornography that only began to emerge in the 1970s. Up until that time, the obscenity approach had been the exclusive way legal efforts to suppress such material were understood and justified.

Not all feminists have favored the MacKinnon-Dworkin ordinance, and some feminists would agree with my view that adults have a broad moral right to produce and consume pornography. Yet, a very wide range of feminists contend that pornography is a cause of serious harm to women and invoke that harm to justify legal restrictions such as those contained in the MacKinnon-Dworkin ordinances. Among those harms are sexual violence, sex discrimination in employment and other social opportunities, and the reinforcement of women's inferior status in society. My focus will be on sexual violence. If a strong case can be made that pornography causes harm to women, then sexual violence will be at the center of the case. Moreover, the strongest justification of laws that block the access of adults to pornography would rest on the claim that pornography causes sexual violence, because the harms of such violence are the most serious harms attributed to pornography and also because the best evidence that currently exists concerns the relation of pornography to sexual violence.

In examining the relation of pornography to sexual violence, it is crucial to disambiguate the statement that pornography causes such violence into two distinct claims. One claim is that there are individual instances in which pornography plays a causal role in explaining why a particular person perpetrated sexual violence on a particular occasion and why the violence took the particular form it did. Another claim is that, at the social level, as the availability of pornography increases, so does sexual violence against women; and, by implication, as the availability decreases, so does such violence. Even if the individual-level claim is correct, it does not follow that the social-level claim is also true. Some advocates of a broad right to pornography have claimed that pornography is entirely harmless. I do not make such a claim. I am convinced that the claim of harm at the individual level is in fact correct, but I am skeptical of the social-level claim and find that the evidence for it is very weak. And when it comes to the justification of laws restricting adult access to pornography, it is the social-level claim that needs to be vindicated.

Moreover, even if the social-level claim were supported by strong evidence, the justification of laws restricting adult access to pornography would still not be made. I will argue that a comparison between alcohol and pornography is helpful in putting the pornography issue into a proper perspective. The evidence that, at the social level, alcohol consumption causes violence, including sexual and nonsexual violence against women, is strong; indeed, as we will see, it is much stronger than the evidence that pornography consumption causes violence against women. But, notwithstanding the alcohol-violence connection, adults have a right to produce, purchase, and consume alcohol. Adults have this right, not because the prevention of all or most alcohol consumption is infeasible—although it is true that, outside of theocratic regimes, such prevention is infeasible—but because deciding to drink alcohol is an exercise of personal liberty by an adult. And the same can be said for pornography. Indeed, the use of pornography is not simply *an* exercise of personal liberty by an adult but the exercise of his freedom to shape his life as a sexual being. If the right of sexual autonomy is an especially important form of personal liberty, more weighty than a right to enjoy alcohol, then the case for a right to pornography will be stronger than the right to alcohol. Conversely, if adults have a moral right to alcohol, then, *a fortiori*, they have a moral right to pornography. At any rate, so I will argue.

Before closing this section, I would like to address briefly a distinction between two forms of individual autonomy. Lori Watson refers to one of those forms, when she characterizes sexual autonomy as a matter of "the ability to direct one's sexual life authentically" (this Volume: 282). Having autonomy in this sense depends on which factors have influenced the formation of one's desires and on whether one endorses those desires in a sufficiently informed and reflective manner. Many feminists, including Watson, hold that a social and cultural system of male domination shapes sexual desires in a way that distorts or unduly limits this form of autonomy. I think that such feminists are right. Watson also correctly points out that I do not examine what this form of autonomy involves.

The reason that I do not explore this first form of autonomy is that I do not think that the state can legitimately use legal prohibitions to enforce a conception of authentic sexuality. A state that enforces any such conception encroaches on a different form of autonomy, namely, the authority of adult citizens to direct their own sexual lives, regardless of whether or not they are achieving authentic sexuality. Put another way, this second form of autonomy includes a right to be wrong about what counts as authentic sexuality and even to not care about whether one's own sexuality is authentic. This is the form of sexual autonomy that is at stake in debates about legal restrictions on the access of adults to pornography that is made using consenting adults. In order to paint a clearer picture of what a right to such autonomy entails, I now turn to an examination of the general idea of a moral right.

1.2 WHAT ARE RIGHTS?

Few doubt that various important aspects of the well-being and freedom of persons should be protected by legal rights that are granted to them as individuals. But the idea that individuals have certain rights—call them "moral rights"— even if the rights are not granted by law, has proved much more controversial. More than a few philosophers have been hostile to the idea of moral rights, particularly utilitarians, whose fundamental moral principle mandates that overall utility be maximized. Historically, many critics of the idea of moral rights rest their case on the ground that empirical confirmation of the existence of such rights, in contrast to legal rights, is lacking. However, the lack of such confirmation is not peculiar to moral rights, as opposed to others sorts of moral demands, whether the demands are formulated in terms of duties, obligations, wrongs, or some such category that expresses the thought that agents are morally bound in some way. One should not expect moral demands to be subject to empirical confirmation: they tell us what *ought to be*, not what actually *is*.

At the same time, one should expect moral demands to cohere with one another and to have appropriate connections to dimensions of life that have deep and abiding significance for us humans. Accordingly, claims regarding rights and other moral demands are not arbitrary stipulations but can be defended and argued about in reasoned ways.

The idea that there are moral rights captures in a direct way an understanding of the normative status of the human individual that, at least in the modern world, is difficult to deny. On that understanding, each individual is owed a certain way of being treated by institutions and other individuals, so that any way of acting that is incompatible with that treatment is not simply wrong but a wrong *to the individual* in question. The individual, in turn, has the moral authority to demand that the wrongful treatment cease. Even utilitarians, whose principle of utility demands that each individual count for one and no more than one in the determination of what maximizes utility, seem to assume a moral right of each individual to the equal consideration of her interests.

Yet, one persistent problem concerning at least some moral rights has been their lack of specificity, or, more exactly, the difficulty of giving them specificity in a way that preserves the plausibility of the idea that each human individual—or, in certain cases, each adult human—is owed a certain sort treatment. In some cases, a relatively well-specified right that does preserve such plausibility can be formulated. The right against torture seems to me to be a case of that kind. But the moral rights to due process of law and to private property are more difficult to specify, because the contours of those rights seem to vary considerably, depending in large measure on the institutional and social framework in which individuals are claiming such rights. The due-process right of a criminal defendant to a lawyer makes sense in contexts where there is a legal profession but not in contexts where there are no institutions of legal training and practice. The right to private property makes sense where there are institutions to define and impartially adjudicate conflicts over property but is unlikely to shed much light on which demands should be met in the absence of such institutions. As we will see in my account of sexual autonomy, the contours of the right of sexual autonomy are partly, but not entirely, determined by the institutional context.

In contending that adults have a moral right to pornography, I am saying that (a) adults should be legally free to produce, exchange, and consume pornographic material; (b) it would be a wrong *to them* for any agent, including the government, to block their voluntary activities in producing and using pornography; and (c) there should be basic legal rights, which can be vindicated in court and cannot be extinguished by legislative action, protecting the freedom of adults to produce and use pornography. Utilitarians could easily endorse (a) and (c). For them, the trickier part is (b). Perhaps the idea of a wrong to a particular person can be elucidated in terms of the utility of giving the person certain legal rights that others would not possess, such as the right to compensation from the wrongdoer. I am skeptical that any such elucidation will prove persuasive. But a utilitarian who agrees that it is important to accommodate (b) would, to that extent, be in position to accept my account of the right of sexual autonomy.

An important part of my argument is that sexual autonomy is a basic liberty, not on a plane with all other liberties but rather one among a small group of liberties that carry special weight. Utilitarians tend to think that there are no basic liberties but rather that (1) there is a general right of liberty insofar as every restriction on any liberty requires justification in order to be permissible, and (2) the same level of justification is needed for restrictions on each and every liberty. However, there are ways in which utilitarians can seek to accommodate the idea of a basic liberty, that is, a liberty whose special weight means that an especially strong justification is needed for its restriction to be permissible. They could argue that legal recognition of certain liberties as having special weight conduces to the greatest overall happiness. For my own part, I wish to remain agnostic on empirical claims about what brings about the greatest happiness. And regardless of whether legal recognition of special rights would lead to the greatest happiness, I think that certain rights do have special weight. I count the right of sexual autonomy among these basic liberties, and I will give an account of why the right is special in the next section. Utilitarians might be able to accept much of my account, but they would do so always with the proviso that, at the deepest level of morality, what counts is nothing other than the greatest happiness. That proviso is where we part company.

If a person exercises his right to view pornography, I do not claim that he is being a moral exemplar. One often has a right to do things that, if done, would be much less than morally ideal. In that sense, one can have a right to do wrong. In order to understand this idea, it is important to keep in mind that there are several parts of morality, involving different ways of assessing persons and their conduct. The realm of rights is an important part, and violating another's rights is always *pro tanto* wrong: just insofar as some act is a rights violation the act is wrong. But I can do wrong in the sense of falling far short of what some moral ideal or principle calls for, without violating anyone's rights. If the action is, nonetheless, one that I have the moral authority to decide to take, or not to take, then I have acted within my rights and also done something wrong.

Suppose there is a moral principle entailing that persons who are economically well off should donate a significant part of their income or effort to organizations that help persons who are economically destitute. If I am well off and refuse to donate anything, then I have done wrong in a perfectly recognizable sense of "wrong": I have not acted as I ought to have acted and can be rightly criticized for it. Yet, I had a right to do wrong, because the decision about what to do with my income is mine to make. I might make it in a very stingy and uncaring way, and other people will end up worse off, that is, harmed, as a result of my decision. But the decision is within my authority to make, and that fact is (part of) what it means to say that I have a right to make it. So when I say that individuals have a moral right to pornography, I do not mean that those who consume pornography are beyond moral criticism or are acting consistently with all moral principles and ideals. But I do mean that they are not necessarily violating anyone else's rights simply in virtue of their being pornography consumers.

I do not think that the right to pornography, or any other right for that matter, is absolute. Nor do I think that social harms and benefits are irrelevant to questions about the exact contours and qualifications of moral rights. Thus, I do not take the view that Susan Brison construes me as holding, namely, that "whatever harm results from pornography is just the price we pay for the right of sexual autonomy" (2014: 326) Rather, my view is that the social harm attributed to pornography has not been sufficiently established to exclude a right to pornography as an aspect of the more general right of sexual autonomy.

As with many other moral rights, the right to pornography concerns the locus of decision-making authority when it comes to certain sorts of matters. In claiming that there is such a right, I am saying that, when it comes to purchasing and using pornography, decision-making authority lies with the individual and not with his family or friends, much less his government. No one other than the individual has the moral authority to make the decision for him about whether or not to consume pornographic materials. The decision is his.

In her argument for civil laws that would greatly restrict the access of adults to pornography, Lori Watson analogizes the right of sexual autonomy to the right of self-defense, pointing out that the latter right is not sensibly thought to include a legitimate claim to acquire any and every weapon that one might desire to defend oneself (this Volume: 289). Why, then, should the right to sexual autonomy be thought to include a right to purchase any and every sexually explicit item one might wish to have? My answer is that I do not deny that there are acceptable limits on the right to purchase pornographic materials. In my view, persons do not have a moral right to purchase child pornography or any pornography made by threats of violence. However, *contra* Watson, I will argue that sexually explicit materials made with consenting adults does fall under the right of sexual autonomy.

But aren't such materials like guns in the harm they cause? Watson rests much of her case for the (civil) legal prohibition of pornography on the evidence of harm to women that it causes. I will argue that the evidence on which she relies is considerably weaker than she claims it to be. But setting that matter aside for the moment, none of the empirical studies that she invokes concludes or even hints that the harm caused by pornography is anywhere near the scale of the harmed causes by guns. Moreover, studies of gun violence have consistently shown that greater access to guns in the United States, as compared to other high-income countries, explains why its rates of death by guns (homicide, suicide, accident, etc.) are ten times that of other countries, amounting to tens of thousands of persons every year (Grinshteyn and Hemenway 2016). And while men are twice as likely as women to die as a result of gun violence, 90% of all women in twenty-two high-income countries who die from such violence are in the United States (2016: 267). That 90% amounts to thousands of American women every year. The law should make access to guns in the United States much more difficult, because the scale of the harm caused by easy access is so enormous. And, to repeat the crucial point: there is no support in the studies Watson cites for the notion that guns and pornography are morally analogous in the scale of the harm that they cause.

1.3 SEXUAL AUTONOMY: PLEASURE, INTIMACY, AND HARDWIRING

In this section, I begin my discussion of the grounds and contours of the moral right of sexual autonomy. Questions about such autonomy are at the center of many of the most controversial legal and political issues of the day, and I do not have any general theory of the right of sexual autonomy. Moreover, most of what I argue about pornography could be accepted by people with very different ideas about the grounds and contours of the right of sexual autonomy. My arguments stand free from a wide range of specific accounts of that right. Any account will fit with those arguments as long as it holds that (a) the right of sexual autonomy is an especially weighty or important personal liberty, and (b) the right to pornography is an aspect of the right to sexual autonomy. Still, it might be helpful in understanding the view I have of pornography for me to offer some additional thoughts regarding sexual autonomy.

A preliminary point. As we have seen, some thinkers hold the view that there is a moral right to liberty in general, and all other liberties are just implications and derivations of this general right to liberty. In contrast, I think that there are rights to certain kinds of liberty, such as sexual autonomy and freedom from torture or other threats to bodily security, and that the rights to these "basic liberties" cannot be adequately explained in terms of a general right to liberty. Rather, the rights must be understood in terms of the central position that the liberties in question play in human life. I do not deny that there is a general right to liberty, but the justified curtailment of that general right does not need to invoke especially weighty considerations. In contrast, the justified curtailment of basic liberties does require especially weighty reasons.

Accordingly, in my view, violating a person's sexual autonomy or freedom from threats to bodily security cannot be sensibly placed on the same plane as violating her liberty to drink alcoholic beverages. The right to have a gin and tonic is an aspect of the general right of freedom, and so its curtailment does not demand especially weighty reasons as the justification. But the right to engage in sexual intercourse with another consenting adult is an aspect of the basic liberty of sexual autonomy. Over the years, various reasons have been cited to justify curtailments of that aspect of sexual autonomy: intercourse between persons of different races would produce degenerate children, allowing same-sex intercourse would lead to the disintegration of society, and so on. The fact that the reasons offered have pointed to extremely bad social outcomes is telling: it shows that even the opponents of sexual autonomy have conceded that especially weighty reasons are needed to justify its curtailment. But the reasons they have invoked rest on falsehood and fear, not on fact, as most people came to realize in the case of race and as more and more people are coming to realize in the case of same-sex relations.

Let me turn now to the right of sexual autonomy. Although few people would contest the special importance of the right, it is not easy to explain why it is important. Any person can, of course, insist that it is important *to him*, but anything can be the object of importance in that way,

and I have rejected the idea that every liberty is on the same
level and simply a part of a general right to liberty. Why is
sexual autonomy a basic liberty, on a different level from
the right to a gin and tonic, even if there are undoubtedly
some individuals for whom sex is less important than their
gin and tonic?

In what follows, I examine several ways of thinking
about the basis for the right of sexual autonomy. I do not
regard these ways of thinking as providing deductions
from first principles or other premises, as Euclid derived
theorems from his axioms. Deduction plays a role in any
sensible way of thinking, but for matters like sex that pose
problems for us about what to do as individuals and how to
organize our common social and political lives, deduction
alone will not get us very far. We need ways of thinking that
show us how various aspects of human life fit together to
form a meaningful whole, or at least how we can make of
life as much of a meaningful whole as its messy materials
admit. And the effort to construe life in this way is invariably shaped by the many assumptions with which one
starts. This feature is especially true when it comes to sex, a
matter about which it would be foolish to think that we can,
or should, entirely escape the cultural meanings and values
within which our minds and bodies have been formed.
Moreover, I doubt that there is any single feature of sexual
activity that can fully account for why the right of sexual
autonomy is a basic liberty. Instead, it seems more likely
that there are a number of features that, in combination,
provide us with an understanding of why sexual autonomy
is properly counted among the basic liberties.

One plausible line of thinking that leads to the idea
that there is a (basic) right to sexual autonomy revolves

around the thought that the pleasures of sex are extraordinarily intense. Richard Mohr states that "in intensity and in kind [sexual pleasure] is unique among human pleasures; it has no passable substitute from other realms of life. For ordinary persons . . . orgasmic sex is the only access that they have to ecstasy" (1998: 113). Thomas Nagel voices a similar view: "Sex is the source of the most intense pleasure of which humans are capable and one of the few sources of human ecstasy" (2002: 46). In much the same vein, the great utilitarian thinker Jeremy Bentham had written in the late eighteenth century that sex provided "the greatest, and perhaps the only real pleasures of mankind" (quoted in Dabhoiwala 2014). Sexual pleasures were, in his estimation, "the most copious source of enjoyment" and "more conducive to happiness" than anything else in human life (quoted in Dabhoiwala 2012: 136). And it might well have been such a view that lay behind the ancient idea that "sexual arousal, activity, and reproduction were . . . immanent divine powers, not simply human forms of energy" (Gaca 2003: 132).

Nevertheless, Alan Soble has criticized the view that the pleasure of sex is uniquely intense. He argues that the view ignores "the multitude of ordinary people who *enjoy* sex but *would die* for their pots, or dances, or stamps, or drugs, for the ecstatic pleasure these things, not sex, make possible" (1996: 19). However, I think that Soble overstates his case. Individuals might well find stamp collecting or dancing to be deeply satisfying in a way that they do not find with sex. And cocaine might be able to light up the pleasure centers of the brain in the same way that an orgasm can do. But for the standard-issue human brain, I seriously doubt that stamps, dances, or pottery are capable of lighting up those centers to the degree that an orgasm does. Nonetheless, we are still left with the question of how the claim that sexual pleasure is unusually, even if not uniquely, intense can lead to the idea that there is a right to sexual autonomy.

Although I do not expect that Nagel or Mohr would agree, I think that the most convincing route from sexual pleasure to a right of sexual autonomy involves a rather pessimistic view of human life. There is a passage, quoted in part by MacKinnon, from George Eliot's *Middlemarch* that beautifully expresses the view:

> [W]e do not expect people to be deeply moved by what is not unusual. That element of tragedy which lies in the very fact of frequency, has not yet wrought itself into the coarser emotion of mankind; and perhaps our frames could hardly bear much of it. If we had keen vision and feeling for all ordinary human life, it would be like hearing the grass grow and the squirrel's heart beat, and we should die of that roar that lies on the other side of silence. As it is, the quickest of us walk about well wadded with stupidity. (Eliot 2003/1871– 1872: 184–185; MacKinnon 1997: 18)

Put more mundanely and elaborated upon a bit, the thought is that human life is ordinarily an agonizing struggle, whose tragic suffering goes largely unnoticed due to the coarseness of our feelings and perceptions. And were we to hear unmuffled the screams of agony—our own and those of others—we would not be able to bear it. What protects us is our dullness and stupidity.

There seems to me to be more than a small measure of truth in such a pessimistic view of life, although I will not argue for the view here. My point is that, if human life is essentially a tragic tale of suffering and struggle, and if sexual pleasure is "one of the few sources of human ecstasy," then it seems that one would have at least the beginnings of a case for the idea that individuals have a right to control their own sexual lives. A key step in developing the case would be to argue that, given such a bleak existence, it would be a wrong to the individual to deny him or her control in one of the few areas of life that can provide ecstatic pleasure to offset to some degree the otherwise relentless misery of being alive. Admittedly, this step is not compelled by the view of life that motivates it. One might simply think that it would be a matter of cruelty to deny an individual such control and leave the idea of a wrong to the individual on the sidelines. But if one thinks that there are wrongs to the individual and that the individual has certain justified claims against such wrongs—in other words, if one accepts the idea of personal rights—then it is plausible to treat the denial of sexual autonomy as the denial of something that is so important to relief from the misery of life that it amounts to a right and one of considerable weight.

Suppose that the pessimistic view is exaggerated, however, and that life is not ordinarily so miserable but rather, under ordinary conditions, can be quite decent. Then I think that the route from sexual ecstasy to a right of sexual autonomy becomes more difficult to make. In order to see why that it so, consider the kind of intense pain that is involved in torture. Avoiding such intense pain *does* seem to me to be sufficiently important to ground an exceptionally weighty right against the deliberate infliction of such pain. If a decent life is ordinarily possible, torture can readily destroy the semblance of such a life or, at a minimum, leave a permanent and large scar on any life. In this connection, Susan Brison quotes the author Jean Amery, who was tortured by the Gestapo and sent to a Nazi forced labor camp: "Whoever was tortured, stays tortured" (2004). And if life is essentially miserable, as the pessimistic view expressed above has it, then torture makes life a living hell. Either way, avoiding torture is an interest of the utmost urgency, and, if one thinks of torture not simply in terms of cruelty but in terms of wrongs to the individual, then the idea of a basic right against torture makes perfect sense. But if we are assuming the ordinary possibility of a decently good human life, then it is unclear to me that enjoying ecstatic pleasure is as crucial for such a life as avoiding intense pain, and so the claim of a basic right to activities—sexual or otherwise—that produce such pleasure seems to me to be less secure.

In any case, the unusual intensity of sexual pleasure is not the only feature of sex that might lead to the conclusion that individuals have a right of sexual autonomy. Another feature is that sexual activity is an expression of the very important human values of intimacy and (romantic) love. The idea is not simply that sexual relations help to bring about intimacy or love, as, say, exercise contributes to good health. Rather, the idea is that sex with another person is—or at least can be—an expression of intimacy and love, that is, a way of manifesting intimacy and showing love. Moreover, we can add to this idea the thought that intimacy and love, as valuable elements of human life, cannot be coerced or forced upon an individual. Intimacy must be chosen, and, even if love is not within the individual's control, the value for two lovers of their relationship will be compromised if the way they manifest their love is subject to the control of a third party.

Starting with those ideas about sex, love, and intimacy, one can plausibly argue that depriving a person of control of her sex life would be to deprive her of elements of human life that have great value. A life without the ecstatic pleasure of sex would be lacking, but my surmise is that most people would judge that a life without intimacy and love would be even more lacking. If a decent life is ordinarily possible, perhaps it would not be possible in the absence of intimacy and love. And if it is not ordinarily possible, then all the more reason why individuals have a claim to control of their sex lives, namely, so that they can enjoy some of the few morsels of good that life offers, and all the more convincing is it for them to assert that they have been seriously wronged when denied such control.

However, there are certain aspects of the right to sexual autonomy that appear to be puzzling when viewed in terms of ecstasy or intimacy/love. Sexual autonomy not only includes the choice of what sexual relations to engage in, and with which willing partners to engage in it; such autonomy also involves the choice to engage in activities without any partner at all, as well as the decision to forego sex entirely. If the right of sexual autonomy is tied to intimacy and love, then it is difficult to see why masturbation is a protected sexual choice. And it is difficult to see how the sexual ecstasy view can explain why being forced to engage in sexual activity, when one wants to remain abstinent, is a violation of the one's right to sexual autonomy.

The right of sexual autonomy gives each individual the authority to decide on the roles that sexual pleasure, intimacy, and love will play in his or her life. It is up to me, not to you or to the community to decide what my sex life will be like, as long as the decisions are consistent with everyone else's equal right. Accordingly, foregoing sexual pleasure entirely is within the scope of the right, as is pursuing the pleasure but in a solitary way or through otherwise meaningless one-night stands.

One might suggest that the choice to forego sexual pleasure gets much of its meaning from the fact that so many people do not make such a choice, and I agree with the suggestion. It is not surprising that various religious radicals have preached and practiced abstinence, for it is a dramatic statement and symbol of devotion to some otherworldly value. If sex were not a big deal for almost everybody, then giving it up as part of one's religious devotions would be no big deal. Nonetheless, noting that abstinence derives its meaning from its contrast with what most humans find irresistibly attractive does not yet give us a good picture of why there is a right to abstinence as part of the right of sexual autonomy in the first place.

Alan Soble proposes a basis for the right of sexual autonomy that is different from either the ecstatic pleasure or the intimacy/love approaches. He does agree that the values of pleasure and intimacy lend some weight to the idea of a right to sexual autonomy, but he goes on to claim that "the strongest argument" for such a right "would be that the 'basic human need' for sex requires, as does eating and breathing, doing what is hardwired into the human design" (1996: 23).

I do not find this argument from hardwiring convincing. Unlike eating and breathing, sex is not necessary for the life of the individual (and in the near future might no longer be necessary for the continuation of the species). No religious ascetic died for lack of sex, but there are some who died due to fasting. Moreover, the hardwiring argument only increases the puzzle of why the right includes the right to be abstinent. Why should people who can muster the will to resist their hardwired sex drive have the right to resist that drive? Finally, and from the other direction, there is this familiar problem: the fact that some drive is hardwired into humans hardly entails that it would wrong an individual to force him to refrain from acting on it. If some connection can be drawn between our sexual hardwiring and our flourishing or our leading a decent life, then the hardwiring might be part of a larger account of the right to sexual autonomy. I will, in fact, make a suggestion about how our human hardwiring plays a role in understanding the right. But the hardwiring that I invoke is, in certain respects, very different from what Soble seems to have in mind.

I do not doubt that a good understanding of why humans have a basic right of sexual autonomy will have a place for the intense pleasures of sex, the love and intimacy that sex can express, and even include something about how the human brain/nervous system is wired. But I think that there is a crucial element missing from those accounts. An important clue to the missing element is provided by the fact that, across cultures and historical periods, one of the central factors distinguishing slaves and other persons subjected to a degraded and subordinate social status has been the denial of their freedom and equality in matters of sex.

1.4 OUR STICKY AND OOZY SELVES

In his study of scores of slave societies across world history, Orlando Patterson writes, "I know of no slaveholding society in which a master, when so inclined, could not exact sexual services from his female slaves" (1982: 173). Moreover, even when an owner did not force sex upon his female slave, the fact that she was living under a system in which it was permitted for her to be treated in that way rendered the slave's status a severely degraded one. A person's status depends not simply on how she is actually treated but on how it is permissible, under existing social norms, for her to be treated. As Nagel puts it, "What actually happens to us is not the only thing we care about: What *may* be done is also important, quite apart from whether or not *is* done to us" (2003: 38). And among the elements of a person's status as a slave—among the "badges and incidents of slavery," to use the US Supreme Court's famous phrase (*Civil Rights Cases* 1883: 20)—are the ways in which it is permissible, under the norms of society, for her to be treated.[3]

For much of history, married women were in the same position with respect to their husbands as female slaves were with respect to their owners, and wives still are in that position in some countries at present. Such wives were under the sexual domination of their husbands and that domination was an unmistakable sign of the degraded and subordinate status of women wherever it appeared. Moreover, it is no accident that, historically, advocates of women's equality often represented marriage as a kind of slavery, for the status of married women has often included this particular badge of slavery. As with slaves, women's lack of sexual autonomy was a dimension of their degraded social status.

The importance that almost all humans across history have attached to having significant control over their own sexual activities and relations helps to explain why the denial of such control became among the "badges and incident of slavery." If humans did not care about whom they had sex with, or what kind of sex, or within what kind of interpersonal relationship they had sex, then the denial of such control would not have been important to them and would not have become among the badges of slavery. And it is difficult to doubt that humans attach so much importance to having significant control over their sex lives in large part because of the intensity of sexual pleasure and the intimacy that sex can express, as well as a strong drive that is hardwired into us.

Yet, the right of sexual autonomy, as I see it, rests on more than the psychological and biological factors that explain why sex is important to almost all members of the human species. The right also rests on the fact that the social worlds we humans have created attach a certain social meaning to control over one's sex life. And just as the denial of sexual autonomy is a badge and incident of slavery or of some analogously degraded status, the acknowledgment of a right of sexual autonomy is part of the recognition of an adult as a free and equal member of society.

But why is the denial of sexual autonomy so uniformly treated as a badge and incident of slavery? What is it about sex that makes one's control of one's own sexual activities such a socially important dimension of life? I don't know that anyone has a good answer to these questions. My own is, admittedly, iconoclastic and no doubt quite incomplete. But it does build on what I regard as a neglected but central truth about the human condition. Martha Nussbaum has put this truth plainly, in her illuminating reflection on the role of disgust in human life. Pointing out that disgust is a response to our animality and mortality, she writes that "perhaps we cannot live easily with too much vivid awareness of the fact that we are made of sticky and oozy substances that will all too soon decay" (2004: 14). I do not presume that Nussbaum would agree with the following analysis, but it coheres well with her thoughts about disgust.

Sex is an activity that characteristically involves the release of sticky and oozy substances and, often times, their transfer onto or into the bodies of others. The normal, hardwired reaction to the sticky substances—semen, vaginal fluids, mucous, saliva, and so on—of a random other person is disgust and repulsion. Sexual attraction can, somehow, cancel that disgust and repulsion, and if this canceling power was not powerfully hardwired into most of us, I think that the reproduction of the species would probably be more precarious than it has been historically. But this hardwiring is not the entire story, because sexual attraction does not, by itself, do the whole job of canceling disgust at another person's sticky substances. There also needs to be an affirmation of the attraction, a kind of second-order endorsement of the first-order impulse. Without that endorsement, the disgust and repulsion will not be extinguished. Such endorsement is what we think of, in more ordinary terms, as consent to having sex with another person.

Lack of control of your own sex life is a sign of your degraded social status, I suggest, because it means that others have social permission to spill their disgusting sticky substances onto or into you without your consent. Aside from the intense pleasure of sex and the value we attach to sexual intimacy—which are perhaps related to the need to cancel disgust at another's sticky substances—the right of sexual autonomy should be understood as a right against others spilling their substances onto or into you without your consent. The right is violated by societies that have slaves and other persons who occupy a radically degraded status.

Admittedly, this understanding of the right to sexual autonomy is not an especially romantic one, but it does help explain why the right includes a right to abstinence: the right to keep another person from exposing you to his sticky substances is a right to decide not to be exposed to those substances and even to decide to keep one's own sticky substances sealed up within (though doing so is not really possible with urine, feces, or probably even saliva; and so, alas, with their disgustingly imperfect bodies, radical ascetics need to settle for something less than ideal). Moreover, my understanding sheds light on why prostitutes historically had been consigned to a degraded status. In the abstract, prostitution can be thought of as just another form of employment. But the human mind does not always operate at such a high level of abstraction, and, perceived in more concrete terms, prostitutes have generally seemed to most people (or at least to most men) like women onto or into whom any random male can decide at will to spill his sticky substances. High-priced prostitutes are an exception, because male access to them is severely limited by economic constraints. But male access to lower-class prostitutes has not been substantially limited by such constraints. Accordingly, the status of such prostitutes has generally been not merely that of a low-wage worker, who still has a socially recognized dignity, but that of a tainted person occupying a radically degraded social position.[4]

My account also helps to explain why it is widely and reasonably thought that sexual assaults are generally more serious incursions on autonomy than other physical assaults. Grabbing a person's crotch without her consent is not the equivalent of grabbing her by the arm; deliberately spilling one's semen on her body is not on a moral par with deliberately spilling a glass of water on her. The differences are not captured simply by appealing to a right to bodily integrity but need to explained in terms of an account of how and why sexual violations of bodily integrity generally constitute more serious violations of that right. One might point out that sexual violations generally have a more deleterious psychological effect, but the point does not account for why they have a more deleterious effect. I believe that it is necessary to introduce an account of cultural meanings that proceeds roughly along the lines I have suggested: a person consistently subjected to sexual violations is thereby marked with a sign of a severely degraded social status. That one is so marked is a source of especially severe psychological distress.

One might object to my account that disgust at another's sticky substances is to be explained by the harmful organisms that they might contain and that, looked at from a logical point of view, in cases where the substances are harmless to another person, there can be no right against being exposed to them. No harm, no foul. But while such a view is unimpeachable as a matter of abstract logic, it is absurd as a matter of human psychological and cultural reality. I would like to see the person who would not object to having the semen, urine, sweat and saliva of strangers spilled onto or into him, as long as he could be sure that they did not carry any pathogens. And if I did see such a person, I would pronounce him so oblivious to human meanings that his fitness for life in common with others would be suspect.

So far, I have examined the basis of a right to sexual autonomy but have not said much about its scope. That free and equal persons, as opposed to slaves, low-class prostitutes, and others who have a degraded social status, have their right to sexual autonomy socially recognized does not yet tell us what is covered by the right. Certain people, for example, might say that the right only extends as far as sex within marriage for purposes of procreation. That view of sex was, of course, the predominant one in Western culture from medieval times until well into the twentieth century, though it had some presence in the pagan worlds of ancient Greece and Rome. But modern societies have largely come to reject such a view and to affirm, instead, that the right of sexual autonomy is a broad one that includes one-night stands, sex before marriage, oral sex, and masturbation, among other forms of non-marital and non-procreative sex. Same-sex relations are also increasingly regarded, at least within liberal democratic societies, as within the scope of the right, as they should be, given that the right rests on considerations stemming from pleasure, intimacy, and the importance of deciding with whom to share sticky substances. This combination of considerations underlies the modern rejection of the earlier view that sex within marriage and for procreation is the only acceptable form of sexual activity.

The right of sexual autonomy is a right held by each adult and includes the rights to engage in, or abstain from, sexual activity, and to choose the type of sexual activity in which to engage, whether alone or with a willing and competent adult partner. At the same time, there are various qualifications and specifications of the right of sexual autonomy that are tied, more or less tightly, to social and institutional context. For example, if there is a moral right to pornography as a dimension of the right to sexual autonomy, as I will argue is the case, then the right to pornography will be connected to the ways in which a given society defines property rights. My right to pornography is not a right to your pornography. And my right to engage in sexual relations with a willing adult partner is not a right to engage in such relations in my local public park.

It will not always be a simple matter to determine whether a given social or legal restriction on sexual activity counts as a violation of the right of sexual autonomy. Laws enforcing monogamy are, I think, a case in point. In the abstract, such laws appear to be a clear violation of the right. In the concrete reality of human life, though, societies permitting polygamy have a far worse track record when it comes to gender equality for reasons linked to their polygamy. My point is not to argue for, or against, enforced monogamy, but only to suggest that the question of whether such a restriction is a violation of the right to sexual autonomy or, in contrast, a legitimate qualification of that right, is a complex question that calls for careful attention to how human life actually works. Matters are no different when it comes to restrictions on pornography.

I turn now from sexual autonomy to sexually explicit words and images and how, since the eighteenth century, the law in the United States and Britain has sought to regulate such words and images.

NOTES

1. It was left to the philosopher Alan Soble to refer approvingly to Schauer's idea that pornography was a matter of sexual autonomy, but Soble did not develop the idea. See Soble 1996.
2. There were several versions of the MacKinnon-Dworkin ordinance. I discuss in some detail its main provisions in Chapter 4.
3. Sexual autonomy involves, not merely the right to engage in or refrain from sexual conduct, but also a variety of rights and powers linked to sexual conduct, such as the right to get married and to raise one's offspring as one's own. Although many slave societies did recognize marriage between slaves, the permission of the master was required. Additionally, "slaves had no custodial claims or powers over their children, and children inherited no claims or obligations to their parents" (Patterson 1982: 6). The denial of these powers to slaves—male and female—were major incursions on their sexual autonomy.
4. I do not mean to weigh in here on the debates over efforts to change the social meaning of prostitution so that a prostitute is seen as just another wage worker.

2

Obscenity and
Pornography

2.1 OBSCENITY

In both American and English law, "obscenity" has traditionally been the preferred term for material with objectionable sexual content. In the early 18th century, British law first recognized "obscene libel" as a common-law crime that could be prosecuted in secular courts. The case involved a book about sexually active nuns. During the middle of the century, the novel *Fanny Hill*, in which a prostitute explicitly relates her sexual activities, was banned in Britain. And the British were not content simply with prosecuting publishers, authors, and sellers of sexually explicit material. An act of Parliament during the mid-19th century empowered police to seize such material and magistrates to order its destruction. The purpose of the statute was that of "more effectually preventing the sale of obscene books, pictures, prints, and other articles" (De Grazia 1969: 5, note 1). The statute did not define "obscenity," but in *Queen v. Hicklin*, the court presented the definition that would remain legally authoritative in Britain for a century: "the test of obscenity is . . . whether the tendency of the matter charged as obscenity is to deprave and corrupt those whose minds are open to such immoral influences" (De Grazia 1969: 9).

The publication at issue in *Hicklin* was a pamphlet attacking the Catholic Church and claiming that priests used the confessional booth to talk about various sexual acts to their female parishioners. The court found that "the minds of those hitherto pure are exposed to the danger of contamination and pollution from the impurity [the pamphlet] contains" and claimed that certain passages described "impure practices, some of them of the most filthy and disgusting and unnatural description it is possible to imagine" (De Grazia 1969: 9).

During the latter part of the 19th and first half of the 20th centuries in Britain, the works of Emile Zola, James Joyce, and D. H. Lawrence, among other celebrated writers, were deemed "obscene" by the authorities due to their sexual content. The works were banned, seized, and burned, and the publishers were subjected to prosecution. And until 1959, in obscenity cases, judges would not permit testimony about the artistic or literary merits of the material.

In the United States, the treatment of sexually explicit material in the 19th and early 20th centuries was not substantially different from its treatment in Britain. In *Commonwealth v. Sharpless* (1815), the defendant was prosecuted for inviting paying customers to see a painting that was displayed in his home. The Philadelphia grand jury described the painting as representing "a man in an obscene, impudent, and indecent posture with a woman" and characterized the artwork as "lewd, wicked, scandalous, infamous, and obscene" (Mackey 2002: 21). The defendant challenged his conviction on the ground that there was no statute specifically outlawing his conduct. However, the state supreme court upheld the conviction, citing a common-law rule prohibiting public indecency and noting that "a picture tends to excite lust as strongly as writing" (Mackey 2002: 21) And in 1821, the Supreme Judicial Court of Massachusetts upheld the conviction of a man for selling copies of *Fanny Hill*. The prosecutor claimed that the novel created in the minds of readers "inordinate and lustful desires" (Mackey 2002: 22)

In the late 19th century, the US Supreme Court heard a case involving a statute that outlawed sending obscene, lewd, and lascivious materials through the mails. The Court held in *Swearingen v. US* that "the words 'obscene', 'lewd', and 'lascivious', as used in the statute, signify that form of immorality which has relation to sexual impurity" (1896: 451). As the Court construed the statute, obscene material was "calculated to corrupt and debauch the minds and morals of those into whose hands it might fall." The Court's emphasis on the "impurity" of such material and its capacity to "corrupt and debauch" the mind is very much in keeping with the English court's opinion in *Hicklin*.

Obscene material was traditionally treated by US courts as beyond the protection of the First Amendment's Free Speech Clause. It was not until 1957, in *Roth v. US*, that the Supreme Court regarded obscenity as raising any free speech issue. Up to that point, it was simply assumed that, when government deemed material to be obscene, the First Amendment was irrelevant. This assumption gave the government considerable discretion to define obscenity however it wished, and publishers and authors of sexually explicit material would need to show that, under the government's definition, the work was not obscene. Yet, the ruling of a federal appellate court in the 1930s did place an important limit on the government's discretion.

In that case, the court ruled against the Customs Service, which had seized copies of James Joyce's *Ulysses* at the border under the authority of a law that banned the importation of "any obscene book, pamphlet, paper, writing, advertisement, circular, print, picture, drawing, or other representation, figure, or image on or of paper or other material" (*US v. One Book* 1934: 706) The Court of Appeals explained:

> That numerous long passages in *Ulysses* contain matter that is obscene under any fair definition of the word cannot be gainsaid; yet they are relevant to the purpose of depicting the thoughts of the characters and are introduced to give meaning to the whole, rather than to promote lust or portray filth for its own sake. . . . The book as a whole is not pornographic, and, while in not a few spots it is coarse, blasphemous, and obscene, it does not, in our opinion, tend to promote lust. (706–707)

Thus, the Court of Appeals emphasized that that the reason why *Ulysses* did not fall into the category of the "obscene" was that, when judged as a whole, the work had literary merit and was not sexually arousing. Accordingly, the judges declared, "[W]e believe that the proper test of whether a given book is obscene is its dominant effect. . . . We think that *Ulysses* is a book of originality and sincerity of treatment and that it has not the effect of promoting lust" (708). This decision made US law more accommodating to sexually explicit material than was British law at the time, which still adhered to the *Hicklin* ruling. However, even in the *Ulysses* case, the First Amendment was treated as an irrelevancy.

Two decades later, in *Roth*, the Supreme Court explicitly addressed the matter of obscenity and the First Amendment. While declaring obscenity to be beyond First Amendment protection, the Court simultaneously decided that it had the authority to place important limits on how obscenity could be defined. In particular, the Court decided that obscenity could not be defined, consistent with the Constitution's protection of freedom of speech, in a way that encompassed material conveying "ideas having even the slightest redeeming social importance" (484). All such ideas, including "unorthodox ideas, controversial ideas, even ideas hateful to the prevailing climate of opinion—have the full protection of the guaranties [of the First Amendment], unless excludable because they encroach upon the limited area of more important interests" (484).

The Court explained that obscenity is not protected because "implicit in the history of the First Amendment is the rejection of obscenity as utterly without redeeming social importance. . . . Obscene material is material which deals with sex in a manner appealing to prurient interest . . ., i.e., material having a tendency to excite lustful thoughts" (487 and n. 20). The word "prurient" derives from the Latin, *prūrīre*, meaning to itch or to be sexually excited. The English word connotes the encouraging of an excessive or inappropriate concern with sexual matters. And the Court in *Roth* approvingly cited the jury instructions which drew the connection between obscenity and sexual arousal: "[t]he words 'obscene, lewd and lascivious' as used in the law, signify that form of immorality which has relation to sexual impurity and has a tendency to excite lustful *thoughts*" (486; emphasis in original).

A decade after *Roth*, the Supreme Court made it clear that material can be constitutionally protected, even if parts of it are sexually arousing. In *Memoirs v. Massachusetts* (1964), the Court overturned a ruling of the state's Supreme Judicial Court that affirmed the 19th-century precedent finding *Fanny Hill* to be obscene. In *Memoirs*, the Supreme Court held that, in order for a work to be obscene, "three elements must coalesce: it must be established that (a) the dominant theme of the material taken as a whole appeals to a prurient interest in sex; (b) the material is patently offensive because it affronts contemporary community standards relating to the description or representation of sexual matters; and (c) the material is utterly without redeeming social value" (418). Although the state court found that the dominant theme of *Fanny Hill* appealed to the prurient interest and that the novel was patently offensive by community standards, that court conceded that the novel had some social value. Because of that concession, the Supreme Court reasoned, the judgment that the work was obscene could not be sustained.

Nonetheless, the Supreme Court added that it would not be "improper under all circumstances" for an American court to find *Fanny Hill* to be obscene. The Court explained, "Evidence that the book was commercially exploited for the sake of prurient appeal, to the exclusion of all other values, might justify the conclusion that the book was utterly without redeeming social importance" (420). In other words, the Court was saying that the sexually oriented marketing of a publication could reasonably lead to the conclusion that the publication was "utterly without redeeming social value."

The Court was as good as its word. In *Ginzburg v. US* (1966), the petitioner had been convicted for violating the federal obscenity statute, by mailing sexually explicit magazines and books. The Court found that "each of the accused publications was originated or sold as stock in trade of the sordid business of pandering—the business of purveying textual or graphic matter openly advertised to appeal to the erotic interest of their customers" (467). Even though the magazine in question contained articles that might be thought to be informational, the Court dismissed the inclusion of such pieces as a "pretense" (470) aimed at helping to protect the publisher against prosecution and found that the magazine was "created, represented and sold solely as a claimed instrument of the sexual stimulation it would bring" (471). Moreover, the advertisements for Ginzburg's publications represented them "as erotically arousing [and] . . . stimulated the reader to accept them as prurient; [the reader] looks for titillation, not for saving intellectual content" (470).

The Supreme Court has never retreated from the position that sexually explicit material that appeals to the "prurient interest," that is, material created, distributed, and used exclusively for the purpose of causing sexual arousal, is socially worthless. In a case that is still good law, the Court presented its authoritative test for obscenity. In *Miller v. California* (1973), the Court held that material was obscene if and only if all of the following conditions were met: (1) the average person, applying contemporary community standards, finds that the material, taken as a whole, appeals to the prurient interest; (2) the material depicts in a patently offensive way sexual acts specifically enumerated in a relevant state or federal law; and (3) the material, taken as a whole, lacks serious literary, artistic, political, or scientific value.

The Court in *Miller* jettisoned the *Roth/Memoirs* provision that obscenity was "utterly without redeeming social value," replacing it with a criterion referring to a lack of "serious literary, artistic, political, or scientific value" (26). Perhaps the Court thought that by this modification, it could suppress the embarrassing question, "Why doesn't material aiming exclusively at arousal have some *social* value and thereby merit free speech protection?" Nonetheless, the question is an obvious one, and the Court simply ignores it.

The Court might have been counting on the linguistic associations among "obscenity," on the one hand, and "filth," "impurity," and "that which is disgusting," on the other. After all, how could what is filthy and disgusting be constitutionally protected? And the word associations in question were reflected in the popular characterization of pornography as "smut" and "dirty pictures." Nonetheless, word association does not an argument make, and the Court never developed an adequate justification for why "dirty pictures" should be deprived of the legal protection that other sorts of pictures received.

Some legal theorists have tried to provide the justification that the Court failed to provide. In particular, Frederick Schauer has argued that certain sorts of sexually explicit materials—specifically, those aimed exclusively or primarily at producing sexual arousal in the viewer—were not reasonably seen as a form of speech, whatever their social value might be. In his view, such materials were what should be labeled "obscene," and because they were not speech, they were not properly covered by the Free Speech Clause of the First Amendment. Schauer suggested, instead, that the use of the materials was better seen as a matter of personal sexual liberty: "the arguments about obscenity parallel the arguments about homosexuality, adultery, and 'unnatural' sexual practices. . . . The issue . . . is not a free speech issue" (1982: 180). In a later section, I argue that Schauer's view is partly right, partly wrong.

While Schauer was trying to salvage obscenity doctrine, anti-pornography feminists were posing a radical challenge to the doctrine. Contrary to a widely voiced view, the feminist approach was not anti-sex. It was obscenity doctrine that was anti-sex. For it was obscenity doctrine that treated all materials aimed exclusively at sexual arousal as appealing to the allegedly objectionable "prurient interest" and as liable to legal suppression for that reason. In the view of anti-pornography feminists such as Catharine MacKinnon and Lori Watson, there is nothing objectionable per se in materials aimed at producing sexual arousal. Thus, MacKinnon wrote, "Obscenity as such probably does little harm" (1985: 22). In other words, material was not harmful simply because it aimed exclusively at arousal and was found offensive by the community. But sexually explicit material did become harmful, in the view of anti-pornography feminists, when it involved the degradation, humiliation, or violation of women. Material of that kind was "pornography," as opposed to obscenity.[1] I now turn to an examination of the various meanings of "pornography."

2.2 THE MEANINGS OF "PORNOGRAPHY"

The word "pornography" was introduced in the 19th century to refer to the ancient Roman depictions with sexually explicit content that had been discovered in the ruins of Pompei starting in the prior century (Kendrick 1987: 11). The word derived from the ancient Greek terms, "pornē," which was a derogatory term for low-class prostitutes and can be translated as "whore," and "graphein," meaning "to write." In one ancient Greek source, "pornographoi" is used to refer to writers or painters who depict such prostitutes (Kendrick 1987: 12).

Anti-pornography feminists were quick to pick up on the etymology of "pornography." Gloria Steinem explained, "Pornography begins with a root 'porno', meaning 'prostitution' or 'female captives', thus letting us know that the subject is not mutual love, or love at all, but domination and violence against women" (1980: 37). Andrea Dworkin declared, "The word pornography does not have any meaning other than . . . the graphic depiction of the lowest whores. Whores exist to serve men sexually; whores exist only in a framework of male sexual domination" (1989: 200). And MacKinnon and Dworkin wrote that "in pornography women are graphically depicted as whores by nature, that is, defined by our status as sexual chattel" (1997: 257). For anti-pornography feminists, the Greek root of the word revealed that pornography was not simply sexually explicit or used for sexual arousal, but rather that it was essentially material that presented women as whores, that is, material implying through its depictions that all women were the socially degraded sexual servants of men and properly so. Of course, this reading of the word was anachronistic: "pornographoi" seems not to have been used much at all by the ancient Greeks, and it did not convey the idea that all woman were whores, even in the extended sense of someone who is properly regarded as a sexual servant of men. Nonetheless, the etymological connection between "pornography" and "pornē" did allow feminists to make a key substantive point about what they saw as intolerable in much of the material that came to be called "pornography" in the modern world: the material was degrading to women.

Anti-pornography feminists clearly distinguished between pornography and other sorts of sexually explicit material. Helen Longino provided one of the first feminist definitions of pornography, according to which it consists in "explicit representations of sexual behavior" that are distinguished by their "*degrading and demeaning portrayal of the role and status of the human female as a mere sexual object to be exploited and manipulated sexually.*" She added that the material must be such as "*to endorse the degradation*" of women (1980: 42–43; emphasis in original). Thus, not all sexually explicit material counts as pornographic, but only that subset—however large in reality—that portrays women as sexual objects and endorses such a view of women.

In a similar vein, MacKinnon and Dworkin pointed out that the definition of pornography contained in their legal ordinance did not include "erotica . . . which is sexually explicit [depictions of] sex premised on equality" (1997: 255). Thus, their ordinance defined pornography as involving "the graphic sexually explicit subordination of women, whether in pictures or words" (1997: 444). This definition went beyond Longino's in an important way: while Longino said that pornographic material depicted and endorsed the sexual degradation and subordination of women, the MacKinnon-Dworkin definition rested on the idea that pornography did not simply depict and endorse the subordination of women but, in so representing them, actually subordinated women. MacKinnon and others have defended this idea, and I examine it later. The main point here is that for MacKinnon and Dworkin, as for Longino and other anti-pornography feminists, sexually explicit material, even if designed and used for purposes of arousal, is not necessarily pornographic.

Feminist definitions of pornography differ from those that do not take the degrading and demeaning portrayal of women to be an essential feature of pornographic material. An example of a non-feminist definition can be found in the 1979 report of the British Committee on Obscenity and Film Censorship. Appointed by the government and led by the prominent philosopher Bernard Williams, the report said, "We take it that, as almost everyone understands the term, a pornographic representation is one that combines two features: it has a certain function or intention, to arouse its audience sexually, and also a certain content, explicit representation of sexual material (organs, postures, activity, etc.). A work has to have both this function and this content to be a piece of pornography" (1981: 103).

The feminist anti-pornography movement was in its early stages when the Williams report was being written and seems not to have had much of an influence on the report. From the feminist point of view, the report omitted the crucial features that made sexually explicit material pornographic, namely, the depiction and endorsement of the sexual subordination of women. And it certainly was not the case that "almost everyone" went along with the report's definition. In addition to feminist definitions, many non-feminist alternatives to Williams's definition were offered.

Among the non-feminist definitions was one given by Fred Berger, who proposed that pornography be understood as material that "explicitly depicts sexual activity or arousal in a manner having little or no artistic or literary value" (1977: 184). More recently, Michael Rae has suggested that material is pornographic if "it is reasonable to believe that [the material] will be used (or treated) as pornography by most of the audience for which it was produced," where being used as pornography involves use for the purpose of sexual arousal or gratification (2001: 120). Rea denies that material must be sexually explicit in order to count as pornographic (122–123).

The number of definitions of pornography could easily be extended into the dozens. But is the disagreement over how "pornography" should be defined anything other than a trivial verbal dispute that can be circumvented simply by stipulation? I think that it is more than a verbal dispute. Our words and how we define them might not determine the basic structure of our thoughts about reality, contrary to a once popular hypothesis among linguists and literary theorists. However, our words and their definitions do make some phenomena relatively salient in our experience and more readily available for thought and discussion. A virtue of feminist definitions is that they mark out a range of material that ought to be of concern to any person or society committed to a principle of the equal status of men and women. I say "of concern" not because I think that there ought to be special laws against such material, but because I think that anyone who dismisses out of hand equality-based worries about the material is not taking equality seriously enough.

Nonetheless, there is a potential drawback with feminist definitions of pornography. Although the Williams Committee was wrong to claim that almost everyone understood the term in the way that the committee understood it, many people do understand it in roughly that way: explicit depictions of sex intended or reasonably expected to be sexually arousing. If it turns out that pornography, as feminists construe it, does have society-wide harmful effects on women but that some forms of pornography, as the Williams Committee defines it, do not have such effects, then the unqualified assertion that pornography has harmful effects on women will be understood by many people to include those instances of Williams-style pornography that do not demean or degrade women. In other words, because the pornography-erotica distinction is not one commonly employed, but rather "pornography" is widely understood in a way that crosses over that distinction, the two forms of sexually explicit material are likely to be conflated.

One might try to protect against the conflation by proposing precise legal definitions, but even if such a strategy would work in court, the conflation is likely to persist in society more generally. If the aim is to make salient in the public mind certain potential problems with a particular kind of sexually explicit material, then the conflation is a problem.

Yet, one might argue that Williams's definition reflects the pre-feminist era and, by itself, does little to highlight a form of sexually explicit material that is both pervasive and prima facie problematic for a society supposedly committed to the equality of men and women. Moreover, the idea that sexually explicit and arousing material is socially problematic is a holdover from the days when such material was widely thought of as "dirty." That way of thinking still has a grip on a significant part of society, but there is reason to avoid lending support to such thinking by defining pornography in a way would make good sense if so-called "obscene" material really were socially problematic. So one could reasonably claim that it is better to define "pornography" in a way that reflects feminist insights, and, as A.W. Eaton writes, "The particularly feminist objection is not that pornography is sinful, obscene, impolite, lewd, shameful, or disgusting but instead that pornography causes harm to women in the sense that it impairs or thwarts their capacity to pursue their interests" (2007: 681).

Even if we were to restrict ourselves to feminist definitions, though, there are conflicting views of what counts as pornography. Eaton seeks to sidestep these definitional disagreements by suggesting that a "sensible" version of anti-pornography feminism "restricts itself to *inegalitarian pornography*: sexually explicit representations that as a whole eroticize relations (acts, scenarios, or postures) characterized by gender inequality" (2007: 676). Erotizing means "making something sexy," that is, giving it sexual appeal (682), and, in eroticizing male dominance, inegalitarian pornography "endorses and recommends women's subordination and degradation" (681).

Eaton's strategy of focusing on inegalitarian pornography is a reasonable one. Notice, however, that by adding the adjective "inegalitarian," she is presupposing that there is a conception of pornography that does not include the feminist element. Yet, in a number of places in her analysis, she also uses "pornography" without the qualifying adjective to refer to the inegalitarian sort. I do not make these points as criticisms. I think that they reflect a dialectically complex situation in which anti-pornography feminists are seeking to change social and linguistic norms without inventing entirely new meanings for words. Such a situation invariably carries with it the risk of linguistic misunderstanding and other problems deriving from the continuing hold that past meanings have on the present.

I doubt that there is any problem-free solution to defining "pornography." My own approach will be to use "pornography," in some contexts, to refer to the broader class of materials picked out by Williams's definition and, in other contexts, to refer to the narrower class of materials picked out by Eaton's "inegalitarian pornography." Some philosophers might want me to distinguish between pornography-1 and pornography-2, but I do not think that such a device is needed. Context will usually make it clear what is being referred to, and when the referent might be unclear, I will refer to pornography in its "broad sense," or to "inegalitarian pornography."

Perhaps over time, feminist definitions will come to better reflect common usage than Williams's definition does, and then it might make sense simply to use "pornography" always to refer to the inegalitarian sort. But in light of my judgment that the Williams's meaning better reflects current common usage, I do not think that it would be wise to rule out using "pornography" to express that meaning.

At the same time, feminist meanings incorporate two insights that argue in favor of using the term in a feminist sense in many contexts. First, as Eaton, Watson, and other anti-pornography feminists have emphasized, the kind of sexually explicit and arousing material that needs to be scrutinized is the inegalitarian sort. Of course, anti-pornography feminists do not simply say that such material needs to be scrutinized; they also argue that it should be legally restricted because it results in society-wide harm to women and poses a serious obstacle to equality between men and women. Those arguments are at the heart of my disagreement with anti-pornography feminists, but I aim to reject the arguments while still agreeing with the point that the availability of inegalitarian materials of a sexually explicit and arousing sort does raise troubling questions for any person or society committed to a principle of the equal status of men and women.

The second feminist insight is that the vast bulk of sexually explicit and arousing material that circulates in contemporary society is in fact inegalitarian. If only a small proportion of sexually explicit and arousing material were inegalitarian, then the availability of that small subset might still raise troubling questions for an egalitarian society, but it would be difficult to make the case for defining "pornography" so as to require the inegalitarian element. Yet, such a definition does make sense, even if it is not the uniquely sensible definition, once we accept the feminist point that most of the material is inegalitarian. And then we can contrast pornography, as MacKinnon does, with "erotica," that is, "sexually explicit materials premised on equality" (1985: 22).

2.3 EROTICIZING INEQUALITY

As we have seen, a major part of the feminist understanding of inegalitarian pornography is that it eroticizes sex inequality. Sometimes the idea is that such pornography makes something "sexy," as Eaton puts it (2007: 682). Making something sexy means taking something that is not sexy and turning it into something that is sexy. Advertising seeks to do this with the products it sells: ordinary consumer goods are "made sexy" by being endorsed by sexy celebrities or attractive actors, or by other psychological associations that the advertising tries to forge between the goods and something that is already sexy. However, I do not think that much of the material that feminists—or anyone else—would regard as pornographic *makes* anything sexy. Pornography of all types deals with what the consumers of it already find sexy. Men seek out sexually explicit depictions in which women are subordinate to men because they already find such depictions arousing. If they did not find the depictions arousing to begin with, they would seek out sexually explicit depictions that did not represent such subordination. And so I agree with Susan Brison, when she writes about "degrading pornography," that "the arousal [men experience] is dependent on the depiction of degradation" (2014: 324). What, then, explains why so many men find inegalitarian pornography arousing? I don't know, but, whatever it is, it has taken hold before males see their first pornography.

I do not find it plausible, then, when MacKinnon writes, "Pornography sexualizes rape, battery, sexual harassment, prostitution, and child sexual abuse. . . . More generally, it eroticizes the dominance and submission that is the dynamic common to them all. It makes hierarchy sexy. . . . Pornography conditions male orgasm to female subordination" (1985: 17 and 58). In my view, pornography does not make hierarchy or female subordination sexy; rather, pornography relies on such subordination being sexy to men in the first place. It might be possible for laboratory experimenters to condition men to find something sexually arousing that they did not initially find so, and some kind of conditioning process is likely at work in sexual fetishisms, such as the fetish that finds shoes a turn on. And I am not claiming that men are genetically predisposed to find female subordination sexy. My point is that exposure to pornography is not what makes men find female subordination sexy. Men do not need to learn from pornography to find pornography sexy, as Pavlov's dogs needed to learn to salivate at the sound of a bell. Men salivate from the start when they view pornography. There is no training period in which young males view pornography in association with non-pornographic materials that they find arousing, eventually coming to find the pornography arousing due to the repeated association. Young males who are old enough to find the viewing of anything sexually arousing find pornography arousing.

One might suggest that certain kinds of sexual representations can be made sexy by associating them with what is already experienced as sexy. I do not wish to rule out such a suggestion, but it does not resonate at all with my own sexual experience. When I first viewed sexually explicit photographs at the age of thirteen or fourteen, from a copy of *Playboy* that a friend of mine had somehow acquired, I did not find the pictures arousing because they were associated with anything else. I just found them arousing, period. Of course, something about my upbringing and/ or genetic make-up made them so; but they certainly were not made so by any pornography I had experienced, as they were the first pornography that I ever saw. And as I had subsequent experiences with various forms of pornography, what I found arousing was not plausibly explained by any process of association with previous pornography. In those experiences, I found some types of scenes arousing, while I was indifferent to or repulsed by many others. But I never began to find a certain type of scene arousing when it was not so for me from the start. If pornography makes things sexy, then I could have been expected to begin to find arousing scenes that were not initially so.

My experience of pornography is thus very much like the experience of sexuality reported by many who engage in same-sex relations: they discover that they are sexually attracted only to persons of the same sex and that nothing subsequently budges them from that initial mode of sexuality. There has, of course, been considerable public controversy over whether sexual preference is genetically determined. I do not intend to weigh-in on those debates here. My point is about how a person's sexuality appears to the person whose sexuality it is, and, more specifically, that my responses to pornographic materials have appeared to me to have the same sort of "given" quality that many who engage in same-sex relations report. I discovered what I found arousing and what I did not find so, and, once the discoveries were made, the range of material that I found arousing remained relatively stable.

One might suggest that pornography can make certain activities much more arousing that are initially only very mildly arousing to start. Perhaps the suggestion is accurate, but if a man has a choice between material that is very mildly arousing and material that is strongly arousing—and the Internet certainly provides men with plenty of choices—then he would have no reason to choose the mildly arousing material. MacKinnon rightly emphasizes that, for male viewers of pornography, the point is arousal and orgasm. So there is no point for a man to choose mildly over strongly arousing material.

Some people claim that whatever men find initially arousing becomes, after a certain amount of exposure, less so and that, as a result, men seek out increasingly extreme forms of pornography for purposes of arousal. The more extreme forms are presumably the forms that depict more extreme forms of female subordination. But one must distinguish between two different forms of habituation. In one form, a man becomes less aroused by viewing the same material over and over again. This form of habituation would not necessarily lead someone to seek out more extreme material, because he might only need to view material of the same degree of extremeness but with new scenes and different female participants. In a second form of habituation, new scenes having the same degree of extremeness as the old become less arousing, but even here, it is not necessarily true that a man will seek out more extreme material. He might seek out less-extreme material and find that it is now more arousing than it used to be. Moreover, for many men, there might be some upper limit to the extremity of the pornography that they will find even mildly arousing. So even if such men were habituated to pornography at the next level down, going to more extreme depictions would only be less arousing for them.

My own experience is that there is an upper limit and that it has proved very stable. Moreover, although habituation is a real phenomenon, in my experience, it has been of the first kind, and I have found that viewing less-extreme forms of pornography was more arousing than resorting to more extreme forms. One might reply that my experience is idiosyncratic, and it might well be so. But I do not find that the scientific literature on male sexuality sheds any better, or more reliable, light on these matters. Another possibility is that I am deluding myself, and I am well aware that the human mind is quite adept at self-deception. Matters of sex are likely to be especially prone to the mind's ability to fool itself. A great virtue of solid scientific studies is their power to correct for such delusions. So I am prepared to be corrected, but I do not think that the research shows that I am deluded in these matters.

I am skeptical, then, of the idea that pornography eroticizes subordination, if that means that it makes sexually arousing what men do not find arousing to begin with or that it makes more arousing that which men find less arousing to begin with. Andrea Dworkin asserts that pornography "behaviorally conditions men to sex as dominance over and violence against women" (1997: 311). And MacKinnon writes, "As society becomes saturated with pornography, what makes for sexual arousal, and the nature of sex itself . . . change" (1993: 25). Yet, if men do not find sex as dominance arousing to begin with, then I do not see how exposure to pornography makes such sex arousing for them.

Yet, it is entirely plausible that, even if pornography does not make things arousing, it does more deeply engrain in the mind the sexual appeal of what is already found very arousing. Thus, if certain forms of the sexual subordination of women are found very arousing from a man's initial experience with pornography, then it would seem that subsequent experiences with pornography could make it more difficult for the subordination-arousal connection to be extinguished or even substantially weakened. Because men generally use pornography to become aroused and reach orgasm, the orgasmic pleasure might well operate as part of a psychological process that entrenches the connection between a man's arousal and whatever representations help to generate that arousal. Even if this process does not make a man aroused by forms of subordination that did not turn him on from the start, it is potentially important, because it could make it more difficult for those social forces to be effective that seek to counteract the initial sexual mindset that finds subordinating material—of whatever sort—sexually arousing. If the aim is to move in the direction of a society in which men and women have equal status and if such a society is impossible without equality in sexual relations, then it is possible that counteracting an initial inegalitarian sexual mindset is essential to such movement. Accordingly, if eroticizing female subordination is taken broadly so as to include a process in which a preexisting connection between such subordination and sexual arousal is strengthened by pornography, then I think that it is likely both true and important that pornography eroticizes female subordination.

2.4 PORNOGRAPHY CONSUMPTION AS A FORM OF SEX

MacKinnon writes, "Pornography is masturbation material. It is used as sex. Therefore, it is sex. Men know this. . . . [T]he materials . . . are part of the sex act" (1993: 17). The main emendation that I would make here to these statements is that sometimes pornography is used as sex by women in heterosexual or same-sex relationships. Malamuth states that "[m]en have been found to be much more likely [than women] to use pornography on their own, often as a stimulant to masturbation. A considerable number of men and women report using pornography in the context of a relationship" (2007: 679). But I do not doubt that the overwhelming use of pornography in film, video, and other visual media is by men and for purposes of masturbation. And MacKinnon's central point here is quite right: using pornography is a form of sexual activity, plain and simple.

Frederick Schauer was perhaps the first major thinker to argue that pornography use was a kind of sexual activity. The argument was a key part of Schauer's view that so-called "hard-core" pornography was properly placed outside the free speech protections of the First Amendment. Although such pornography might appear at first to be an instance of the communicative material that the amendment protects from legal suppression, Schauer maintained that "the prototypical pornographic item on closer analysis shares more of the characteristics of sexual activity than of the communicative process. The pornographic item is in a real sense a sexual surrogate. . . . It takes pictorial or linguistic form only because some individuals achieve sexual gratification by those means" (1979: 922–923).

Schauer goes on to compare pornography to "rubber, plastic, or leather sex aids. It is hard to find any free speech aspects in their sale or use. . . . The purveyor of . . . pornography is in the business solely of providing sexual pleasure [and] . . . there is no reason to believe that the recipient desires anything other than sexual stimulation" (1979: 923). To vividly make his case that pornography is a sexual aid and not a form of speech, Schauer writes,

> Let us suppose a hypothetical example of . . . 'hard core pornography'. Imagine a motion picture of ten minutes duration whose entire content consists of a close-up colour depiction of the sexual organs of a male and female who are engaged in sexual intercourse. The film contains no variety, no dialogue, no music, no attempt at artistic depictions, and not even any view of the faces of the participants. The film is shown to paying customers who, observing the film, either reach orgasm instantly or are led to masturbate while the film is being shown. . . . [A]ny definition of speech . . . that includes this film in this setting is being bizarrely literal or formalistic. (1982: 181)

Schauer's film is similar to the short, 8mm movies called "stag films" that circulated on college campuses, among other places, in the days before video players and personal computers. It is also similar to some Internet pornography, especially in the lack of any effort at displaying artistic quality. However, it is not like feature-length pornographic movies, which typically contain scenes that are close-up images of a penis repeatedly penetrating a vagina but also include dialogue, music, images of the faces of the participants, and, as I have mentioned, even some efforts at humor. Even pornographic video clips on the Internet often contain dialogue, shots of faces, and music.

In order to make his case that pornography is not a matter of freedom of speech, Schauer needs to argue that actual "hard-core" pornography is more like his hypothetical film than it is like other sexually explicit material that is protected by the First Amendment. Not only does he not develop any such argument, Schauer has described his hypothetical film in a way that makes it doubtful that any argument along those lines would be convincing. A great deal of the pornography that he apparently thinks can be legally suppressed consistent with freedom of speech—such as the classic pornographic movies of the 1970s—is not at all like a film that "contains no variety, no dialogue, no music, no attempt at artistic depictions, and not even any view of the faces of the participants."

I suggest that we disentangle two elements of Schauer's view: his claim that "hard-core" pornography is not protected by free speech principles and his claim that pornography is used for sex. Even if we reject the first claim, or adopt an agnostic position with respect to it, the second claim can still be accepted. And the second claim is, I think, correct. Whether or not the production, circulation, and use of pornography are a matter of freedom of speech, they are a matter of sexual autonomy, because pornography is generally used for sex.

Yet, in his efforts to exclude pornography from First Amendment protection, Schauer gives us a very distorted picture of pornography's use for sex. Because he is intent on making that exclusion, he pushes too hard on the analogy between pornography and physical sexual aids like dildos. Schauer writes, "If pornography is viewed merely as a type of aid to sexual satisfaction, any distinction between pornography and so-called 'rubber products' is meaningless. The mere fact that in pornography the stimulating experience is initiated by visual rather than tactile means is irrelevant, if every other aspect of the experience is the same" (1979: 923).

It is never the case, however, that "every other aspect of the experience is the same." Pornography is a sex aid, but it is a type of sex aid that operates much differently than do rubber products. The arousal brought about by pornography is not a matter of producing a certain sort of friction in its physical contact with a person's sex organs. Pornography causes arousal through the mind and the meanings that the mind perceives in what it is viewing or reading. If MacKinnon and other feminists are right, and I think they are, most men are aroused by pornography because they perceive pornographic images and scenes as presenting female sexual subordination.

Schauer states that "[t]he point is that the use of pornography may be treated conceptually as a purely physical rather than mental experience. This is of course an oversimplification. Physical sensations have mental elements." Nonetheless, he insists, the physical "predominates" over the mental in the use of pornography (1979: 923).

I do not understand the sense in which the physical "predominates." Sexual activity *is* physical, but its mental component is essential and no less important when a man is masturbating to some pornographic image of a woman than when he is having sexual relations with a woman. Pornographic images do not physically generate a pleasurable friction on a man's penis, as some rubber or leather products might do. The images need to be interpreted by the mind in order to produce arousal. The leather product does not need to be interpreted but only applied to the right spot with the right pressure and motion.

Accordingly, I think that Andrea Dworkin expresses a more accurate understanding of pornography than does Schauer when she writes that "[s]peech and action are

meshed" in pornography (1997: 310). If pornography is
to be denied the protection of free speech principles, then
the reason is not that, in pornography use, the physical
"predominates" over the mental, but because of the distinctive way in which the physical and the mental mesh with
one another and the effects of that distinctive meshing.

I do not wish to delve into the question of whether
pornography, particularly the material typically found on
pornographic Internet sites, is protected by free speech
principles properly understood. Although those pornographic materials are different from Schauer's hypothetical film, they are also different from the kind of sexually
explicit material that, in the 1960s, democratic societies
began to protect as a matter of freedom of speech. Much
of that material clearly possessed artistic, literary, and political value. It was not used mainly, much less exclusively,
for sex. But even if material that is used mainly or exclusively for sex is beyond the right of freedom of speech, it
still could fall within the right of sexual autonomy.

Because pornography is used for sex, there is a presumptive case for regarding it as within the right of sexual
autonomy. Sexual activity that involves pornography is,
after all, a certain kind of sex. However, the presumptive
case needs to be developed in order to respond to feminist
anti-pornography arguments. In particular, the argument
needs to be addressed that pornography causes a range of
serious harms to women and that legally suppressing male
access and exposure to pornography would substantially
lower the overall amount of harm done to women. If the
claim is correct, we have the makings of a good argument
for concluding that the right of sexual autonomy does not
protect a person's choice to use pornography.[2]

NOTES

1. Aside from their position on pornography, another factor that prompted the judgment that (many) feminists were anti-sex was their criticism of the sexual revolution and its unreserved enthusiasm for greater sexual freedom. But that criticism was aimed, not at the greater sexual freedom as such, but rather at the gender inequalities that, in the view of the critics, permitted men to sexual exploit and oppress women in the name of sexual freedom. On this feminist view, the sexual revolution essentially served male pleasure by making women more sexually accessible than ever before but failed to adequately empower women to protect their own interests.

2. I say the "makings" of a good argument, because much will depend on how much harm would be averted by legal restrictions on pornography. As will become clear in my discussion of alcohol, the existence of rights goes along with the toleration of some increased level of harm.

3

Evidence and Harm

3.1 PERSONAL TESTIMONY AND THE QUESTION OF CAUSALITY

There is a wealth of personal testimony from women indicating a causal link between pornography and sexual violence against women. Much of this testimony was presented before government bodies during hearings in several cities on the MacKinnon-Dworkin legal ordinances. And I think that any fair reading of the testimony would conclude that there is a real causal connection in the particular instances related by the women who testified. For example, the testimony told of how male partners coerced the women into sexual activities that the men had seen in pornographic materials. The testimony is entirely credible. However, several additional points need to be kept in mind, and they show that one cannot move from such personal testimony to the conclusion that the suppression of pornography would lead to less overall sexual violence and other egregious harms to women.

First, even if a particular man's pornography consumption causally explains a certain type of sexual violence perpetrated by him against a certain woman on a certain occasion, so that he would not have perpetrated that kind of violence against that woman on that occasion but for his pornography consumption, it does not follow that he would have refrained from perpetrating some other kind of sexual violence against that woman, or some other woman, on a different occasion. Without access to pornography, the man might still have committed sexual violence, even if the sexual violence would have been of a different kind or against a different woman or at a different time. It should not be forgotten that there is an abundance of movies, photographs, novels, and so on that are not sexually explicit but that represent sexual violence against women. If pornography had been unavailable to the men who committed the violence described at the MacKinnon-Dworkin hearings, some non-pornographic material might have prompted the same men to perpetrate sexual violence, albeit at a different time or in a different way. The drawback of personal testimony about causality is that it is limited to particular episodes and does not by itself admit of inferences to conclusions about the overall social effects of pornography.

A second problem with moving from the testimony of women victimized by pornography consumers to conclusions about overall social effects is that one cannot assume that the male partners of the women are representative of male pornography consumers. Indeed, the partners are often portrayed by the women as psychologically quite abnormal and even deranged. One women testified that "sex [with her ex-husband] became especially abusive after he started using pornography. He got his ideas from it." She later went on to say about the man, "If he decided that I liked something, he would try to kill it, like dogs we had" (1997: 263). A number of the women testified that, while they were children, their pornography-inspired fathers or other adult males had sexually abused them. One woman said, "My father incestuously molested me for a period of ten years when I was ages 8 to 18. During the early stages of molestations, some of the things he used to coerce me into having sex with him were pornographic materials" (1997: 240). Another woman testified, "Starting at age 4, old Mr. Edwards up the street used pornography to entice me into taking baths so he could watch, had me wearing his wife's clothes and eventually having oral sex and being penetrated by him. This went on for five years" (1997: 264). Still another woman testified to abuse at the hands of her father: "[B]y age eight I was forced into my first pornographic movies. . . . At home I was raped nightly" (1997: 265). On one occasion, this woman said, her father became enraged at her for crying while being anally penetrated during a movie he was filming: "He dragged me into a basement room. He locked the metal door and began beating me. He ripped off my clothes . . . then I saw the knife. . . . [H]e thrusted it into my vagina" (1997: 222). And, testifying about a series of sexually abuse male partners, another woman said, "Carl was a bisexual child molester. . . . Jim stole porn magazines and books by the boxload [from his place of employment]. . . . Michael . . . tied me up and blew strawfuls of cocaine up into my nose and then would rape me" (1997: 372–375).

One might claim that these men are on a psychological continuum with more typical pornography consumers, possessing essentially the same mentality when it comes to sex but extended a few steps further. But what is the basis for such a claim? None of the psychological experts who testified in favor of the MacKinnon-Dworkin ordinance suggested that the typical pornography consumer had the same basic sexual mentality as men who rape their daughters and force pornography on four-year-old girls. Indeed, in discussing his experiments, MacKinnon's own expert witness said, "In our research we are not talking about rapists. We are talking about normal, healthy, young males" (1997: 51). Even assuming for the sake of argument that these young males are typical of pornography consumers, the difference between the typical viewer of pornography and the deranged men described above is not a difference of degree but one of kind. And there is no evidence that the majority of pornography consumers, or even a large minority, have raped and made pornography with their daughters, killed pet dogs that their female partners were fond of, and so on. Nor is there reason to believe that the men who did these things would have refrained from committing sexual atrocities, or committed fewer such atrocities, had pornography not been freely available to them as a consumer product. Like the one father, these morally deranged men might have made their own private pornography with their children or unwilling partners, or searched out underground pornography, or have committed an equal number of rapes of their partners or children, with or without pornography.

MacKinnon does claim that laboratory research shows that exposure to pornography "makes normal men more closely resemble convicted rapists attitudinally, although as a group they don't look all that different from them to start with" (1985: 53). She is referring to the experimental findings that men exposed to pornography become more calloused than control groups not so exposed in their attitudes toward rape victims and that, as reported in a study by Malamuth et al., "over half of the [male] sample do not rule out the possibility that they would engage in sexual assault if they could not be caught. These findings may be interpreted as providing some support for the contention that rape is an extension of normal attitudes and socialization practices in our society rather than totally the product of a sick and aberrant mind" (1980: 134).

Someone might suggest that such a study gives credibility to the idea that there is a psychological continuum between the men in the lives of the women who testified at the hearings on the MacKinnon-Dworkin ordinance and "normal" men. However, Malamuth goes on to say, "It would seem highly inappropriate to argue that those subjects who indicated a possibility of engaging in rape, particularly under the hypothetical circumstances of being assured of not being caught, are actually likely to rape. This self-report, however, may be an indication of a tendency that in combination with other factors and in an exaggerated form may indeed be predictive of such assaults" (1980: 134). Nothing in Malamuth's analysis provides grounds for thinking that the men who raped their own children, killed pet dogs, and so on did things that "were an extension of normal attitudes and socialization practices." Additionally, we will see in the next section that MacKinnon's claim that normal men "as a group . . . don't look all that different" from convicted rapists is not persuasively supported by laboratory experiments, because the subjects in those studies were not randomly chosen from a sample of "normal men."

The third problem with inferring that there would be less overall sexual violence against women if pornography were unavailable is this: in the hypothetical absence of access to pornography, the man whose actual sexual aggression can be causally explained by pornography might commit more acts of sexual aggression than he actually does perpetrate. How could that be? One popular answer is the "safety-value" (or "catharsis") hypothesis: men's masturbating to pornography serves as a release of their sexual aggression, similar to a safety valve releasing steam that is building up to dangerous levels in a boiler. MacKinnon has called the hypothesis "fantasy" (1985: 59).

In my view, the safety-valve hypothesis probably presents an oversimplified view of male sexual psychology. Sexual desire in men is not, I think, so straightforward or mechanical that it can be modeled on the physical phenomenon of steam pressure, though there might be some similarity. Rather, such desire is freighted with ambiguities, conflicting tendencies, obscurities, and paradoxes that render it less like steam pressure and more like a text written in a language and form that is understood only in a fragmentary way. Even so, it could still be the case that, for some men, pornography serves as a substitute for sexual abuse, shifting their conduct in a direction that is less harmful to women. The studies that Lori Watson cites as a refutation of the safety-valve hypothesis would, it is true, also disconfirm my somewhat more-nuanced representation of male sexual desire (this Volume: 230). However, those studies simply establish correlations, not causal connections, between pornography use and aggressive behaviors and attitudes toward women.

3.2 THE EXPERIMENTAL STUDIES

Up until the late 1960s, there was little scientific research done on pornography and its effects (Byrne and Kelley

1984: 2). Then president Lyndon B. Johnson established a commission to examine the matter. Studies were conducted under its auspices, and the commission reviewed the studies in its report. Among the commission's conclusions was that "findings of available research cast considerable doubt on the thesis that erotica is a determinant of either the extent or nature of individuals' habitual sexual behavior. Such behavioral effects as were observed were short-lived" (quoted in Donnerstein et al. 1987: 30). Additionally, the commission found that "the data do not appear to support the thesis of a causal connection between increased availability of erotica and the commission of sex offenses; the data, however, do not conclusively disprove such a connection" (quoted in Donnerstein et al. 1987: 33).

The commission's report proved to be controversial and was subjected to a variety of criticisms by social scientists. They pointed out that some of the studies relied on by the commission used sloppy scientific methodology and that the type of sexually explicit materials examined were from a period when pornography as a whole was not as violent and degrading as it would become over the course of the 1970s and later.

Research into pornography continued during the 1970s and '80s, and a different picture began to emerge than the one presented by the presidential commission. Studies began to consistently show that exposure to at least some varieties of pornography affected the attitudes and dispositions of men in ways that could prove harmful to women. These studies showed that men who are exposed to pornography are, subsequent to the exposure, more likely to accept the myth that women enjoy being raped, to report that they would commit a rape if they were not caught, and to aggress against women in laboratory arrangements in which the men believed that they were actually hurting women with electric shocks and other noxious stimuli (MacKinnon and Dworkin 1997: 48). Summarizing the results of laboratory experiments run through the mid-1980s, Donnerstein and his coauthors wrote that the studies "have found that individuals exposed to certain types of materials respond with blunted sensitivity to violence against women, calloused attitudes about rape, and sexual arousal to rape depictions and laboratory simulations of aggression against women" (1987: 5). But what types of materials? Did the results apply to men across the board or only to a subset of men with distinctive psychological characteristics? And have the results been consistently confirmed since then?

Donnerstein et al. concluded that "[to] date the evidence supporting the contention that so-called degrading pornographic materials, as long as they are not violent, are harmful is sparse and inconsistent" (1987: 171). Elaborating on the matter, they wrote that "the research . . . clearly indicates that when males are exposed to violent pornography they will display heightened levels of aggression against a woman in a laboratory setting. Whether this laboratory aggression is representative of real-world aggression, such as rape, is still a matter for considerable debate" (174). These judgments are difficult to square with the confident assertions made by anti-pornography feminists throughout the 1980s and later that scientific studies subsequent to the flawed studies relied on by the presidential commission had conclusively demonstrated that pornography caused harm to women. Thus, Robin Morgan had declared in a letter submitted as testimony to hearings on the MacKinnon-Dworkin ordinance that studies "utterly refute the 'pornography-as-a-harmless-outlet for sexual aggression' theory promulgated by pornographers" (MacKinnon and Dworkin 1997: 222). And in the 1990s MacKinnon had written that the "false statement that scientific evidence on the harmful effects of the exposure to pornography is mixed and inconclusive is now repeated like a mantra, even in court" (1997: 22). In her judgment, once the flawed studies from the presidential commission were discarded, the scientific evidence consistently confirmed that pornography does harm to women.

One might suspect Donnerstein of bias against the feminist anti-pornography position. But he was one of the main experts used by MacKinnon to support her ordinance at the hearings. And he has long been considered among the leading scientific figures in the study of the effects of pornography. Undoubtedly, Donnerstein did believe that there was good experimental evidence that some kinds of pornography harm women. But he apparently did not think that the evidence was unambiguous and conclusive. We do not need to go into detail as to how MacKinnon managed, through her questioning of him at the hearings, to make it appear that he was much more certain that pornography harms women than he actually was. The point is that the evidence was not as cut-and-dried as she and other anti-pornography feminists claimed.

Before proceeding to what the evidence has shown since the 1980s, I would like to make some points about the laboratory experiments conducted by Donnerstein and the other leading figures in the study of the effects of pornography. I do not doubt that their experiments provide some evidence that less pornography would result in fewer harms to women at the social level. But I am more skeptical than Donnerstein about the strength of the evidence.

The first point to note is that, while the experiments expose subjects to pornographic material and then seek to measure their level of aggressiveness, callousness, and so on, the experiments do not have the subjects masturbate to climax before measuring those variables. I find this lack rather surprising. MacKinnon writes, "With pornography, men masturbate to women being exposed, humiliated, violated, degraded, mutilated, dismembered, bound, gagged, tortured, and killed" (1993: 17). But with the experiments calculated to detect the effects of pornography, men do not masturbate at all. This feature of the experiments seems to me to present a serious problem in reasoning from their results to conclusions about real-world effects. It means that the experiments fail to reflect how pornography is actually used by men and so provide scant grounds for concluding that pornography consumption increases the total amount of aggression against women or for ruling out the counter-hypothesis that such consumption decreases that total.

The second point is that the experiments do not involve a random sample of men. Most of the subjects are college-age males. In fact, many of the experiments, like Malamuth's that found more than half the male subjects saying that they might commit rape if they could not be caught, involve volunteers from Introduction to Psychology courses. Such courses are typically taken in the first two years of college, and so we are talking about a population of experimental subjects skewed toward 18–20-year-olds. Neurological studies show that the part of the brain that is the substrate for reasoning and executive control, the prefrontal cortex, does not generally mature until approximately the age of 25. Moreover, sociological factors related to the pacifying effects of marriage and family make it unreasonable to expect that the study subjects can serve as a representative sample of men. The subjects are disproportionately unmarried and without children to support.

Donnerstein points out that males of the18–22 age group are the most likely individuals in the overall population to perpetrate sexual offenses, so studying the effects of pornography on its members can provide data useful for purposes of law and policy. And Watson points out that, just because young men are more likely than older ones to perpetrate certain harmful acts, it does not follow that society should refrain from having laws against the acts in question. These points made by Donnerstein and Watson are fair enough. Yet, it should be noted that the same points can be made about young men and the harms resulting from alcohol consumption: young males are the individuals most likely to drive recklessly, get into brawls, and engage in a whole range of antisocial behavior. Few people defend a general ban on alcohol on the ground that young males are more likely than other demographic sectors to drink to excess.

However, setting aside for the moment the alcohol-pornography comparison, I am dubious that the subjects in the pornography experiments are even a random sample of the 18–22 age group. The published studies often say little or nothing about what the subjects were told about the experiment, and in particular whether they were told that it involved viewing sexually explicit material, before they agreed to sign up.[1] Yet, such information is important. It is problematic to assume that college-age males who volunteer for studies that they know will involve viewing sexual material are a representative sample of that age group.

Third, the extrapolation from increased aggression in the laboratory to increased aggression in the outside world is problematic, not because the subjects fail to believe that they really are delivering shocks or other noxious stimuli, but because it is quite possible that they understand a laboratory setting as (a) giving them permission to aggress and (b) assuring them that no lasting harm will be done to the women to whom they deliver the shocks. Donnerstein et al. refer to the possible "permission giving" effects at some points in their analysis (1987: 84) but fail to do so when defending the idea that increased laboratory aggression is likely to be reflected in the outside world. And they make no mention of the possibility that the subjects interpret the setting to mean that their shocks might cause transitory hurt but no real harm. It could hardly be surprising if the subjects thought that the experimenter would intervene to stop the proceedings, were the shocks to become so severe that the victims would require hospitalization or suffer long-term damage to their health.

Fourth, the extrapolation from the laboratory to the outside world is further rendered problematic by the fact that the laboratory aggression does not involve any physical contact with the (supposed) victim. I find it quite odd that this form of aggression is taken as an indicator of a propensity for *sexual* aggression, as if there were no important psychological differences between touching and not touching another human being, especially when the issue is a touching that is sexual and likely to produce serious harm. I would have expected experts in human psychology to have been psychologically more astute about such matters.

What, then, do the more recent studies indicate about the effects of pornography? Here is Malamuth's summary of the body of studies:

> Overall, it seems that no simple generalizations are justified but that the effects [of exposure to pornography] depend largely on the type of person . . . as well as the content of the material. . . . [T]he research suggests that if a man already has relatively strong tendencies to be aggressive toward women, then heavy pornography consumption may increase his aggressive tendencies. This seems to be particularly likely if he is sexually aroused by pornography that includes violent content. Conversely, if a man has little risk for being aggressive toward women, then whether or not he consumes pornography does not appear to significantly affect his risk of being aggressive toward women." (2012: 679–680).

I do not quarrel with Malamuth's summary, and it would be foolish to declare that his conclusions are wrong or even unsupported by evidence. But I take the experimental results with a grain of salt, in part because the experiments still suffer from the deficiencies I noted in connection with the studies from the late 1970s and '80s. Additionally, even if we were to accept the statement that there is good evidence showing that if a man already has relatively strong tendencies to be aggressive toward women, then heavy pornography consumption will likely increase his aggressive tendencies—and such a statement is more ambitious than what Malamuth himself claims—it would still fail to undermine the idea that the right of sexual autonomy covers the use of pornography. And it would still leave the case for the legal suppression of even violent pornography on very weak grounds.

In order to see why the experimental results do not undermine the case for a right to use pornography, there are four main areas to examine: (1) population-level studies of the relations between pornography and harm to women, (2) the large decline in rates of reported rape over the past twenty years, (3) the relation of alcohol use to violence against women; and (4) the pervasive presence of violence against women in material that is not sexually explicit and so not pornographic.

Before turning to those four topics, I would like to address a recent statistical meta-analysis in which Watson places great stock (this Volume: 222). The analysis examines the association between pornography and aggressive behavior and looks at twenty-two first-order studies. Most of those studies suffer from the defects I pointed out earlier in criticizing pornography studies. But let me set that issue aside, and ask, how impressive is it that a meta-analysis of twenty-two studies finds an association between pornography and aggressive behavior? My answer is: Not very impressive.

To see matters in perspective, consider a recent literature review of studies of the link between alcohol consumption and violence, examining eighteen such studies *that were themselves meta-analyses* (Duke et al. 2018). In other words, the number of *meta-analyses* was nearly as many as the number of first-order studies in the single pornography meta-analysis on which Watson places so much reliance. Moreover, an additional five meta-analyses examined in the review of the alcohol-violence literature looked at the relation between alcohol consumption and being a victim of violence (for example, the matter of whether drinking by women made them more likely to be victims of intimate partner violence), and still another eight meta-analyses looked at the combined effect of alcohol and drug use on the perpetration of violence. The analysis of these more than thirty meta-analyses showed a strong link between alcohol consumption and violence. That is what I call an impressive body of empirical research. By comparison, Watson's lonely pornography meta-analysis looks meager, at best, and insufficient to alter summary of pornography research that "no simple generalizations are justified but that the effects depend largely on the type of person . . . as well as the content of the material" (Malamuth 2007: 679–680).

3.3 POPULATION-LEVEL STUDIES

A.W. Eaton has argued that the hypothesis that (inegalitarian) pornography causes harm to women "should construe the causal relation . . . not in terms of necessary and sufficient conditions but rather as (a) probabilistic, (b) holding ceteris paribus, and (c) one salient component of a complex causal mechanism" (2007: 703). As Eaton explains, when construed in such a way, the hypothesized causal relation is like the relation that we know obtains between cigarette smoking and cancer, where smoking is neither necessary nor sufficient for getting cancer, but a relation in which, other variables held constant, smoking raises the probability of getting cancer and plays a key role in the complex physiological processes that produce cancer. Accordingly, the claim that pornography causes harm to women should be construed as the assertion that "exposure to pornography is a salient risk factor for a variety of harms" to women (702).

I think that Eaton is exactly right on this matter. The key causal claim about pornography that needs to be assessed for general questions about law, policy, and social practice is not about whether particular men were incited by particular pieces of pornography to perpetrate a particular harm but whether, other variables held constant, more pornography in society increases harms to women and less pornography decreases such harms. Eaton's probabilistic model captures the crucial claim of causality. She proceeds to point out that there is a major lacuna in the evidence for the claim that pornography causes harms to women: the dearth of population-level studies.

The case establishing that smoking causes cancer relied to an important extent on population-level studies. Such studies were not laboratory experiments that gave cigarettes to some random group of subjects and had them smoke, while having another random group not smoke. Instead, the studies tracked over many years very large groups of persons and how much they smoked and compared the proportion of the smokers who developed cancer with the proportion of nonsmokers who came down with the disease. The population-level studies of smoking and cancer consistently found that smokers developed cancer at higher rates and that, among smokers, those who smoked more developed cancer at higher rates than those who smoked less. The body of these consistent findings was sufficient to convince any reasonable person that smoking causes cancer.

There are some population-level studies of pornography and harm, but, as Eaton notes, they are methodologically deficient as well as being inconsistent with one another in their findings. For example, one of the first population-level studies of pornography, conducted by Ben-Veniste and used by the 1970 Presidential Commission, examined rates of reported sex crimes in Copenhagen between 1958 and 1969. Danish laws had been liberalized in mid-1967, exempting sexually explicit literature from the nation's obscenity laws, and liberalized again in 1969, eliminating the obscenity laws entirely. Reported sex crimes fell dramatically in the last three years of the period that Ben-Veniste examined. He concluded that "pornography of the type disseminated in Denmark apparently has caused no increase in the rate of sex crime" (n.d.: 252). However, the decline in 1967 is unlikely to be explained by a legal change that took effect in the middle of that year, and there had been previous major declines in 1960 and 1962. Additionally, the big legal change was in 1969, the last year of the study. It might be true that increased pornography consumption did not cause rises in sex crimes in 1967 through 1969—there were no rises in those years—but that is slim grounds for thinking that there would not be increases subsequently or that any such increases would not be due even in part to increased exposure to pornography.

Moreover, Ben-Veniste's qualification that his conclusion concerned "pornography of the type disseminated in Denmark" is an important one. The "pornography" legalized by the 1967 legislation consisted in works of literature, while the material legalized in 1969 included sexually explicit magazines and movies. These are very different types of sexually explicit material, with potentially very different effects. Finally, although Ben-Veniste mentions some factors other than pornography that might be connected to the fall in sex crimes, such as more liberal attitudes toward sex, he provides no systematic analysis of their influence.

In another early population-level study, John Court concluded that there was "a positive correlation with some significance" (1976: 152) between increased exposure to pornography and sex crimes. He examined sex crime data from eight international jurisdictions, mostly in Western liberal democracies, from 1958 to 1974, finding an "upward trend" in reported rape rates. Court concluded that the trend "appears to coincide with, or closely follow, the availability of pornography in the community" and that there was no upward trend in the one jurisdiction (Singapore) in which pornography remained under legal suppression (152–153). However, Court did not provide any specific dates regarding the legalization or greater availability of pornography in the countries with the upward trends in rape rates. He simply asserted, "Pornography is more readily available in numerous Western countries than it was a decade ago" (152). Such an analysis is not sufficiently fine-grained to yield helpful conclusions about correlations.

Subsequent population-level studies have not provided any clear picture of the relation of pornography to sexual aggression against women. After reviewing a body of studies of pornography in the United States and other countries, Bauserman concluded that "the nonexperimental evidence for a causal role of exposure to sexually explicit material in sex crimes is ambiguous and often contradictory" (1996: 422). Accordingly, Eaton seems to me to be quite reasonable when she writes, "In order for the harm hypothesis to become more than a hypothesis, we need more careful ecologic [i.e., population-based] studies" (2007: 706).

Donnerstein is dismissive of population-level studies as a way of establishing causality, even stating that some of his "good colleagues" would say that the evidence from laboratory experiments for aggression against women caused by sexually violent images is stronger than the evidence that smoking causes cancer (MacKinnon and Dworkin 1997: 52) He insists that "the only way that you can determine causality . . . is through experimental research" (MacKinnon and Dworkin 1997: 301). But by that standard, it is impossible in practice to determine by laboratory experiments that pornography causes the sort of harm that is perpetrated against women outside of the laboratory. As Donnerstein himself admits, "we can't expose the [pornographic] material to [the subjects] and see if they go out and rape" (MacKinnon and Dworkin 1997: 57). And, of course, no one is interested in whether pornography consumption causes men outside the laboratory to give electric shocks to women. Donnerstein's dismissal, not just of the particular, very flawed population-level studies of pornography that were done, but of that kind of study for determining causality, is myopic and unreasonable.

3.4 RATES OF REPORTED RAPE IN THE INTERNET ERA

In the mid-1980s, MacKinnon wrote, "If you understand that pornography literally means what it says, you might conclude that sexuality has become the fascism of contemporary America and we are moving into the last days of Weimar" (1987: 15). In her view, pornography literally means that women are the sexual servants of men, and she appeared to be anticipating a drastic turn for the worse in the situation of women, the emergence of a sexual Nazism that would reduce women to the level of sex slaves for men. Even if her reference to Germany is a rhetorical flourish, one can understand the source of her concern. Access to pornography was increasing substantially in the 1980s due to the introduction and spread of home video players and of rental outlets for the distribution of videos. Pornographic videos were very popular. The new technology was MacKinnon's worst nightmare: if she was right in thinking that increasing pornography consumption caused increasing sexual violence and other serious harms to women, one would expect that the inevitable spread of technology would lead to large increases in such violence. Yet, the anticipated increases did not materialize. They did not even materialize when it turned out that an even worse nightmare for MacKinnon was around the corner: the emergence in the 1990s of the Web and the huge increase in access to pornography that would follow.

From 1994 to 2012, reported rape rates in the United States dropped from 39.3 to 26.9 per 100,000, a 34% decline. The decrease was fairly steady over the whole period, and since 2005, the rate has declined about 15.4% (F.B.I. 2012: Offenses, Table 1). The World Wide Web went online in 1991. By 1997, it had about 900 pornography sites, and, by 2013, the number of such sites was in the range of 2 million or more (Ogas and Gaddam 2011: 8). It has been estimated that, in 2008, 100 million males in the United States and Canada accessed online pornography (Ogas and Gaddam: 8). And starting around 2007, pornography sites have emulated YouTube by posting video clips but showing sexually explicit scenes. Of the million most popular websites, approximately 42,000 contain sexually explicit material (Ogas and Gaddam: 31). There is little question that over the period in which reported rape rates were declining substantially, access to pornography of every kind was rising exponentially. It is not easy to see how this fact squares with the idea that increased pornography consumption causes increases in sexual aggression against women, and it is notable that the social psychologists who have done laboratory experiments on pornography and claim that there is a causal link to aggression against women do not bother to explain what is going on. It is true that rates of reported rates notoriously underestimate the actual number of rapes, due to the social stigma of being a rape victim, police mistreatment of rape victims, and related factors. But there is no reason to think that in the two decades since 1994 those factors have worsened, and attributing the decline in reported rates to an increased unwillingness of women to report the crime is grasping at straws.

Let me be clear: I do *not* take the figures on reported rapes to be an accurate measure of the actual sexual abuse of women. But I *do* assume that a dramatic drop in the number of reported rapes over a period of decades is not compatible with a substantial rise in such abuse over that same period, and I do not see how any contrary assumption is remotely plausible. In my view, then, what happened with reported rape rates is very different from what one would be led to think would happen with those rates, if the crucial hypothesis of MacKinnon, Watson, and other anti-pornography feminists that pornography is a "powerful mechanism through which sex inequality is imposed and maintained" (this Volume: 151) were true. The hypothesis would lead one to expect that reported rape rates would rise, probably by a great deal (given the vast increase in accessibility to pornography due to the Internet); in no case would one expect a dramatic decrease.

Watson says that pornography causes harm that does not directly involve sexual abuse, such as lower pay for women. But are we then to believe that the "powerful mechanism" of pornography only has its effects when it comes to matters other than sexual attacks? Such a belief strains credulity and illustrates how implausible the premises are that would be needed to save the MacKinnon/Watson hypothesis from the facts about reported rapes.

The fall in reported rape rates has led some commentators to claim that pornography causally contributes to the lowering of rape rates. After providing some statistics about rape at the state and national levels and noting that correlation is not the same as causation, Anthony D'Amato suggests that "pornography is the most important causal factor in the decline of rape" (2006: 6). His statistical analysis is woefully incomplete, however, and his concluding suggestion is made without any effort to control for other variables that might be associated with rape rates, such as the general decline in violent crime or other factors that could have brought about the fall in the rates of reported rape. So D'Amato's analysis is worth little if anything.

At hearings on the MacKinnon-Dworkin ordinance held in Minneapolis in 1983, one of the expert witnesses, Dr. Pauline Bart, testified: "If indeed it were true that the cartharsis [i.e., safety-value] model is successful, then since we have had a proliferation of pornography, we should have a diminution of sexual assault and rape, and that is certainly not the case" (MacKinnon and Dworkin 1997: 74). She was seeking to debunk the safety-valve model as part of her presentation supporting the ordinance. Bart's mistake was the same one that D'Amato would make three decades later: one cannot draw any conclusions about the causal effects of pornography simply by looking at the correlation over time between changes in consumption and changes in rates of sexual violence.

Nonetheless, the large decline in rates of reported rapes should give serious pause to anyone who thinks that they understand the causal effects on society of the increasing availability of pornography. There are, no doubt, ways to explain that decline in a way that is consistent with feminist anti-pornography claims about harm to women. For example, one might point out that the decline in rape rates was not as precipitous as the decline in (nonsexual) aggravated assault, which dropped from 440 to 242 per 100,000 over that period (a 45% decline, in comparison to the 34% decline rape) (F.B.I. 2012: Offenses, Table 1). So one might claim that rape rates would have fallen more precipitously than they actually did had it not been for pornography. And nothing in the data I have cited establishes otherwise. Indeed, the data on reported rape rates do not, by themselves, amount to a serious statistical analysis. What is needed are statistically rigorous population-level studies that look at rape rates and control for a range of variables.

Even if it turns out that pornography does not cause (in the relevant sense of causality) rape or sexual assault, it could still be very harmful to women in the other ways that

Watson identifies. Yet, the evidence of a causal connection to those other forms of harm is no better than it is for the hypothesis that pornography causes rape and other sexual attacks against women. And as the evidence stands, it is too weak and inconsistent to mount a successful case for the legal suppression of pornography.

3.5 ALCOHOL AND ITS SOCIAL HARMS

The causal connection between alcohol consumption and violence against women has been recognized since before Prohibition, and, although the connection was not among the main reasons for outlawing alcohol, it was one of the reasons cited by women who favored Prohibition. An historian of the movement writes, "Temperance reformers found links between alcohol and domestic violence" (Rose 1996: 23). And Annie Wittenmeyer, a prominent pro-temperance figure of the late 19th century, declared, "No pen can portray the utter hopelessness of the women into whose homes the drink curse had come. The men who had sworn at the altar to protect them had become demons from whom they fled in fear" (1882: 30).

Alcohol-induced violence against women was seen by Prohibitionists as one aspect of a more general problem; as a pro-temperance encyclopedia of the late 19th century put it: "The influence of alcohol . . . torpifies the moral instincts and weakens the faculty of logical inference, while at the same time it stimulates the propensity of combativeness." The encyclopedia went on to cite the experimental work of a German scientist: "a half-ounce dose of strong rye-brandy . . . excited an unusually gentle deerhound to a pitch of fury which came near endangering the life of the experimenter" (Oswald 1891: 141). And for good measure the encyclopedia quoted a prison chaplain, stating that he had heard "more than 15,000 prisoners declare that the enticements of ale and beer houses had been their ruin" (142).

Scientific studies of alcohol consumption and aggression in humans have since confirmed what the Prohibitionists thought. As I pointed out in a previous section, a recent analysis of more than two dozen *meta-analyses* found a consistent association of alcohol consumption and aggression (Duke et al. 2018). Those meta-analyses included the analysis of experimental studies, finding that "there is strong evidence to suggest that low doses of CNS depressants [including alcohol] cause aggressive behavior in humans" (Bushman 1993: 150). Additionally, population-level studies "indicate a causal relationship between alcohol and violence" (Babor 2010: 61). Such studies have found that rates of violence, including homicide, rise with increased per capita consumption, which is exactly what one would expect if alcohol is a causal factor contributing to violence. Moreover, "violence against intimate partners is strongly associated with the amount of alcohol consumed" (Babor 2010: 61), and a number of studies provide evidence that alcohol consumption by female college students increases the probability of their being raped (Messman-Moore et al. 2008: 1741–1742; Mouilso and Fischer 2012). In a review and analysis of the evidence, Room and Rossow state that "there is no doubt that the impact of alcohol consumption on rates of violence is substantial, and that incidents of violence can be prevented by significant reduction in the overall intake of alcohol and/or heavy drinking episodes" (2001: 221).

It is true that the strength of the link between alcohol consumption and violence has been found to vary across countries (Babor 2010: 62). It is stronger in the United States, Australia, and certain Northern European countries than in Southern Europe. Based on statistical analyses of population-level data, it has been estimated that in the United States, a 1% rise in per capita consumption of alcohol is accompanied by a 9% increase in the homicide rate; for Australia the figure is 8% (Graham 2011: 453). These increases are considerably higher than for most European countries.

Rather than undermining the hypothesis of a causal link between alcohol consumption and violence, the differences across countries is what one would expect for a phenomenon that is deeply embedded in webs of social meanings and practices. One would have had to suspect that something was awry if the studies had shown that the connection was the same strength across societies. As Kai Pernanan, a prominent researcher in the field puts it: "[N]o *single* causal model will explain why alcohol is implicated in so much violence . . . Alcohol, drinking, and drunkenness are too much a part of the symbolic fabric of society to have remained on an innocent, uncontaminated, natural-scientific level, where only its pharmacological properties determine the behavioral outcomes of its ingestion" (1991: 222; emphasis in original).

In addition to causing violent behavior, alcohol consumption has a range of other socially harmful effects, from serious diseases to automobile and machinery accidents to impaired performance at work. Yet, adults have a right to produce and consume alcohol. Given the host of harmful effects flowing from alcohol consumption, it is difficult to think that there are stronger grounds against a right to pornography than there are against a right to alcohol consumption. Indeed, it is difficult to think that the grounds are as strong in the case of pornography. The reason is not simply that the harmful effects of alcohol are of so many different kinds beyond its propensity to trigger violence. Rather, the reason also involves the relative strength of the evidence of population-wide effects of alcohol, in comparison with the evidence regarding pornography's population-wide effects.

The body of studies of that link alcohol consumption to increased levels of violence in society is substantially more convincing than the studies of the pornography-harm connection. Alcohol studies include many statistically rigorous analyses of population-level data, confirming that, as alcohol consumption increases in society, so does violence. As we have seen, it was this kind of population-level study that proved crucial to establishing that smoking causes cancer. And pornography research suffers from a dearth of such studies.

There is another consideration to examine in comparing pornography and alcohol consumption. Drinking alcohol is not a basic liberty: it is part of the weaker general right to liberty, and it seems that, even so, the right to one's gin and tonic is not nullified by the fact that some people abuse alcohol and end up doing grievous harm to others. In contrast, sexual autonomy is a basic liberty and pornography use is an element of that liberty. So in comparing pornography with alcohol consumption, pornography consumption involves a stronger right combined with weaker evidence of social harm. It is difficult for me to see, then, how a right to one's gin and tonic is not nullified but a right to pornography is so.

Watson contends that there is an important difference between the two forms of consumption: the harm from pornography falls mainly on women, while the harm from alcohol is more even spread across men and women. And I agree with her that, other factors held constant, diminishing the harm-gap between women and men is an important consideration. But the absolute level of personal safety for women is also an important factor, a point not lost on the women advocates of Prohibition, and increasing that level substantially should be an important priority, even when that increase can be accomplished by means that do not reduce the harm-gap. The population-level studies of alcohol provide good evidence that curtailing alcohol use would in fact produce a significant absolute improvement in women's safety. And yet the relatively weak general right to liberty still seems sufficient to ground a person's right to his gin and tonic. If that right survives and curtailing alcohol use must be accomplished by education and other means that do not involve legal prohibition, then I do not see how a right to the basic liberty involved in pornography use can be extinguished, even if extra weight is given to reducing gender inequality. Additionally, in sizing up the morally wrongful harm that results from alcohol, it is important to ask, not just who is harmed, but also whether those who are harmed bear any responsibility for the harm they suffer. Even if harm to blameworthy parties is not to be entirely disregarded, it should not carry the same weight as the harm wrongfully done to persons who are not to blame. And it might well be true that the harm caused by alcohol consumption to those who are not to blame falls disproportionately on women. Let me explain.

Drunken men beat up other drunken men, who are sometimes all too willing to engage in battle. But such men also beat up women who do not wish to engage in battle and who bear no responsibility for the violent conduct to which they are subjected. And it is no accident that drunken men, when stimulated to violence by the alcohol they have consumed, often choose women to beat up rather than to physically attack other men. On average, women are not only smaller and have less muscle mass than men; they are often living with the man who has become inebriated and so they can be beaten up in the privacy of the home. Starting a physical fight with another man, by contrast, would typically require a battle against a more evenly matched opponent in a public setting like a street or bar. So there is some reason to think that women do suffer disproportionately from the wrongful harm caused by alcohol and, to that extent, curtailing alcohol consumption would reduce the morally relevant harm-gap between men and women.

One might deny that there is any right to consume alcohol and so my whole argument falls through. But why is there no such right, even a weak one as part of a general right to liberty? It would seem that, by itself, the abuse of alcohol by some cannot extinguish the right for all. Going down that argumentative path makes it difficult to see how anyone can have a right to anything. Even tableware can be used to commit murder. And the point remains that the evidence of social harm, and of harm to women, is much stronger in the case of alcohol.

3.6 SLASHER MOVIES AND
THE ROLLING STONES

Donnerstein and his coauthors assert that "the most well-documented finding in the social science literature [regarding the connection between violence and depictions of sex] is that all sexually violent material in our society, whether sexually *explicit* or not, tends to promote aggression against women" (1987: 179). And a commission established by U.S. Attorney General Edward Meese found that "so-called 'slasher films', which depict a great deal of violence connected with an undeniably sexual theme but less sexual explicitness than materials that are truly pornographic, are likely to produce [harmful] consequences . . . to a greater extent than most materials available in 'adults only' pornographic outlets." The Commission found that "once a certain level of sexual content is reached, increases in this variable are not as important as increases in violence. In other words, increasing violence results in more harmful consequences than increasing sexual explicitness" (Donnerstein et al. 1987: 175).

For reasons explained earlier, I am much more skeptical of the social science findings than are Donnerstein and his colleagues. The empirical evidence for regarding the sex-violence combination as harmful at the societal level is still lacking. There is a dearth of adequate population-level studies of the matter, and, in the laboratory, violence alone has all of the effects that the sex-violence combination displays: increased aggression against women, increased acceptance of the rape myth, increased callousness toward female victims of rape, and so on (Donnerstein et al.

109–112 and 123–135). It might be asserted that the sex-violence combination increases these effects even more than violence alone, but this assertion remains a piece of speculation.

However, Donnerstein's conclusions seem to me to be quite plausible and better supported than the claims commonly made by anti-pornography feminists that sexually explicit material that is degrading to women causes a range of social harms to women. Notwithstanding those claims, Donnerstein and his colleagues write, "To date, the evidence supporting the contention that so-called degrading [but nonviolent] pornographic materials . . . are harmful is sparse and inconsistent" (171). So should we conclude that, even if it would be wrong to legally suppress all pornography, the suppression of material that combines sex with violence should be subject to such suppression? I do not think so. Let me explain why, beginning with the Rolling Stones and then turning to slasher movies.

In the mid-1970s, a billboard was put up in Hollywood, triggering a protracted feminist protest (Bronstein 2011: 93–122). The billboard advertised the Rolling Stones's album *Black and Blue* and showed a scantily clad woman, hands tied up over her head, breasts partially exposed but not showing the nipples, bruised legs spread and straddling the facial images of Mick Jagger and the other band members. Pubic hair and genitalia were not visible. The woman's countenance suggested that she was sexually aroused, and the words on the billboard reinforced that suggestion: "I'm 'Black and Blue' from the Rolling Stones and I love it." This billboard was not sexually explicit; it was sexually suggestive. The same goes for its violent character: the violence was implied but not shown.

Jagger was not depicted whipping or hitting the woman, but the image suggested that we were looking at the aftermath of such violence.

On Susan Brison's view, material that is "violent, degrading [and] misogynistic" (2014: 321) is legitimately subject to legal suppression, because individuals have no moral right to the material. The Stones's image seems clearly to count as such material. So it would seem that Brison is committed to the claim, not simply that the Stones could be properly criticized for using the image, but that they had no right to do so. In contrast, I claim that, even though the Stones were rightly criticized for their gross indifference to violence against women and for effectively condoning such violence, they had a right to use the image. Let us examine in more detail the disagreement between Brison and me by turning to the more graphic violence of slasher films.

Such films are horrifically and explicitly violent; the violence is uniformly directed against women; there is a sexual dimension to the violence; and it is difficult for me think that the films do not express a misogynistic attitude. Because these movies are aimed primarily at general entertainment and not at being used for sex, I do not include the right to see them under the right of sexual autonomy. Instead, it seems to me that the claim to view them lies straightforwardly under a different basic liberty, namely, freedom of speech and expression.

On my view, the decision about whether to view these movies rightly lies with the individual. No other person or group has decision-making authority in this respect: not the individual's family or friends or neighbors, not the community at large. Others are at liberty to dissuade the individual from viewing the films and to modify or break off personal relations with him if they see fit. But they are not at liberty to block him from entering the theater showing the films or to seize his video copies of the films or to program his computer so that he cannot get access to them. Decision-making authority lies with him. That is what having a moral right to view the films amounts to.

If Brison wishes to challenge my view, then she must explain where decision-making authority lies, if not with the individual. She can point to the social harm done by such films and assert such harm nullifies any claim of a right to view them. But she needs to say where decision-making authority lies. If not the individual, who, then has the authority to decide whether the individual gets to view the films? I do not think that there is any answer to that question that does not contradict the principles of a society committed to freedom of speech and expression. Even if one accepts the view of the evidence presented by the social scientists most supportive of the idea that slasher films cause social harm to women, it does not follow that the individual lacks decision-making authority. It is telling that Donnerstein and his colleagues do not support taking decisions out of the hands of the individual but rather call for "educational programs that enable viewers to make wiser choices about the media to which they expose themselves" (1987: 179). Such an approach is perfectly consistent with the position that there is a moral right to see slasher films, and, in my judgment, provides a more reasonable view of the issues than one that would insist that there is no such right and that some agent other than the individual has the moral authority to determine whether such films are seen.

NOTE

1. Malamuth's studies are the exception in explicitly indicating that the subjects were told that they would be viewing material of a sexual nature.

4

The MacKinnon-Dworkin Ordinance

SEVERAL DECADES AGO, CATHARINE MACKINNON and Andrea Dworkin drafted legislation to embody and implement their idea that pornography should be treated as a civil rights issue for women. They wrote, "Pornography is a discriminatory practice based on sex which denies women equal opportunities in society" (1997: 439). The legislation went on to define pornography as:

> the graphic sexually explicit subordination of women, whether in pictures or in words, that also includes one or more of the following:
> 1. Women are presented as sexual objects who enjoy pain or humiliation; or
> 2. Women are presented as sexual objects who experience sexual pleasure in being raped; or
> 3. Women are presented as sexual objects tied up or cut up or mutilated or bruised or physically hurt, or as dismembered or truncated or fragmented or severed into body parts; or
> 4. Women are presented as being penetrated by objects or animals; or
> 5. Women are presented in scenarios of degradation, injury, abusement, torture, shown as filthy or inferior,

bleeding or bruised, or hurt in a context that makes
these conditions sexual; [or]
6. Women are presented as sexual objects for domination, conquest, violation, exploitation, possession, or
   use, or through postures of servility and submission
   or display. (1997: 444)

The legislation empowered women to bring civil lawsuits
against persons involved in the production, circulation,
or display of pornography for having committed one or
more of the following violations: (a) trafficking in pornography, (b) coercing a person into pornographic performance, (c) forcing pornography on a person, and (d) assault
or physical attack directly caused by specific pornographic
material.

The legislation was vociferously criticized in a number
of quarters as a form of censorship and declared unconstitutional by the highest federal court to hear a challenge to
it. But MacKinnon and Dworkin rejected the notion that the
ordinance imposed censorship. MacKinnon testified at the
hearings on the ordinance in Indianapolis, "Classically,
[the ordinance] is not censorship or a ban in a way that
the state, that is the government, is involved actively
in [taking] actions to enforce it. It is a civil rights law, a law
that allows those people who have been harmed . . . to bring
actions against the people who have done that harm, including . . . the people who profit from it" (MacKinnon and
Dworkin 1997: 271). Later, she wrote, "Neither the ordinance nor the hearings have anything in common with censorship. . . . [They] freed previously suppressed speech" (8).

The idea that the ordinance is not a matter of censorship because the government is not "involved actively" in

enforcing it is wholly unpersuasive. The government *would* have been actively involved in enforcing the ordinance, because courts and other government bodies would have issued orders and injunctions and would have imposed fines pursuant to the law. It is true that the government bodies would have been acting in response to complaints brought by citizens, but that fact hardly means that the government would have been a passive bystander.

Moreover, the history of censorship shows that nongovernmental organizations can take the initiative in the suppression of published material. The New York Society for the Suppression of Vice, founded by Anthony Comstock in 1873, was chartered by the state to help enforce its antiobscenity laws. Magistrates were required by law to issue search warrants upon the complaint of the Society, and the Society was entitled to a portion of the fines imposed by the courts against individuals or companies convicted of violating anti-obscenity laws (De Grazia 1992: 119). At the Society's instigation, many works of literature, including *Ulyssses*, were found obscene in judicial proceedings. So the argument that the MacKinnon-Dworkin ordinance does not establish censorship because government does not take the initiative in enforcing the terms of the ordinance rests on a non sequitur.

MacKinnon also claims that the ordinance (and the hearings on it) "freed previously suppressed speech." Yet, it fails to follow that the ordinance does not establish censorship. Freeing speech that was previously suppressed is not incompatible with suppressing other speech that was previously free. If the ordinance were to do both things, then its suppressive aspect would seem to be a matter of censorship, even if its liberatory aspect was not so. And even if the ordinance would have freed more speech than it suppressed, assuming that such a judgment makes sense, the suppressive aspect would still seem to be censorious. Additionally, I do not see how the suppressive aspect of the ordinance can be reasonably denied. The ordinance aimed to put into the hands of women legal tools by which the women, in conjunction with government enforcement bodies, could suppress the circulation of pornography. MacKinnon herself states that the ordinance was "the first effective threat to [pornography's] existence" (1997: 20). I think that the claim was hyperbolic, even ignoring the subsequent development of the Internet. But the claim does show that suppression was not some unintended side effect of the ordinance but its raison d'être.

I think that MacKinnon's most basic reason for denying that the ordinance has "anything in common with censorship" is that she conceives of censorship as something that the powerful in society impose on the weak and vulnerable. Thus, she writes, "These days, censorship occurs less through explicit state policy than through official and unofficial privileging of powerful groups and viewpoints" (1993: 77). As she sees the matter, her ordinance is a legal tool for the weak and vulnerable to protect themselves against the powerful, that is, the pornography industry and its apologists. But even if we accept that important point and also conceive of censorship as an act of the powerful, it still does not follow that her ordinance has *nothing* in common with censorship. What it has in common is that it is designed to suppress the production, circulation, and consumption of a certain kind of published material.

I do not insist on claiming that the MacKinnon-Dworkin law imposes censorship. What matters is that the law aims, and can be reasonably foreseen, to suppress a certain sort of sexual material. The principal engine of suppression would have been the trafficking provision, which outlaws "the production, sale, exhibition, or distribution of pornography" and provides that "any woman may file a complaint as a woman acting against the subordination of women" (1997: 449). In other words, a women who files a complaint under the trafficking provision need not show that she was personally harmed by the pornographic material against which she brings the complaint or specify the way in which she was harmed. It is, as it were, indefeasibly assumed that she was harmed just by being a woman.

MacKinnon and Dworkin did take some significant steps to limit the broad sweep that the trafficking provision would otherwise have had. For example, in the Indianapolis version of the ordinance, the provision would not apply to materials that were pornographic solely in virtue of element (6) of their definition, namely, that "[w]omen are presented as sexual objects for domination, conquest, violation, exploitation, possession, or use, or through postures of servility and submission or display." Depending on how the other five elements are interpreted, this limitation could make a significant difference to how suppressive the law would be. But I think that MacKinnon overstates matters when she claims that the limitation "requires that violence be shown or done for the materials to be actionable under the trafficking provision" (1997: 8 n. 23). Violence is not necessarily shown or done in presenting a woman as enjoying humiliation (1), as being penetrated by an object (4), or even as being sexually degraded (5).

A great deal of sexually explicit material that men use as part of sex fits under elements (1)–(5) of the

MacKinnon-Dworkin definition. And so the trafficking provision is a central to making the ordinance "the first effective threat to [pornography's] existence" (1997: 20). It is for that very reason that I regard their ordinance as transgressing the right to sexual autonomy. In previous sections, I have already explained why I do not accept the idea that the right to pornography for which I argue is overridden or nullified by the harm that pornography is said to do. I will not repeat my reasoning here but simply point to the extensive way in which the MacKinnon-Dworkin ordinance oversteps the boundaries of that right.

At the Indianapolis hearings, MacKinnon pointed out that the law does not apply to any material that is not sexually explicit. Addressing the city council and defending the law against detractors who complained that it would cover great works of art and literature, she went on to explain, "Very few grand masters, old classics, all the things that everyone is going to try to tell you are so legitimate and yet would be covered by this law—on the whole, they are not sexually explicit. If the sex is not explicit, we are not talking about this law" (1997: 275).

But the fact is that many "grand masters" painted and sculpted works every bit as sexually explicit as forms of contemporary pornography to which MacKinnon objects. A.W. Eaton has a more accurate understanding of Western art history, pointing out that the female nude is an entire genre of Western art, a genre that sexually objectifies women. Eaton cites many examples of great artworks that are not only sexually explicit but are also sexually objectifying. She writes that the works, painted by, among others, Titian, Velasquez, Ingres, Giorgione, and Manet, are "quite beautiful and compelling and display dazzling skill and creativity" (2012: 307).

But at the same time, the paintings "promote women's subordination to men" (308) by representing women as sexually vulnerable, soft, and weak. These works and their reproductions would arguably be subject to the MacKinnon-Dworkin ordinance. Even if they would not be subject to the trafficking provision, because they satisfy only element (6) of the ordinance's definition of pornography, they would still fall under the prohibition against "the forcing of pornography on any man, woman, child, or transsexual in any place of employment, in education, in a home, or in any public place" (1997: 443). The same goes for photographs of classical statutes of Aphrodite and images of the sexually explicit artwork on ancient Greek and Roman vases and the celebrated sculptures by Bernini representing the rapes of Persephone and Daphne.

There is, in short, a considerable amount of great Western art that would have counted as actionable pornography under the terms of the ordinance. I do not think that such art serves as masturbation material for men much anymore: there is more effective material readily available for that purpose. Accordingly, I do not think that sexual autonomy is an issue in this regard. But freedom of expression certainly is an issue here, and the implications of the ordinance for great works of art show that it goes much too far in limiting the right of freedom of expression. Those works are not unproblematic, as Eaton shows, but they should not be subjected to the legal prohibition imposed on them by the MacKinnon-Dworkin ordinance. Subjecting them to such a prohibition is the result, in my view, of a decided lack of perspective that fails to register their aesthetic value while simultaneously overestimating the role they play in perpetuating women's inequality.

One of the controversial features of the Mackinnon-Dworkin ordinance concerns its implications for lesbian pornography. Much of the controversy has focused on the way in which Canadian authorities have treated such pornography. In 1992, the Canadian Supreme Court issued a landmark ruling upholding a conviction under a provision of the national criminal code that deemed "obscene" and outlawed any material characterized by "an undue exploitation of sex" (*R. v. Butler* 1992: para. 42). What made the ruling so important was its explicit recognition and validation of the concern that pornography harms women. The Court held that material is obscene "not because it offends against morals but because it is perceived by public opinion to be harmful to society, particularly women" (para. 50). Elaborating on the kind of material that would count as obscene, the Court went on to say that "[t]he portrayal of sex coupled with violence will almost always constitute the undue exploitation of sex" (para. 60). And the Court ruled that criminal prohibitions on material that unduly exploited sex did not violate the nation's *Charter of Rights and Freedoms*, which guarantees "freedom of thought, belief, opinion and expression, including freedom of the press and other media of communication" (sec. 2b).

MacKinnon wrote favorably of the Canadian Supreme Court's analysis in *Butler*. She lauded the Court for understanding that "harm to women . . . *was* harm to society as a whole" (1993: 101) and for recognizing "the reality of inequality in the issues before it" (103). And she contrasted the Canadian Supreme Court's approach with that of the US federal appeals court that struck down her ordinance as a violation of the Free Speech Clause of the First Amendment.

Unlike the Canadian court, the US court failed to take seriously women's inequality and the role of pornography in producing that inequality.

At the same time that the Canadian Supreme Court incorporated feminist concerns about pornography in its free speech doctrine, the Canadian Customs Service was engaged in targeting gay and lesbian pornography for seizure at the border. Those seizures provoked outrage and legal action from the Canadian gay and lesbian community. Because MacKinnon had written favorably of the opinion in *Butler*, some persons evidently came to the conclusion that her legal approach was responsible for what Canadian Customs was doing. She and Dworkin issued a press release in which they pointed out that Canada had not adopted their ordinance and that there were substantial differences between Canada's legal approach and their own: "Canada . . . has not adopted our statutory definition of pornography; it has not adopted our civil (as opposed to criminal) approach to pornography; nor has Canada adopted any of the five civil causes of action we proposed (coercion, assault, force, trafficking, defamation)" (1994). Importantly, MacKinnon and Dworkin noted that Canadian Customs had been targeting gay and lesbian materials well before *Butler*: "Canada Customs has a long record of homophobic seizures, producing an equally long record of loud and justifiable outrage from the Canadian lesbian and gay community. There is no evidence that whatever is happening at the border now is different from what happened before the *Butler* decision" (1994).

MacKinnon and Dworkin are surely right in saying that the discriminatory policies of Canadian Customs cannot be sensibly attributed to their legal approach. However, it does not follow that their approach raises no legitimate concerns from the perspective of lesbian pornography consumers. Lesbian pornography would be subject to the same legal restrictions under the MacKinnon-Dworkin ordinance as heterosexual pornography. Women can be "presented as sex objects for domination, conquest, violation, exploitation, possession, or use, or through postures of servility and submission or display" (MacKinnon-Dworkin 1997: 444), even when it is other women who are doing the dominating and no men are involved. Such pornography would be subject to suppression by the MacKinnon-Dworkin ordinance, and, yet, there is virtually no social scientific evidence regarding the societal effects of lesbian pornography of that kind. Accordingly, the ordinance should be regarded as overbroad, even setting aside my arguments in Chapter 3 that question the adequacy of the studies purporting to show that, at the macro-social level, heterosexual pornography causes harm to women.

5

Pornography
as Subordinating Speech

I POINTED OUT IN CHAPTER 2 that the MacKinnon-Dworkin definition of pornography does not simply stipulate that pornography depicts the subordination of women but that it *does subordinate* women. Explaining her view, MacKinnon writes that "authoritatively *saying* someone is inferior is largely how structures of status and differential treatment are demarcated and actualized. Words and images are how people are placed in hierarchies" (1993: 31). In her view, pornography authoritatively says that women are inferior to men and are to be the sexual servants of men. Put another way, the idea is that pornography is regarded as having the authority to prescribe norms of sexual conduct and that it prescribes a norm that deems women to be the sexual servants of men. Of course, this authority is not truly normative in the sense that pornographers have a moral right to prescribe such norms. But it is *de facto* authority insofar as people accept the norms prescribed by pornography because (i.e., on the grounds that) they are prescribed by pornography.

I am skeptical about the claim that pornography "authoritatively says" anything. Let's start with the authority that pornography is alleged to possess. Leslie Green rejects MacKinnon's view that pornography authoritatively deems women to be the sexual inferiors of men, and he contends that "[i]n a society which endorses freedom of expression, pornography is private, non-authoritative speech" (1998: 298). I think that he is right. Rae Langton defends MacKinnon's view and thinks that Green is wrong. Let's examine the issue.

Green says that, to be *de facto* authoritative, norms must be "generally accepted as setting binding standards of behavior," and he argues that the norms prescribed by pornography are not generally accepted. Langton counters that there can be authoritative norms that are only "locally accepted" in a given community: the norms might not have "general perceived legitimacy" but they would have "local perceived legitimacy" (2009: 97–98). And if a person is a member of such a local community, then the norms are *de facto* authoritative relative to him, even if it deems him to be subordinate in the local hierarchy. Moreover, if those persons in the local community who accept the norm have considerable power, then the norm might be effective in subordinating him: "Where he is, he is subordinate" (98).

Langton's claims about the possibility of local authority/ perceived legitimacy are true. One can easily imagine a local community having its own authoritative norms that are not accepted by the rest of society. Amish communities are like that. But where is the local community that is the pornographic equivalent of the Amish, so that the norms of pornography are locally authoritative in the way that Amish norms are authoritative in their communities? Langton does not say where these pornography communities are.

One might suggest that she could assert that pornography is so pervasive that every local community is the pornographic equivalent of the Amish, but then it is puzzling why she makes so much of the distinction between general and local perceived legitimacy.

Langton insists, though, that if "those in [a woman's] community who accept the norms of pornography . . . have the power to hire and fire her, control her education, affect her civil rights, and they sometimes exercise that power . . . [then] it is not true that 'in these circumstances, pornography . . . has a character of a private view'" (2009: 100). I beg to differ. First, just because a man accepts the norms of pornography, it does not follow that he regards pornography as authoritative. He must accept the norms *because* (i.e., on the ground that) they are prescribed by pornography. Second, even if some male employers, educators, or politicians in a given community accept pornographic norms because the norms are prescribed by pornography, it does not follow that a belief in the validity of pornography's norms is something other than a private view. Rather, such a belief is a private view that motivates those men to do things that run contrary to public law. Consider the analogy with religion. Some religions involve racist views, and there are men and women in local communities who subscribe to those racist views because their religion tells them that the views are right. Some of these men and women are employers, educators, or politicians, and sometimes they exercise their powers in a racist way. These facts do not give their racist religious views the mantle of public authority. It is the laws that have the mantle of authority, and the laws declare their conduct illegal.

Langton points to "an interesting thought" (2009: 100) that Green expresses in passing near the end of his piece: perhaps pornography is not speech at all and so it makes no sense to think of pornography as saying anything, authoritatively or not. But if pornography is not speech, she reasons, then *"free speech* does not protect pornography" (101), contrary to what Green had apparently been arguing. However, I am not troubled by the implications of the thought that there is much pornography that is not speech and thus is unprotected by the principle of freedom of expression. As I have argued, such pornography is covered by the right of sexual autonomy, and the remainder of sexually explicit materials—Joyce's *Ulysses*, Bernini's statute of the rape of Daphne, and other less notable examples of literature and art—clearly are covered by the principle of free expression.

Additionally, I do not think that Langton or anyone else has explained how pornography *says* anything. The philosopher J. L. Austin has explained how you can do many things with *words*: make promises, render verdicts, issue warnings, and so on (1962). Words are governed by a complicated set of rules that enable us to do such things, and linguists and philosophers have made explicit and analyzed those rules. But no one has told us what the analogous rules are for pornography. To my mind, rather than thinking of pornography as saying anything, much less anything authoritative, it makes more sense to think of it as *showing* something. What pornography shows is sex, and most pornography shows sex in which men are dominant and women subordinate. I do not doubt that the showing of such sex might lead some men to think that sexual relations between men and women ought to

be that way, or—more likely—that the showing can reinforce a preexisting belief that sex ought to be that way.
But we do not need the idea that pornography says anything to understand such effects.

MacKinnon is right to say that "[w]ords and images
are how people are placed in hierarchies" (1993: 31). But
words and images accomplish this placement in different
ways, words by saying and images by showing. So then
can we simply modify MacKinnon's formulation and assert that pornography authoritatively shows that women
are the sexual subordinates of men? I do not think so, because pornography is not regarded as authoritative by society generally or by any local community within society.
MacKinnon might argue that the saturation of society
by pornography shows that it has "general perceived legitimacy," to use Langton's phrase. But something can be
widespread in society without being authoritative within
the society. Being (*de facto*) authoritative in a society is a
matter of how something is generally regarded: something
is authoritative when what it shows (or says—for words) is
regarded as right because that is what it shows. "Because"
here means "on the grounds that"; it refers to a logical relation involving considerations that provide rational support;
it does not refer to a causal relation involving stimulus and
effect. That there is widespread use of pornography among
men does not establish that men regard women's sexual
subordination as right because—that is, on the grounds
that—pornography shows sex that way. Widespread use
does confirm the obvious, however: men get turned on by
pornography.

Confusion arises due to the ambiguity of "because" between its logical and causal senses. Even if pornography

caused many men to think that women are properly their sexual subordinates, it would not follow that there are many men who take what pornography shows as rational support for holding such a view of women. It is true that some of the male partners of the women who testified at the hearings on the MacKinnon-Dworkin ordinance seem to have regarded pornography as authoritative. But, as I argued, those male partners can hardly be considered as representative of men in society generally.

I remember a pornographic movie that I saw around 1970, in which the sex scenes were introduced by a (pretend) physician, wearing a white lab coat and explaining that the scenes to follow provided scientific insight into human sexuality. I was a naïve college student at the time, but even so, I understood that the scenes involving the physician were not to be taken seriously. I would be very surprised if anyone in the audience took them as anything other than ludicrous.

If there is sexually explicit material that carries authority in the way that MacKinnon and Langton suggest, then it is not the run-of-the-mill pornography on which their attention is focused. Rather, it is the great works of art that Eaton examines in her critical analysis of the female nude as a genre of art in the Western tradition. She writes,

> Many of the works . . . are quite beautiful and compelling and display dazzling skill and creativity. This not only makes the message of female inferiority and male superiority more compelling, but . . . protects it from feminist criticism. . . . Art's venerated status invests this message . . . with special authority, making it an especially effective way of promoting sex inequality. (2012: 307–308)

Run-of-the-mill pornography lacks such a "venerated status," and, notwithstanding its widespread use by men, pornography retains even in our sexually liberated society the foul odor of something impure, dirty, and disreputable. In general, men do not proudly and publicly proclaim their use of pornography, and one of the reasons for the popularity of Internet pornography is that, unlike an "adult" bookstore or movie theater, a man does not need to appear in public in order to get access to the material. It should not be surprising, then, that polls have consistently shown that the large majority of Americans have a dim attitude toward pornography. Even as recently as 2011 and 2012, more than twice as many Americans thought that pornography was "morally wrong" than found it "morally acceptable." The figures for 2011 were 66% *v.* 30% and for 2012, 64% *v.* 31% (Newport 2013: 189 and 2014: 228). The MacKinnon-Langton view of pornography's authority is difficult to square with this view of pornography as disreputable.

By contrast, the great works of art that Eaton discusses do not have a disreputable side, in the eyes of society. The works are proudly displayed in museums and publicly honored in many ways; not only is there no foul odor of impurity or dirtiness that attaches to the works, they are regarded as among the most magnificent achievements of the human creative capacity. And, as Eaton points out, there is good reason for them to be so regarded. It is these works, not pornography, that have a plausible claim to *de facto* authority in matters of sexuality.

6

Conclusion: The Big Historical Picture

FOR MANY CENTURIES, SEXUALLY EXPLICIT representations adorned the public and private places of the centers of Western civilization. Ancient Greek vases and cups were decorated with images of various forms of sexual activity, including anal and oral sex and orgies, and were likely used, not simply for drinking, but for sexual arousal as well. In ancient Greece and Rome, there were nude statutes of females, which were apparently visited by young men for the purpose of masturbating (Stearns 2009: 35). According to one story, a sailor was so aroused by a famous nude statute of the goddess of sexual desire and pleasure, Aphrodite, that he had "intercourse" with it and left semen stains on the statute as evidence of his lovemaking. In Rome, depictions of the god Priapus, showing him sporting a gigantic erection, were common in homes and public places. The Emperor Tiberius was said to have been given a painting portraying the Greek heroine Atalanta performing fellatio (Suetonius: "Tiberius" secs. 43–45). And lamps with explicit sexual scenes depicted on them seem to have adorned many middle-class Roman bedrooms, undoubtedly placed there for purposes of arousing sexual appetites.

Such sexually explicit representations raised no social controversies. The representations were not judged to be filthy or corrosive of moral character. There was no debate about whether they should be made illegal. There were certainly no condemnations charging that they promoted inequality between men and women. The representations were socially accepted as a matter of course. If there was a time in Western history when pornography was regarded as authoritative, it was in ancient Greece and Rome.

However, the social acceptance of sexually explicit representations disappeared entirely when Christianity came to dominate Western culture in the early middle ages. The new religion brought with it a sexual revolution. Although the French philosopher Michel Foucault suggested that there was no great change from pagan to Christian sexual morality (1990), Kathy Gaca makes a much stronger case that a "sharp and irreconcilable divide" (2003: 293) separated pagan and Christian culture on matters of sex. Foucault might have been led astray by the fact that many ancient philosophers were advocates of sexual restraint, apparently placing them closer to the Church fathers than to the common view within pagan culture. And indeed there were ancient pagan thinkers who argued that sex should only be practiced within marriage and strictly for purposes of procreation, a position that would become part of the orthodox Christian view. Thus, a Pythagorean thinker writing under the name Charondas insisted that "into nothing else [but his wife] should [a man] ejaculate the seed of his children. . . . Nature had made seed for the sake [of] producing children" (Gaca: 108). And the Stoic philosophers Seneca and Musonius maintained that the only acceptable form of sex was marital and reproductive (Gaca: 93, 111, and 114). Some pagans also advocated restraint, on the ground that excessive sexual emissions by men would weaken them (Foucault 1990: 15–17).

Yet, Christian attitudes toward sex were quite different than even those held by these very sexually restrained pagan philosophers, and pagan culture was far more permissive in sexual matters than Christian civilization would turn out to be. It is a mistake to draw the distinction by claiming that, in contrast to Christian culture, "among the ancients, sex was unashamedly joyous, in reading as in practice" (Loth 1961: 47). The ancients had plenty of room for sexual shame: being penetrated by a sexual act was treated as shameful for males (and an element of the degraded status of all women), which is why intercrural sex was deemed the proper form of sexual activity between male lovers. Moreover, much sex in the ancient world was forced upon slaves by their owners. But any fair portrait of the ancient pagan sexual world would show it to be quite alien to what Christianity would construct. The Greeks and Romans practiced pederasty, with the Greeks, especially, taking it for granted that older males would have sexual relations with young teenage boys as part of the process by which boys were mentored by the older men about the role that adult male citizens were expected to play. Prostitution was pervasive and legal, while divorce, abortion, contraception, and infanticide were regarded as simple matters of expedience and not as morally charged issues (Hubbard 2010; Richlin 2010). Moreover, as I have noted, in both Greek and Roman culture, depictions of naked bodies and sexual activity were part of the everyday visible environment. The

Christian sexual revolution would radically change all of these facets of pagan sexual life.

In the name of their new religion, many early Christians renounced sex entirely. Tatian held that even spouses who have sex with one another are "enslaved to fornication, and to the devil" (Gaca: 225). Julius Cassianus rejected sexual intercourse per se, holding that Satan was responsible for introducing humans to the practice (Pagels: 27). Similarly, St. Jerome declared that "all sexual intercourse is unclean" and that Adam and Eve were virgins before the Fall (Pagels: 94). But even Christian thinkers who did not go to such extremes still had a much darker view of sexuality than the most sexually restrained pagans. Clement held that sexual pleasure within or outside of marriage was evil and that the mere desire for such pleasure was a form of defiance against God. In Clement's view, Christ had made it possible, through his grace, for married Christians to have intercourse, and thereby to procreate, without experiencing any pleasure (Gaca: 264). In the end, orthodox Christianity settled on a sexual morality that was more moderate than the views of Clement and Tatian but was still quite different from pagan sexual ideas and practices.

The more moderate Christian sexual morality was expressed in some of St. Paul's writings and later developed by St. Augustine. Paul regarded abstinence as the preferred path for Christians, but he recommended to unmarried Christians who could not pursue such a path that they get married, "for it is better to marry than to burn with passion." He also advised married Christians to have sexual intercourse "so that Satan will not tempt you because of your lack of self-control" (1 Corinthians 7). The temptations that Paul had in mind were practices central to pagan sexual morality, including prostitution, same-sex relations, and other non-marital and non-procreative sexual activities.

Augustine, too, denounced pagan sexual morality, without demanding complete abstinence. He wrote that "marital intercourse makes something good out of the evil of lust," by channeling lust into "the honorable task of begetting children" (1996: 46). Still, Augustine held that "continence from all intercourse is certainly better than marital intercourse which takes place for the purposes of begetting children" (48). Abstinence was thus the preferred path for those Christians who were capable of successfully pursuing it. And marital intercourse not aimed at procreation was a sin, though a pardonable one, while "adultery or fornication is . . . a mortal sin" (48). Additionally, Augustine characterized as "evil" the sexual pleasure that Christian married couples experienced during sexual intercourse aimed at procreation, even though he also insisted that such pleasure was not "immodest" (92) because it was being put to a good use.

Augustine's dim view of sexual desire and pleasure stemmed from the idea that, in our fallen world, human sex organs—specifically penises—did not respond to the individual's will and reason but rather to his lust. Among evil desires, "lust is baser than others, and if not resisted it commits horrible impurities" (1996: 91–92). Augustine allowed for the possibility that, prior to the Fall, there was sexual desire in paradise, but added that, in such a scenario, sexual desire "would never even be present unless there were a need; it would never force itself into a person's conscious thoughts with its inordinate and illicit attraction . . . [and] would have followed the person's will with ready and obedient compliance. But . . . this is definitely *not* the way concupiscence is now" (104).

For a millennium and more, Christian morality and culture would condemn any form of sex other than intercourse within marriage and for the sake of having children. Sex for pleasure was an anathema, a surrender to the evil of lust. Christian morality would also sternly disapprove of the portrayal of the unclothed human body, a disapproval that even the artistic geniuses of the Renaissance could not entirely defeat. A Church Council of the mid-16th century ordered that nude figures in Michelangelo's monumental painting in the Sistine Chapel, *The Last Judgment*, be painted over to cover the sex organs. A Vatican official had complained that "it was a very disgraceful thing to have made in so honorable a place all those nude figures showing their nakedness so shamelessly, and that it was a work not for the chapel of a Pope, but for a brothel or tavern" (Vasari 69–70).

Two centuries later the king of Naples locked away sexually explicit works by Michelangelo and Titian, among others, in a museum's secret room, safeguarded by three locks. The king had the room sealed off with bricks for good measure (Rowland: 8). In addition to works by great Renaissance artists, the room contained sexually explicit depictions found in wall paintings, pottery, sculpture, and other artifacts from the ancient Roman city of Pompeii. Those artifacts had been unearthed in excavations starting in the 18th century and had been the original impetus for creating the "Cabinet of Obscene Objects," as it was initially called. The term "pornography" was coined in the 19th century by art catalogers to refer to those objects (Kendrick: 11). Although some access to the objects was permitted in the late 19th and early 20th centuries, as late as 1931, the fascist government in Italy tried to deny all access to the "Pornographic Collection," as it had come to be called. But the ban was ignored and so the government resorted to restricting access to "artists bearing valid documents testifying to their profession" and "personnel on official visits who shall make application" (De Simone: 169).

However, social, political, and economic forces that began to take hold in the West starting around the 18th century virtually ensured that questions about sexually explicit material would become a matter of broad public concern. Modernization and liberalization entailed that pornography could not be locked away in some special cabinet. Modernization involved the spread of markets, literacy, printed matter, and the formation of a public that would discuss matters of common interest. Liberalization involved the idea that individual liberty was not incompatible with modern life but an essential and valued feature of it. So it is not surprising that pornography started to become a public issue in the 18th century, when sexually explicit novels began to have wide circulation in France and, to a lesser extent, in England.

But the history of modern society is not a story of steady, uniform advance. The sexually explicit novels were not welcomed with open arms by governmental and religious authorities. The novels were read by many in the educated classes but were also legally banned. It was in the context of widening circulation of pornographic material along with official censure of such material that the legal doctrine of obscenity was formed and developed. The law was deployed by officials and their allies–men like Anthony

Comstock and the other members of the New York Society for the Suppression of Vice—to stem and reverse the tide of sexually explicit representations that seemed to them to be flooding society and threatening to undermine its very foundations. Such representations were declared obscene– filthy materials that corrupted the moral character of those into whose hands they fell—and were banned and burned.

This regime kept a lid on the circulation of sexually explicit material but was not entirely successful. Even when legally prohibited, much material still circulated underground, and, in a few instances, like the *Ulysses* case in American federal court, prohibitions were judicially overturned. Yet it was not until the sexual revolution of the 1960s that the lid came off almost entirely, and society started to become "saturated with pornography," as MacKinnon puts it (1993: 7 and 25) A dramatic increase in the circulation of pornography accompanied a new sexual morality that repudiated many of the restrictions of traditional Christian sexual ethics. Sex for pleasure and even some forms of sex outside of marriage became socially accepted. And pornography seemed to fit well into the new morality and particularly its acceptance of sex for pleasure.

Anti-pornography feminists point out that their arguments are not to be conflated with those resting on the idea of obscenity. MacKinnon has put the point by saying that pornography "is not a moral issue" (1987). She means that the issue, for feminists, is not about whether pornography corrupts the inner character of persons who are exposed to it or whether pornographic images and words are filthy. Rather, the issue of pornography is about inequality between men and women and the role that pornography plays in perpetuating that inequality. As MacKinnon writes, "What is wrong with pornography is that it hurts women and their equality. What is wrong with obscenity law is that this reality has no role in it" (1993: 88).

Nonetheless, I think that anti-pornography feminists might not have escaped the shadow of the idea of obscenity quite as neatly and cleanly as they might have thought. The social science experiments that they invoke to show that inegalitarian pornography harms women purportedly show that exposure to such pornography alters the attitudes of men toward women for the worse, making men more indifferent to the interests of women and more callous about the harm suffered by women in scenarios of sexual assault. I fail to see why such changes in attitudes are not a matter of men's moral character. To be sure, the changes, if they occur to the extent that anti-pornography feminists think, would have social consequences bearing on the inequality of men and women. And there are perfectly good uses of "morality" that restrict the term to matters of the inner character. But then one should say that pornography is not *only* a moral issue. One should not say that it is not a moral issue.

Moreover, the "obscenity" idea that certain sorts of sexually explicit material is filthy has found its way into anti-pornography feminist discourse. Here is what MacKinnon says: "Pornography offers [two] types of generic of sex: for those who want to wallow in filth without getting their hands dirty and for those who want to violate the pure and get only their hands wet" (1993: 24–25). I do not think that these words are some kind of slip on MacKinnon's part. She is deliberately conveying to the reader that she regards inegalitarian pornography as repulsive and dirty. At the same time, one should acknowledge that such repulsion is not the basis that anti-pornography feminists have for their condemnation of inegalitarian pornography. That basis is the harm that is said to be done to women.

I have argued that the evidence for such harm at the societal level is weak and inconsistent and so insufficient to defeat the idea that there is a moral right to pornography. There is much stronger evidence that alcohol consumption causes considerable harm to women (and men) than there is that pornography consumption does so. Yet, even though a person's right to drink alcohol is not sensibly regarded as a basic liberty, an adult still has the moral right to decide to drink: the choice is his or hers. It can be no less true with pornography, which does involve the basic liberty of sexual autonomy: the choice properly belongs to the individual.

REFERENCES

Augustine. 1996. *St. Augustine on Marriage and Sexuality.* Elizabeth A. Clark, ed. Washington, DC: Catholic University of America Press.

Austin, J. L. 1962. *How to Do Things with Words.* Cambridge, MA: Harvard University Press.

Babor, Thomas. 2010. *Alcohol: No Ordinary Commodity,* 2nd ed. Oxford, UK: Oxford University Press.

Bauserman, R. 1996. "Sexual Aggression and Pornography." *Basic and Applied Social Psychology* 8: 405–427.

Ben-Veniste, Richard. n.d. "Pornography and Sex Crime: The Danish Experience." *Technical Report of the Commission on Obscenity and Pornography* VII. Washington, DC: US Government Printing Office, pp. 245–261.

Berger, Fred R. 1977. "Pornography, Sex, and Censorship." *Social Theory and Practice* 4: 183–209.

Brison, Susan J. 2014. "'The Price We Pay'? Pornography and Harm." Andrew I. Cohen and Christopher H. Wellman, eds. *Contemporary Debates in Applied Ethics,* 2nd ed. Malden, MA: Wiley Blackwell, pp. 319–332.

———. 2004. "Torture, or 'Good Old American Pornography'." *Chronicle of Higher Education, Chronicle Review.* June 4. B10–11.

Bronstein, Carolyn. 2011. *Battling Pornography*. Cambridge, UK: Cambridge University Press.

Brownmiller, Susan. 1975. *Against Our Will: Men, Women, and Rape*. New York: Simon and Shuster.

Bushman, Brad J. 1993. "Human Aggression While Under the Influence of Alcohol and Other Drugs: An Integrative Research Review." *Current Directions in Psychological Science* 2: 148–152.

Byrne, Donn, and Kathryn Kelley. 1984. "Introduction: Pornography and Sex Research." Neil M. Malamuth and Edward Donnerstein, eds. *Pornography and Sexual Aggression*. New York: Academic Press, pp. 1–15.

Court, John H. 1976. "Pornography and Sex-Crimes: A Re-evaluation in the Light of Recent Trends Around the World." *International Journal of Criminology and Penology* 5: 129–157.

Dabhoiwala, Faramerz. 2014. "*Of Sexual Irregularities* by Jeremy Bentham—A Review." *The Guardian*. June 26. Available at http://www.theguardian.com/books/2014/jun/26/sexual-irregularities-morality-jeremy-bentham-review.

———. 2012. *The Origins of Sex*. Oxford, UK: Oxford University Press.

D'Amato, Anthony. 2006. "Porn Up, Rape Down." *Northwestern Public Law Research Paper 913013*. Available at http://papers.ssrn.com/sol3/papers.cfm?abstract_id=913013.

De Grazia, Edward. 1992. *Girls Lean Back Everywhere*. New York: Random House.

———. 1969. *Censorship Landmarks*. New York: Bowker.

De Simone, Antonio. 1975. "The History of the Museum and the Collection." Michael Grant et al., eds. *Eros in Pompeii*. New York: William Morrow, pp. 167–169.

Donnerstein, Edward, Daniel Linz, and Steven Penrod. 1987. *The Question of Pornography*. New York: Free Press.

Downs, Donald A. 1989. *The New Politics of Pornography*. Chicago: University of Chicago Press.

Dworkin, Andrea. 1997. "Brief *Amicus Curiae* of Andrea Dworkin." Catharine MacKinnon and Andrea Dworkin, eds. *In Harm's Way: The Pornography Civil Rights Hearings*. Cambridge, MA: Harvard University Press, pp. 310–320.

———. 1989. *Pornography: Men Possessing Women*. New York: Dutton.

Duke, A. A., K. M. Z. Smith, L. M. S. Oberleitner, A. Westphal, and S. A. McKee. 2018. "Alcohol, Drugs, and Violence: A Meta-Meta-Analysis." *Psychology of Violence* 8: 238–249.

Eaton, A. W. 2012. "What's Wrong with the (Female) Nude? A Feminist Perspective on Art and Pornography." Hans Maes and Jerrold Levinson, eds. *Art and Pornography: Philosophical Essays*. Oxford, UK: Oxford University Press, pp. 277–308.

———. 2007. "A Sensible Antiporn Feminism." *Ethics* 117: 674–715.

Eliot, George. 2003/1871–72. *Middlemarch*. New York: Barnes and Noble Classics.

F.B.I. 2012. *Uniform Crime Reports*. Available at http://www.fbi.gov/about-us/cjis/ucr/crime-in-the-u.s/2012/crime-in-the-u.s.-2012/tables/1tabledatadecoverviewpdf/table_1_crime_in_the_united_states_by_volume_and_rate_per_100000_inhabitants_1993-2012.xls.

Foucault, Michel. 1990. *History of Sexuality, Vol. 2: The Use of Pleasure*. New York: Vintage.

———. 1984. *The Foucault Reader*. Paul Rabinow, ed. New York: Pantheon.

Gaca, Kathy L. 2003. *The Making of Fornication*. Berkeley: University of California Press.

Graham, Kathryn. 2011. "The Relationship Between Alcohol and Violence: Population, Contextual, and Individual Research Approaches." *Drug and Alcohol Review* 30: 453–457.

Grant, Michael. 1975. *Eros in Pompeii*. New York: William Morrow.

Green, Leslie. 1998. "Pornographizing, Subordinating, and Silencing." Robert Post, ed. *Censorship and Silencing: Practices of Cultural Regulation*. Los Angeles, CA: Getty Research Institute, pp. 285–311.

Kendrick, Walter. 1987. *The Secret Museum: Pornography in Modern Culture*. New York: Viking.

Hubbard, Thomas K. 2010. "Sexuality, Greek." Michael Gargarin, ed. *Oxford Encyclopedia of Ancient Greece and Rome*. Oxford University Press. Online.

Langton, Rae. 2009. *Sexual Solipsism*. Oxford, UK: Oxford University Press.

Lefkowitz, Mary. 1985. "Sex and Civilization." *Partisan Review* 52: 460–466.

Longino, Helen E. 1980. "Pornography, Oppression, and Freedom." Laura Lederer, ed. *Take Back the Night*. New York: William Morrow, pp. 40–54.

Loth, David. 1961. *The Erotic in Literature*. New York: J. Messner.

Mackey, Thomas C. 2002. *Pornography on Trial*. Santa Barbara, CA: ABC-CLIO.

MacKinnon, Catharine A. 1997. "The Roar on the Other Side of Silence." Catharine MacKinnon and Andrea Dworkin, eds. *In Harm's Way: The Pornography Civil Rights Hearings*. Cambridge, MA: Harvard University Press, pp. 3–24.

———. 1993. *Only Words*. Cambridge, MA: Harvard University Press.

———. 1987. *Feminism Unmodified*. Cambridge, MA: Harvard University Press.

———. 1985. "Pornography, Civil Rights, and Speech." *Harvard Civil Rights Civil- Liberties Law Review* 20: 2–70.

MacKinnon, Catharine A., and Andrea Dworkin. 1994. "Statement by Catharine A. MacKinnon and Andrea Dworkin Regarding Canadian Customs and Legal Approaches to Pornography." August 26. Available at http://www.nostatusquo.com/ACLU/dworkin/OrdinanceCanada.html.

———, eds. 1997. *In Harm's Way: The Pornography Civil Rights Hearings*. Cambridge, MA: Harvard University Press.

Malamuth, Neil M. 2007. "Pornography." Roy F. Baumeister and Kathleen D. Vohs, eds. *Encyclopedia of Social Psychology*. London: SAGE, pp. 678–680.

Malamuth, Neil M., Scott Haber, and Seymour Feschbach. 1980. "Testing Hypotheses Regarding Rape." *Journal of Research in Personality* 14: 121–137.

Messman-Moore, Terri L., Aubrey A. Coates, Kathryn J. Gaffey, and Carrie F. Johnson. 2008. "Sexuality, Substance Use, and Susceptibility to Victimization: Risk of Women for Rape and Sexual Coercion in a Prospective Study of College Women." *Journal of Interpersonal Violence* 23: 1730–1746.

Mohr, Richard. 1988. *Gays/Justice*. New York: Columbia University Press.

Mouilso, E. R., S. Fischer, and K. S. Calhoun. 2012. "A Prospective Study of Sexual Assault and Alcohol Use Among First-Year College Women." *Violence and Victims* 27: 78–94.

Nagel, Thomas. 2002. *Concealment and Exposure*. New York: Oxford University Press.

Newport, Frank, ed. 2014. *The Gallup Poll: Public Opinion 2012*. Lanham, MD: Rowman and Littlefield.

——, ed. 2013. *The Gallup Poll: Public Opinion 2011*. Lanham, MD: Rowman and Littlefield.

Nussbaum, Martha. 2004. *Hiding from Humanity: Disgust, Shame, and the Law*. Princeton, NJ: Princeton University Press.

Ogas, Ogi, and Sai Gaddam. 2011. *A Billion Wicked Thoughts*. New York: Dutton.

Oswald, Felix L. 1891. "Crime." *The Cyclopedia of Temperance and Prohibition*. New York: Funk and Wagnalls, pp. 141–143.

Pagels, Elaine. 1998. *Adam, Eve, and the Serpent*. New York: Random House.

Patterson, Orlando. 1982. *Slavery and Social Death*. Cambridge, MA: Harvard University Press.

Pernanen, Kai. 1991. *Alcohol in Human Violence*. New York: Guilford Press.

Rae, Michael. 2001. "What Is Pornography?" *Noûs* 35: 118–145.

Richlin, Amy. 2010. "Sexuality, Roman." Michael Gargarin, ed. *Oxford Encyclopedia of Ancient Greece and Rome*. Oxford University Press. Online.

Room R., and I. Rossow. 2001. "The Share of Violence Attributable to Drinking." *Journal of Substance Abuse* 6: 218–228.

Rose, Kenneth D. 1996. *American Women and the Repeal of Prohibition*. New York: New York University Press.

Rowland, Ingrid D. 2013. "The Local, Universal Master." *New York Review of Books* LX: November 7, 8–12.

Schauer, Frederick. 1982. *Free Speech: A Philosophical Inquiry*. Cambridge, UK: Cambridge University Press.

——. 1979. "Speech and 'Speech'—Obscenity and 'Obscenity': An Exercise in the Interpretation of Constitutional Language." *Georgetown Law Review* 67: 899–933.

Soble, Alan. 1996. *Sexual Investigations.* New York: New York University Press.

Stearns, Peter N. 2009. *Sexuality in World History.* New York: Routledge.

Steinem, Gloria. 1980. "Erotica and Pornography: A Clear and Present Difference." Laura Lederer, ed. *Take Back the Night.* New York: William Morrow, pp. 35–39.

Strossen, Nadine. 1995. *Defending Pornography.* New York: Scribner.

Suetonius. 2007. *The Twelve Caesars.* James Rives, ed. New York: Penguin.

Vasari, Giorgio. 2003. *Life of Michelangelo.* Gaston du C. de Vere, trans. New York: St. Pauls.

Williams, Bernard. 1981. *Obscenity and Film Censorship: An Abridgement of the Williams Report.* Cambridge, UK: Cambridge University Press.

Wittenmyer, Annie. 1882. *History of the Woman's Temperance Crusade.* Boston: James H. Earle.

Legal Materials

Cases

Civil Rights Cases, 109 U.S. 3. (1883).

Commonwealth v. Sharpless, 2 Sergeant and Rawle 91 (Sup. Ct. of Penn., 1815).

Ginzburg v. U.S., 383 U.S. 463 (1966).

Memoirs v. Massachusetts, 383 U.S. 413 (1966).

Miller v. California, 413 U.S. 15 (1973).

Regina v. Butler, [Canada] S.C.J. No. 15 (1992).

Regina v. Hicklin, 2 Q.B. 360 (1868).

Roth v. U.S., 354 U.S. 476 (1957).

Swearingen v. U.S., 161 U.S. 446 (1896).

U.S. v. One Book Entitled Ulysses, 72 F.2d. 705 (1934).

Statutory and Constitutional Materials

Charter of Rights and Freedoms [Canada]. 1982. Available at http://laws-lois.justice.gc.ca/eng/const/page-15.html.

Criminal Code [Canada]. 1985. RSC 1985, c C-46. Available at http://canlii.ca/t/52cjj.

Criminal Justice and Immigration Act [United Kingdom]. *2008.* Available at http://www.legislation.gov.uk/ukpga/2008/4/section/63.

PART II

A DEFENSE OF A SEX
EQUALITY APPROACH
TO PORNOGRAPHY

LORI WATSON

Pornography permits men to have whatever they want sexually. It is their "truth about sex."[1]

7

Sex, Equality, and Pornography

CRITICIZING PORNOGRAPHY AS A SIGNIFICANT social practice that is a site of gender-based inequality—centered on the role pornography plays in sex inequality, primarily but not exclusively the inequality of women to men—takes a sex equality approach to the issue. It builds on evidence showing the many ways in which pornography is a central manifestation of, and powerful mechanism through which, sex inequality is imposed and maintained. In this analysis, pornography is a key social location of the subordination of women to men. The evidence for such claims includes: scientific empirical evidence and studies of the harms of pornography, both in its making and its use; the testimony of women and girls (and some men and boys and trans persons) harmed through pornography; and, an analysis of the way in which inequality is eroticized in pornography and affects social status. Given this evidence, a sex equality approach to pornography aims to directly address those harms as part of a systematic approach to bringing about a more sex equal world. The sex equality approach to pornography fits a vast body of empirical evidence; connects with legal and policy discourses on inequality; and, situates pornography's harms in the context of the harms of sex inequality, specifically of sexual abuse.

The aim of my contribution is to explain, develop, and defend a sex equality approach to pornography, in which pornography is understood as a practice of sex-based inequality and sex discrimination. I first lay out the substantive basis for the view. This requires a brief overview of the concept of equality, especially in its competing legal interpretations. It also requires an analysis of the way gender is socially constructed as a relationship of inequality.

Next, I turn to the civil rights ordinances, authored by Catharine A. MacKinnon and Andrea Dworkin (in the early 1980s) at the request of localities, in which pornography is defined as a systematic practice of the subordination of women. The meaning and aims of the ordinances are carefully explained. They have been widely misinterpreted and distorted; as a result, many baseless criticisms continue to circulate. Following the presentation of the ordinances, I present the empirical evidence of the harms of pornography in the literature of several social sciences.

I then consider criticisms of the sex equality approach from those who argue that pornography is a right flowing from a right to freedom of expression—the free speech defense of pornography. Next, I examine criticisms of the sex equality approach to pornography offered by self-styled feminists, who claim that pornography (its making and its use) is a part of sexual liberation for women, and for gays and lesbians insofar as they allege it plays an important role in the communities of sexual minorities. Finally, I examine the arguments to those, like Altman, who locate a "right to pornography" in the right to sexual autonomy. I argue none of these arguments sufficiently establishes their conclusions. There is no "right" to pornography either in a broader right to freedom of speech or in a right of sexual autonomy. Moreover, pornography harms both rights. Neither does pornography embody a liberation project for women, gays and lesbians, or other sexual minorities.

7.1 EQUALITY

The meaning and application of equality are disputed by philosophers, legal scholars, political scientists, judges, legislators, and many others engaged in social and political criticism.[2] Western democratic legal systems enshrine a dominant conception of equality in legal interpretation. Drawing on Aristotle's formulation, equality is defined in terms of sameness and difference.[3] Equality, on this view, requires the same treatment for similar persons and can allow different treatment for different persons. It is effectively summed up as "treat likes alike, and unlikes unalike."[4] In application, in order to determine whether two persons, or two groups of persons, deserve equal treatment, understood as the same treatment, one must first determine if they are "alike" in the relevant sense. In practice, "the relevant sense" carries a lot of weight. Legally, "the relevant sense" has to do with how and why a law in question makes distinctions among groups.

Laws typically classify persons into groups for the purpose of the law. So, for example, the law specifying the legal driving age as 16 creates a legal classification of two groups—those 16 years of age and over and those under the age of 16. The law also grants opportunities to those 16 years of age and over (the ability to get a driver's license provided certain requirements are met) and denies that same opportunity to anyone under the age of 16. Supposing some 15-year-old wanted to challenge the law as unfair (or unequal), one way they might do that is to argue that the distinction between those 16 and over and those under 16 is arbitrary or irrelevant to the purpose of the law. Making this argument in a US court, the plaintiff would likely allege that insofar as the legal classification is arbitrary, it violates their right to equality, probably equal protection of the laws under the US Constitution or state constitutions. Put simply, this just means that this individual would claim that the law does not treat them as an equal under the law because the distinction relied on in the law is not warranted—there is no relevant difference between 15- and 16-year-olds, they would allege. Fifteen-year-olds are just as capable of driving as 16-year-olds.

Seeing why such a challenge is likely to be unsuccessful produces a clearer understanding of legal interpretations of equality, and in particular, the equal protection doctrine as understood in US law (and often similarly in other countries). So long as the government can show that the legal classification drawn (in this case, those 16 and over and those under 16) bears a "rational relationship" to the purpose of the law, and that the purpose of the law reflects a legitimate governmental interest (regulating driver's licenses for the purpose of traffic safety), the law does not violate the equality rights of those under 16. Put simply, "the rational relationship test" is a method for determining whether "like cases are treated alike"—that is, whether there is a relevant difference between those 16 and over and those under 16. If a relevant difference is determined to exist, meaning the distinction is supported by any reasons, and the purpose of the law is judged to reflect a legitimate interest of the state, then there is no violation of equality in treating the two groups differently.

Early challenges to laws that used racial classifications, after the passage of the 14th Amendment with its equal protection clause (1868), raised important debates in the interpretation of US constitutional law, including, for example, whether its equality guarantee was intended to apply only to racial distinctions, and whether that clause was confined to facial distinctions, those that showed race on their face, or whether it also applied to disadvantageous racial consequences in the laws' effects, even if they were neutral as written. Over the course of the last 145 years or so, the Court's interpretation of equal protection has largely centered on a formal interpretation of equality, in which equality was understood to be denied only in cases in which similarly situated persons or groups were treated differently than relevant others.

Two important developments concern the introduction and interpretation of the doctrine of strict scrutiny (or intermediate scrutiny as applied to gender) as it concerns race- and sex-based distinctions in the law. Simplifying greatly and omitting the historical details, race- and sex-based distinctions are, respectively, deemed "suspect classifications" and "quasi-suspect classifications." Thus, any law that classifies on the basis of race or sex is subject to heightened judicial scrutiny, meaning it requires a stronger justification than simply "rational," because courts suspect that it may be discriminatory. This is important for our analysis of the legal concept of equality because underlying this "inherent" suspicion for legal classifications based on race is the claim that equality requires the same treatment for similar persons. This vision of equality combined with the now widely held (legal) view that persons are equal citizens regardless of race (i.e., they are not relevantly different), means that, for the most part, racial equality, as guaranteed by the equal protection clause, demands the same treatment of persons as members of racial groups. The upholding of affirmative action policies represents an exception to this general rule. Of course, the view that racial groups are relevantly similar for legal purposes is a very recent phenomenon. The same legal reasoning underlying the equal protection clause, noted here as requiring the same treatment of similar persons, permits and justifies different treatment for those judged to be "unalike" in the relevant sense.

So, *Plessy v. Ferguson*, the famous "separate but equal" case in which the Supreme Court ruled that a law requiring separate railcars for blacks and whites in Louisiana did not violate the equal protection clause, was decided under this approach to equality.[5] The shift in the treatment of blacks in America, under the auspices of the equal protection clause itself, was a result of a shift from seeing "the races" as essentially different to seeing them as essentially the same. In other words, social equality, in some sense, was a necessary precondition to legal equality. So long as "the races" were seen as different "in the relevant sense," equal protection jurisprudence, with its emphasis on formal equality, was not an effective tool for bringing about equality. Whether it is effective for racial discrimination when "sameness" is both seen and required, especially when racism is structural, both remain to be seen and is beyond the scope of this book.

The ineffectiveness of a sameness/difference approach to equality for bringing about genuine equality for socially unequal groups is starkly apparent in considerations of sex equality. Sex or gender is defined in terms of difference. When men and women are similar or the same, in some respect, that is precisely not what sex or gender is. Difference defines sex distinctions.[6] Because of this understanding of sex, sex-based distinctions in law are subject to a lower, but still "heightened," level of judicial review. They are "quasi-suspect" rather than "inherently" suspect. Presently, the Court requires that distinctions based on sex must be given "an exceedingly persuasive justification" to survive judicial review.[7] In one sense, this is cause for celebration: baseless sex distinctions, which serve to harm women or limit their opportunities, are not likely to survive such scrutiny. However, reliance on such a formal model of equality also means that when laws rely on sex-based distinctions to ameliorate the various forms of social subordination women experience as women, they are not likely to survive such scrutiny either. It also means that many of the forms of social inequality (subordination) that women face as women, such as vastly disproportionate sexual assault because they are women, don't even register as legal equality concerns at all. Fewer men are subject to these conditions, and it is not seen as due to their gender even if it is, so there are no "likes" to be treated "unalike," only "unlikes" treated "unalike," that is, equally.

To the latter point, that under formal models of equality many forms of social inequality that persons experience as members of groups do not register as equality concerns at all, consider: Rape law is under the auspices of the criminal law and not seen to raise equality issues. Nor is prostitution seen to be an issue that gives rise to concerns about equality; it too is a matter of criminal law. Nor is pornography, traditionally understood, thought to give rise to equality concerns. Rather, it is under the auspices of the First Amendment. Similarly, reproductive rights (e.g., abortion and contraception) are not matters of equality within the current legal framework; instead they are matters of privacy. Thus, many of the social practices, policies, and laws that directly concern women's equality fail to even register as equality matters under dominant modes of thinking, especially dominant modes of thinking about equality.

In contrast to a formal model of equality like Aristotle's as embodied in legal conceptions of equality, a substantive model of equality does not rely on an understanding of equality in terms of sameness and difference, but, rather, is focused in terms of social status and rank. Here inequalities mark lower status or lower rank within a social hierarchy. Those who are unequal, or treated unequally, are not merely treated differently, but are treated worse and ranked lower than relevant others. Given that hierarchically structured social practices, including group categorizations, function to sort persons into groups for whom status is enjoyed and those for whom status is denigrated, inequality, so understood, is a matter of social subordination relative to the supremacy enjoyed by members of dominant social groups.

Thus, examining a particular law or social practice from the point of view of concern for substantive equality, one is led to ask whether the law or practice serves to subordinate (rank as lower) some persons relative to others, and not merely whether those who are similar are treated the same or differently. To see this contrast between formal

SEX, EQUALITY, AND PORNOGRAPHY | **159**

and substantive models of equality, consider the way the Supreme Court addressed anti-miscegenation laws in the well-known case of *Loving v. Virginia* (1967).

As late as 1967, twenty-two states in the United States still had anti-miscegenation laws barring certain forms of interracial marriage, notably marriage between whites and blacks.[8] The Lovings married in the District of Columbia in 1958. Mr. Loving was white and Mrs. Loving was black. They moved to Virginia not long after getting married and were indicted for violating Virginia's ban on interracial marriage. They were convicted and each sentenced to a year in jail, which was suspended provided they leave Virginia and not return for twenty-five years.[9] The Lovings challenged the constitutionality of Virginia's law, on the ground that it violated the 14th Amendment, and they won. The Supreme Court of the United States recognized in their decision in the case that the clear purpose of Virginia's statutes was to "maintain White Supremacy," thus legally to give effect to an invidious social hierarchy based on race.

The *Loving* decision is exceptional for prohibiting what amounts to substantive inequality by establishing through its ruling that a social hierarchy that maintained the supremacy of whites over blacks, premised as it was on the belief that the "integrity" of the "white race" required prohibition on marriage with those of African heritage, violated the equal protection clause. Defenders of such laws, relying on the logic of formal legal equality, argued that insofar as the laws treated likes alike—meaning that just as whites could not marry blacks, blacks could not marry whites, and each could marry within their own racial group—the law did not violate the equal protection clause.[10] In invalidating this law, the Supreme Court effectively rejected the sameness/

difference analysis of equality, in favor of a substantive analysis in which rejection of hierarchy, not requirement of same treatment, was the salient analysis.

Loving is one of a few exceptional decisions in US jurisprudence that breaks from the formal model of equality that has served to uphold substantively unequal practices in the name of equality, as it did in *Plessy*. Where the formal model of equality has worked to strike down race- or sex-based classifications, or laws and official state policies that had a disparate (unequal) impact, it has largely been because the social group in question had already achieved a level of social equality such that they could be seen to be the same or sufficiently similar to dominant groups, and thus granted equality on those grounds. Or, the plaintiffs are members of dominant groups themselves.

Thus on a formal model of equality, in 1872, the Supreme Court could reject Myra Bradwell's challenge of an Illinois law prohibiting women from taking the bar as a denial of equality on the grounds that women were "essentially different" than men, stating that "God designed the sexes to occupy different spheres of action."[11] And, close to a hundred years later, in *Reed v. Reed* (1971), relying on the very same equality reasoning, the Supreme Court could strike down an Idaho statute giving preference to males as administrators of estates on the grounds that this sex-based classification bore no "rational relationship to the state objective."[12] The difference between 1872 and 1971 was that over the interim ninety-nine years, women, as a group, had achieved some measure of social equality such that the latter Court could see them as "the same" for purposes of administering estates. But a formal model of equality could do nothing for Ms. Bradwell given the social interpretation of women at the time—women were seen as essentially different such that they could not possibly effectively practice law. It is when society does not already grant equality that legal equality guarantees are most needed. Genuine equality—equality in substance, not just in form—especially for historically subordinated and marginalized groups, requires the use of law to change legal and social practices through which subordination is manifest and maintained. Doing that requires the legal tools to allow the legal recognition of practices of inequality—hierarchical practices—as practices of inequality. An important first step to opening up the legal framework is moving toward an understanding of equality as not primarily about sameness and difference but about the elimination of hierarchy and rank: of social arrangements of privilege over deprivation, worth over worthlessness.

7.2 GENDER AS POWER

Central to understanding the sex equality approach to pornography, as embodied in the civil rights ordinances, and its aim to bring about substantive sex equality in law and in life, is the analysis of dominant social forms of gender and sexuality as hierarchical relations of inequality.

Contrast two pictures of gender. One picture sees gender as primarily a set of *differences* between men and women captured by "the masculine" and "the feminine." Here gender tracks "the sex difference." Accounts vary as to the source of such differences, some emphasizing reproduction, others brain organization, others socialization, and others all of these and more. Thus, seeing gender as primarily a difference, a distinction, the work of theorizing about gender involves sorting out which of these differences are "real" in some way and which are illusory. Whatever ways in which men and women are the same is not gender; whatever ways in which they are different is gender—the gender difference.

Another picture of gender sees gender, in its dominant social form, not as about "difference"—although it doesn't deny that there are gender differences—but as about power. Here gender is a distinction by and through which people are socially organized into two groups that form a hierarchy—those for whom social power is a right, conferred based upon their masculinity; and those for whom social power is denied on the basis of their femininity. Gender, so understood, is a hierarchical hence invidious ordering, not a benign difference.

To grasp this claim about gender, start by trying to figure out what "masculinity" and "femininity" mean. What do they mark out? How do they function socially and politically? The first thing to observe is that masculinity and femininity are defined relationally: relative to each other. To be masculine is to not be feminine. To be feminine is to not be masculine. Social masculinity is expressed and embodied through dominating others. It's not hard to think of examples, beginning with examples of displays of "hyper-masculinity." Take a particularly hard hit on a football field, after which the guy administering the hit celebrates to further emphasize his power over the guy laying on the field. He might celebrate by flexing his biceps, displaying his strength. He might celebrate by pointing to the guy who received the hit, suggesting, "I own you." Or take the ways in which boys, teen boys, and even adult men rely on the comparison of the size of their penises, or the size of their testicles, as evidence of their masculinity and power. Or consider the masculine imperative to never show "weakness" through displays of emotion, such as crying, expressing one's emotional pain, or even emotional effusion. The phrase "man up" captures the sense in which normative masculinity demands that human men take on a posture of stoicism and strength in the face of normal contexts in which human feelings and emotions might be seen as warranted.

Even more revealing are the ways one can be emasculated. Emasculation is accomplished through a loss of power. A boy or man failing to do the proper "masculine" thing, as judged by other men, and sometimes by women, is said to "have no balls," to have a "tiny dick," or to be "a pussy," "a fag," "to be acting a like a "girl." Failing to dominate, or worse being dominated, marks one with a badge of inferiority—a badge of femininity. Women's so-called power to emasculate a man lies in their exercising power over a man in some specific instance. One way this can be imagined to happen is when a woman "bosses" a man, or tells him what to do, even if she is actually his boss. It is a supposed disruption of the "natural" order and carries a cloak of shame for the man or men denied the exercise or recognition of their superiority as men. Public emasculation can and does lead men to aggression and violence as a means to "restore" their masculinity—their standing as dominant beings. Many careful and compelling analyses of the pattern of mass shootings in the United States, overwhelmingly carried out by men, explain the way in which, for many of these men, such acts of violence are a reaction to feeling of loss of masculinity.[13] Violence and aggression are displays of masculinity, culturally not biologically, and thus function as a restorative act in the minds of these men who are inflicting the horror and terror of mass violence. "I win," "I dominate you all," is the message they seek to convey through these acts of violence.

Femininity, in contrast, is accomplished by displaying a lack of power, being "properly" submissive, signaling weakness. Hallmarks of "proper femininity" include: displays of sexual availability to men (but only up to a point); nurturing, caring, acts of selflessness; presentation of self as a beautiful object; avoiding confrontation; and, deference to men, often understood as staying in one's place. As caring, nurturing, and empathic connection to others are the quintessential feminine virtues, orientation to the needs of others, selflessness, and subordination of one's self characterize the stereotypical "virtues" of women.

Displays of power, strength, and domination by women threaten one's femininity, culturally speaking. The ongoing and sustained critiques of Serena Williams illustrate and embody this point. Serena Williams, considered by many the greatest female athlete of all time, and by some simply the greatest athlete of all time (GOAT), has been subjected to racist and sexist critiques of her body, performance, and attitude since she became a public figure in the late 1990s. In part because of her exceptional performance in tennis, fools have made claims, based on no evidence, that she is "really" a man. (Her pregnancy ended that.) But, those same fools, have dissected her body in criticism: "she is too muscular," "too strong," and "too black" (whatever that might mean, they do not say). Such cultural fears of "masculine" women, meaning considered masculine because of her athletic prowess, or that actual men would compete as women, lay behind the "gender test" in sports that only very recently was eliminated from international sports governing bodies.[14]

The imperative that women "stay in their place" and display culturally normative femininity—including polite passivity and unchallenging submission—is not limited to the sports world. Women in employment contexts are routinely faced with the double bind of reconciling femininity with displays of competence and success at work. Where women have been "too successful"—by leading, engaging in "cold," meaning effective, management styles, and outperforming their male counterparts—they have been judged "bitchy," "too masculine," "overly aggressive," and in need of "charm school."[15] Or "bossy."

Empirical studies reveal that when women out-earn their male companions, often husbands, they compensate for this transgression of gender norms by doing more housework, child care, and general domestic labor.[16] This over-functioning on the part of women is sometimes driven by the imperative to fulfill one's feminine role and to maintain the role expectations that women service the men in their lives, thus protecting the masculinity of their companions. Sometimes it happens simply because men refuse to do their fair share of the work of maintaining a shared life, thinking it is a woman's role to serve and service and a man's role to be served and serviced.

Gender norms and roles, in other words, embody a hierarchical structure, in which masculinity is defined in terms of its relational superiority to femininity. Socially, gender is a difference of sorts, but it is not simply a distinction. It entails marking out classes of persons on the basis of perceived sex characteristics in which superior status is expressed through displays of masculinity and inferior status through displays of femininity. There is a separation here, but it is not an equal one. "Separate, but equal" is a myth proclaimed by those who claim gender is a mere difference, properly reflected in the organization of social life.

Of course, gender as just described intersects with other social divisions in ways that manifest hierarchies within gender groups as well. So, for example, the imperatives of femininity in conjunction with racialized norms create further hierarchies between white women, black women, Latina women, Asian women, native and aboriginal women, and so on. These, too, are inequalities in substance. Black women, for example, have been socially penalized—ranked as inferior—for their "failure" to be "properly feminine" as judged by a white-woman standard. Patricia Hill Collins provides a compelling account of the historical and ongoing social construction of black women's and men's identities, and cultural interpretation and appropriation of their bodies, in her important book *Black Sexual Politics*.[17] Hill Collins carefully reconstructs and narrates the ways in which black women are socially constructed as "too strong," "bitchy," and "less attractive" as well as "promiscuous" and "bad mothers," against dominant white norms of femininity. Latina women are represented as "hot and fiery," oversexualized, and promiscuous. Asian women are represented as submissive and subordinate, passive, and demure. Thus, gender becomes raced and race becomes gendered, creating and reinforcing hierarchies within gender groups as well as across them. Kimberlé Crenshaw's pioneering work on intersectionality makes this point.[18] As she states: "In examining the intersections of race and gender, I engaged the dominant assumptions that these are essentially separate; by tracing the categories to their intersections, I hope to . . . disrupt the tendencies to see race and gender an exclusive or separable categories."[19] Misogyny intersects with racism across cultural practices, and this is starkly apparent in pornography where women's sexuality defines them—even as it takes particularized racial forms—as inferior.

7.3 SEXUALITY, GENDER, AND POWER

The central organizing mechanism of gender—as a set of social roles, practices, and norms—can be found in sexuality. Much scholarly work examining and uncovering the source of gender hierarchy, as just described, locates it in sexuality. In this analysis, sexuality is what determines gender, not the other way around. In other words, the content of gendered positions, "the masculine" and "the feminine," is determined by the structure of those roles within heterosexuality, the dominant form of sexual roles and expression. Identifying and understanding the ways the norms of heterosexuality shape, define, and embody inequality between men as a class and women as a class is ground zero for understanding sex/gender inequality in all its forms.

How is masculinity achieved within sexuality? In other words, within sexuality, what acts, behaviors, and attitudes are constitutive of "playing the masculine role" in the stereotypically imposed sense? Masculinity is achieved by power, where that means being the sexual actor—that is, being the initiator and the penetrator, as well as having the authority to determine what sex is, whether it happened, and what is erotic.

When asked "what counts as having sex?," people typically define it in terms of vaginal penetration by a penis. Does this mean lesbians or gay men do not have sex? Some think gay men have sex because it involves penile penetration. But what to say about lesbian sex? If lesbian sex counts as "sex," then oral sex among heterosexual sex partners seems to count as sex as well, which many want to deny. Oral sex among heterosexual partners is a frequent form of "hooking up," but it is not, according to some, sex. Lesbian sex, in this stereotypical view, is a kind of "sexual activity" but, strictly speaking, it is not sex. Sex, by these lights, must involve a penis, and it must involve penetration. These intuitions reveal a deep truth about dominant cultural conceptions of sex: sex is about what men do.

Amassing a large number of sex partners is an achievement of masculinity. The more sex a man has, the more he is a "man!" Back slapping, high fiving, thumbs ups, head nods, and other expressions of admiration flow from men to men as sexual "conquests" are racked up. In contrast, women are often viciously punished for sexual activity outside a monogamous relationship. Men are "players," "pimps," "studs." Women are "whores," "sluts," "easy," and "dirty," if they engage in "too much" sex—even in cases where the sex is unwanted, forced, coerced, or extracted by threats, that is, even when they are raped.

Within this asymmetrical structure, defined as it is by inequality, hierarchy itself is eroticized along gender lines. What it is to be "sexy" is divided by relations of domination and subordination, as those track masculinity and femininity. A photo essay by Rion Sabean makes this uniquely visible. This project, Sabean calls, the "Men-Ups Project."[20] Sabean photographed men in traditional pin-up girl postures and poses. The images reveal the ways in which social femininity demands servility and display of sexual availability as sexual objects for men's pleasure. The images are effective at revealing this precisely because they are of men performing femininity. Given the experience of cognitive dissonance between male bodies performing femininity, the viewer can actually see the servility and sexual availability that constitute the imperatives of femininity. Were these images of women, as they typically are, that is often missed—precisely because the fusion of women's bodies with sexual availability, as defined by masculine heterosexual desire, is so complete. Women, posed as such, just look "natural," according to social definitions of nature in sexual forms.

The eroticization of inequality is nowhere more apparent than in pornography. In addition to the inequality between men and women, any social inequality you can think of has a subgenre of pornography devoted to it. Racial inequality is sexualized in white-master/black-slave genres, in Asian-themed subgenres drawing on stereotypes about submissive Asian women and geishas, and in depictions of Latina women as "oversexed" and "hot and fiery." Age inequality is sexualized in teen-porn genres, with depictions of school-aged girls as virgins having their first "encounter" with older men. Child pornography eroticizes the vulnerability of children, as does pornography of small women said to be over the age of majority but presented as if they are children, eager for male sexual attention. Incest porn is a popular subgenre capturing both the inequality of youth and of the parent/child relationship. Age inequality is also sexualized through subgenres, where older women are made into "grandma porn." Physical disability and inequality are sexualized in genres of pornography that depict persons (largely women) with physical disabilities, including missing limbs and dwarfism. Obesity is an inequality that is sexualized in "fat porn." Nazi/Jew pornography exists, sometimes presenting Jewish women eager to enter concentration camps for sexual purposes. The inequality between nonhuman animals and humans is sexualized in bestiality and "crush" videos, where women in high heels crush small rodents, puppies, and kittens to death by stepping on them as they shriek. For any social inequality and hierarchy that exists, you can count on finding a subgenre of pornography that sexualizes that particular form of inequality. Think about it.

Some think that women will enjoy sexual liberation by simply becoming sexual dominators. This idea is reflected in pop culture often. In the popular Jay-Z song, "Dirt off your shoulder," Jay-Z raps: "If you feeling like a pimp Nigga, go and brush your shoulders off. Ladies is pimps too, go and brush your shoulders off." One imagines Jay-Z, or his listeners, thinking that this is an expression of egalitarianism, if one hears it as embodying the claim that women too can express the kind of power that men do in taking up the persona of "being a pimp," meaning selling others for sexual use. Whether this role of dominance is improved by gender switches from the usual arrangement, or made gender neutral hence "egalitarian," or is no less gendered whatever sex performs it and serves to divert attention from the gendered realities that prevail in the real world that are not changed if the sexes are reversed, is a matter of one's view of equality.

Consider other systems of inequality such as slavery based on race. Racism, the institutionalization of racial inequality, supported by widespread belief that whites are superior to blacks, is the bedrock of slavery's functioning. Would blacks owning slaves too do anything to upend the logic of this system in the sense of making it less a system of inequality? The answer is obviously "No." The same is true for the subordination of women. Advocating for women's liberation by claiming that women should be more like men in the sense of adopting the masculine posture of domination, continues to depend on others being socially located in a subordinate position.

Equality cannot include relationships of domination and subordination. That some women may occupy the position of a dominator does nothing for women as a class. In other words, some women becoming "social men" through acts of domination still requires the subordination of other women, or other groups of persons. Maintaining hierarchy is an illusory vision of liberation.

7.4 THE ORDINANCES

The most well-developed sex equality approach to pornography is found in the work and legal activism of Catharine A. MacKinnon. In 1983 Andrea Dworkin and Catharine A. MacKinnon developed a novel legal approach to pornography. The ordinances that embody this legal approach have been subjected to sustained misunderstandings and distortions, and criticisms based upon them. To engage the criticisms, it is necessary to accurately understand the ordinances themselves.

As Altman carefully and accurately describes in his contribution to this volume, the United States adopts an obscenity-based approach to the regulation of pornography. *Miller* does not aim to regulate pornography; it aims to regulate obscenity understood as material showing sexual conduct that appeals to the prurient interest, violates community standards, and fails to have other socially redeeming value that satisfies the *Miller* test. Thus, pornography and obscenity are conceptually distinct, though some pornography may be (but only very seldom is) deemed obscene. *Miller*'s largely normative approach—prohibiting appeals to the "prurient interest" that "patently offensive[ly]" shows sex without other "serious . . . value"—has stated the controlling constitutional standard for obscenity since 1973.[21] Since that time, the pornography industry has grown to a 13–14 billion-dollar-a-year industry in the United States. Globally, pornography is estimated to be a 97-billion-dollar-a-year industry.[22]

Clearly, *Miller*'s conceptual approach is limited both in the kinds of material it reaches and in the way it conceives of that material. The primary evil conceptualized in an obscenity-based approach is "patent offense," specifically offense to community values. This frames the concern with pornography in terms of undermining conventional and traditional values concerning sexuality. If existing community values are misogynistic, for example, they would not be offended by pornography that is misogynistic. Moreover, in a social context in which sexual material, including pornography, is pervasive, fewer and fewer such representations will turn out to "offend" community values, since they are setting community standards. In other words, the more pornographic our world is, the more pornography represents as well as creates community values. Nowhere in this approach is there a concern for inequality, or sex-based inequality, or concrete harms of sexual abuse.

Liberals like Altman reject obscenity-based approaches to pornography, on the grounds that they unduly burden freedom of expression, violate sexual autonomy, or impose particular and partial conceptions of the good on others. Extrapolating from these values, liberals typically develop a further argument in favor of more freedom to buy, consume, and sell pornography. The sex equality critique of the typical obscenity-based approach to pornography agrees that it functions as illicit moralism, but it does not reason from this claim to a conclusion that greater freedom entails unfettered markets in pornography. Rather, advocates of taking a sex equality approach to pornography emphasize that the harm of pornography is not found in a corruption of morality, offense, or an affront to community values, but rather in the concrete physical harms of the sexual abuse required to make it and demonstrably promoted through its use, and in its enforcement of a subordinate status for women—that is, in its role as an institution of sex inequality.

The ordinances begin with the legislative findings that motivate the law. As with all laws, this statute begins with empirical findings that the legislature (in this case the city council) claims warrant the introduction of the law. The Minneapolis statute begins by documenting "special findings on pornography" as follows:

> The Council finds that pornography is central in maintaining the civil inequality of the sexes. Pornography is a systematic practice of exploitation and subordination based on sex

which differentially harms women. The bigotry and contempt it promotes, with the acts of aggression it fosters, harm women's opportunities for equality rights in employment, education, property rights, public accommodations and public services; create public harassment and private denigration; promote injury and degradation such as rape, battery and prostitution and inhibit the just enforcement of laws against these acts; contribute significantly to restricting women from full exercise of citizenship and participation in public life, including in neighborhoods; damage relations between the sexes; and undermine women's equal rights to speech and action guaranteed to all citizens under the Constitutions and laws of the United States and the state of Minnesota.[23]

As this passage shows, the ordinance is crafted as a civil rights law. Its aims are to address, through the civil law, the ways in which pornography concretely violates those used to make it and abused through its use, and effectively constructs and enacts the second-class status of women. Because of these harms of pornography, women's citizenship rights and status, including access to laws against sexual abuse, are not secured on an equal footing with men's. After laying out and interpreting the ordinances in their specificity, the wealth of empirical literature establishing some of the key claims here, for example, the way in which pornography promotes acts of rape and sexual violence, will be examined.

However, critically important to understanding and appreciating the aims and purpose of the ordinances as documented in these findings are claims that have received less attention, such as the connection between pornography and the failure of the just enforcement of laws against acts of sexual violence against women. From the perspective of concern with civil equality, and so women's equal citizenship rights, this harm is significant. Rape is the least reported, prosecuted, and convicted of all violent crimes. Rape myths function in the public eye, but crucially also in the minds of police officers, prosecutors, juries, and judges: people who hold the power to initiate investigations, bring charges, find guilt or acquit, and impose penalties upon convicted perpetrators. The precise gap between actual rapes and those reported to police is disputed, but even the most conservative estimates show that the gap is striking. The FBI Uniform Crime reports provide data for reported crimes across the United States in a given year. For the years 2010–2015, the following table records the number of reported rapes, the number of arrests, and the number of rapes (according to the National Crime Victimization Survey).[24]

Year	Number of reported rapes	Number of arrests	Number of rapes (NCVS)	Percentage of arrests to reports	Percentage of arrests to NCVS data
2010	84,767	15,586	268,514	18	5
2011	83,425	14,943	244,188	17.9	6
2012	84,376	13,971	346,830	16.5	4
2013	79,770[25]	13,617	300,165	17	4.5
2014	84,041	16,473	284,345	19.6	5.7
2015	90,185	17,504	431,837	19.4	4

According to RAINN (Rape, Abuse and Incest National Network), the largest anti-sexual abuse organization in the United States, the numbers of actual rapes compared to reported rapes is much greater than the data presented here. Drawing on a larger pool of data, RAINN states that "only 344 of every 1000 rapes are reported to police."[26]

The disparity between the FBI's data on reported rapes and the NCVS data on the number of rapes is significant, as the tables show. The actual incidences of rape and sexual assault are far greater than even what the NVCS show, as it is methodologically limited in a number of significant ways. One serious limitation of its methodology, which also plagues other studies on the prevalence of rape, is that it relies on rape victims self-identifying as such.[27] Diana E. H. Russell and Rebecca M. Bolen emphasize: ". . . many women do not conceptualize as rape many sexual attacks that meet the legal definition of rape. Hence, requiring that rape victims self-identify as such would result in a considerable underestimation of the prevalence of rape, particularly that perpetrated in intimate relationships."[28] Additionally, the NCVS employs a limited model for counting the incidents of rape, which leads to undercounting.[29] As Russell and Bolen report, in some cases, such as when one person is raped serially by another person multiple times with in a six-month period, the NCVS counts this as one rape.[30] The methodological decision concerning how to "count" multiple and repeated rapes has a significant impact on any given study's results, and methodological differences on this issue explains some of the variation across studies. Russell's research on rape incidence and prevalence remain the most methodologically sound studies documenting the true data on rape in the United States. In her groundbreaking study of rape in the United States using a large probability sample, Russell found that that 44% of women were victims of at least one completed or attempted rape.[31] Fifty percent of the "women who disclosed an experience of completed or attempted rape had been raped more than once."[32]

Catharine A. MacKinnon carefully and thoroughly summarizes a vast body of empirical research on rape, both within the United States and globally, in her legal textbook *Sex Equality*. Beyond documenting the empirical evidence of the incidence and prevalence of rape, MacKinnon documents the facts concerning the ways in which layered or intersectional forms of inequality combine to produce higher levels of sexual abuse among women of color, Jewish women, American Indian women, Native Alaskan women, and trans women.[33] Women in these groups face additional obstacles for reporting the violence, including sexual violence, they experience. Policing of communities of color is disproportionally violent and perpetuates structural racism. That women in communities of color may not see the police as their ally, to put it mildly, is hardly surprising.

Even when women report rape, they often face hostile questioning and disbelief from investigating officers. Jon Krakhauer's recent exposé of the federal investigation into the University of Montana's and the City of Missoula's handling of rape accusations documents patterns of police dismissal and disbelief of the testimony of rape victims.[34] The City of Missoula Police Department regularly asked women, reporting rape, if they had a boyfriend. If women answered affirmatively, this was taken as evidence that they were lying about being raped. The prosecutors' office had a policy of not prosecuting in such cases—despite clear evidence that rape is no more frequently falsely reported than any other crime[35] and that there is no demonstrated relation between having a boyfriend and falsely reporting a rape by someone else.

Even if rape charges are brought, convictions are difficult to achieve. According to RAINN (Rape, Abuse and Incest National Network), for every 1000 rapes committed, 994 perpetrators "will walk free."[36] That means that roughly 1% of perpetrators of rape are convicted for their crime, making rape the least convicted of all violent crimes.

And even when perpetrators are convicted, in too many cases judges show leniency. Of course, such leniency is much more likely when the defendant is young, white, and wealthy. The sentence of Brock Turner, the Stanford University student convicted of raping an unconscious woman behind a dumpster at a party, was given a sentence of only six months, of which he served three. Public outcry ensued, and a campaign to recall Judge Persky followed. Persky issued the following statement in defense of the six-month sentence: "As a prosecutor, I fought vigorously for victims. As a judge, my role is to consider both sides. California law requires every judge to consider rehabilitation and probation for first-time offenders. It's not always popular, but it's the law, and I took an oath to follow it without regard to public opinion or my opinions as a former prosecutor."[37] His emphasis on a duty to "consider both sides" rings hollow given the severity of trauma and damage to the victim.

The woman sexually assaulted by Brock Turner wrote a powerful letter, which she read aloud at his sentencing hearing. It is worth quoting at length:

Sometimes I think, if I hadn't gone, then this never would've happened. But then I realized, it would have happened, just to somebody else. You were about to enter four years of access to drunk girls and parties, and if this is the foot you started off on, then it is right you did not continue. The night after it happened, he said he thought I liked it because I rubbed his back. A back rub.

Never mentioned me voicing consent, never mentioned us even speaking, a back rub. One more time, in public news, I learned that my ass and vagina were completely exposed outside, my breasts had been groped, fingers had been jabbed inside me along with pine needles and debris, my bare skin and head had been rubbing against the ground behind a dumpster, while an erect freshman was humping my half naked, unconscious body. But I don't remember, so how do I prove I didn't like it.

I thought there's no way this is going to trial; there were witnesses, there was dirt in my body, he ran but was caught. He's going to settle, formally apologize, and we will both move on. Instead, I was told he hired a powerful attorney, expert witnesses, private investigators who were going to try and find details about my personal life to use against me, find loopholes in my story to invalidate me and my sister, in order to show that this sexual assault was in fact a misunderstanding. That he was going to go to any length to convince the world he had simply been confused.

I was not only told that I was assaulted, I was told that because I couldn't remember, I technically could not prove it was unwanted. And that distorted me, damaged me, almost broke me. It is the saddest type of confusion to be told I was assaulted and nearly raped, blatantly out in the open, but we don't know if it counts as assault yet. I had to fight for an entire year to make it clear that there was something wrong with this situation.[38]

And yet, Turner received six months, and, again only served three. Judge Persky is not alone in unjustly issuing a light sentence in cases of rape. In 2013 a Montana judge issued a thirty-one-day sentence for a teacher convicted of raping a student (the sentence was for fifteen years with all but thirty-one days suspended). In that case a higher court overruled the judge's decision after public outcry. If one Googles "teacher given probation for raping student," pages and pages of similar stories populate the search. Recently, the total was 646,000 results. Surely many would be stories on the same attacks but many would not be.

As shown below, when the full scope of the empirical evidence of the harms of pornography is faced, there is a clear causal connection between the consumption of pornography and the acceptance of rape myths. Just this aspect of the way pornography consumption affects users' beliefs and attitudes about women, and interferes with, or undermines, women's ability to secure justice through the just enforcement of laws criminalizing sexual violence, is significant enough to warrant legal intervention aimed at limiting pornography's effects. But the harms of pornography are not restricted to this grievous form of injustice and inequality, as will be documented.

The definition of pornography in the ordinances is written to capture the materials that do the specific harms the ordinances target, and only those harms.

The ordinances define pornography as "the graphic sexually explicit subordination of women, whether in pictures or words, that also includes one or more of the following:

(1) Women are presented as sexual objects who enjoy pain or humiliation; or

(2) Women are presented as sexual objects who experience pleasure in being raped; or

(3) Women are presented as sexual objects tied up or cut up or mutilated or bruised or physically hurt, or as dismembered or truncated or fragmented or severed into body parts; or

(4) Women are presented being penetrated by objects or animals; or

(5) Women are presented in scenarios of degradation, injury, abasement, torture, shown as filthy or inferior, bleeding, bruised, or hurt in a context that makes these conditions sexual; [or]

(6) Women are presented as sexual objects for domination, conquest, violation, exploitation, possession, or use, or through postures or positions of servility or submission or display.

The use of men, children, or transsexuals in the place of women in paragraphs (1) through (6) above shall also constitute pornography under this section."[39]

There are four elements to the definition of pornography in the ordinances. In order to fall under the definition, the material in question must: (1) be graphic, (2) be sexually explicit, (3) subordinate women (or men or children or trans persons), and (4) contain at least one of the enumerated elements listed. All four of these elements must be in the material for the material to be pornography under the law.

It is critical to emphasize that this is just the legal definition of pornography in the ordinance. The causes of action—the grounds for which one may initiate a complaint or civil action—are enumerated in another section, examined in more detail below. This definition, in other words, is simply a definition. It is not, by itself, a legal claim or a crime. One must have a cause of action—a ground for a suit as defined by a particular harm—against actions by people to fall within the purview of the ordinance. The definition itself is not actionable. What this means is the mere fact that some material meets this definition does not itself provide legal ground for action. Many critics have failed to understand this, or obscured it, and so have charged, wrongly, that the definition alone states an illegality. That is false.

Additionally, it is crucial to understand that this is what philosophers call a stipulative definition of pornography. A stipulative definition is one in which the meaning of the word in question—here "pornography"—is given precise meaning for a particular context, in this case the law. Some have criticized the definition of "pornography" in the ordinances on the grounds that it doesn't fully track the ordinary language use of the term. So, for example, many people think of pornography as any sexually explicit image aimed at arousing its viewer.[40] The definition of pornography in the ordinance doesn't encompass this as pornography within the purview of the law, apart from the fact that it would be massively overbroad legally, because this law's definition is limited to the materials that cause the harms the law aims to address. Not all sexually explicit materials cause harm.

Whether one thinks that the definition in the ordinances ought to be broader or narrower to track ordinary usage may be of interest to philosophers or other social theorists, or to those who experience the harm of sexism from mainstream television or advertisements, but there is an important reason the ordinance relies on a narrow stipulative definition. The reason is that laws are precise. A vague law, a law that lacks precision, is a bad law, particularly in this legal area. Persons subject to the law, regular citizens, persons required to interpret the law (judges), and those charged with executing the law (police or other officials) must be provided with a clear and relatively unambiguous meaning for a law to proscribe behavior. One reason vague laws are found unconstitutional is that they violate due process guarantees. Citizens must have notice of what is required or forbidden as a matter of law, and so laws must be sufficiently precise so as to provide adequate information about what constitutes their violation. Without such information, laws are considered potentially arbitrary and can be subject to multiple and conflicting interpretations. This is a particular hazard to be avoided in an area of legal regulation that could, without this kind of care, violate rights of freedom of speech.

Although this definition of "pornography" is stipulative, it is not detached from common meaning or usage. MacKinnon and Dworkin crafted the definition from an examination of pornography in the world and the empirical evidence of its harms. Pornographers, who form a discrete industry, know how to make the materials, and only those materials, they profit so handsomely from selling.

The ordinance provides legal remedy for the specific harms pornography, and only pornography, causes. The definition thus aims to capture the material that harms women, and others, in only the way pornography does.

7.4.1 The Causes of Action

The ordinance evolved slightly as it was introduced in different jurisdictions, according to their specific requests, both in its definition and in its causes of action. The Indianapolis ordinance is often discussed because it was passed into law and adjudicated.[41] The Model Ordinance provides for five civil causes of action: coercion into pornography, forcing pornography on a person, assault or physical attack due to specific pornography, trafficking in pornography, and defamation through pornography.[42]

Coercion into pornography provides that it violates one's civil rights to be coerced, intimidated, or fraudulently induced into sex acts so that pornography, as defined, can be made of them.[43] A canonical example of coercion into a pornography is the experience of Linda Boreman, whose married name was Linda Marchiano and was referred to in the pornography world as "Linda Lovelace." Linda testified at the Minneapolis hearings on the ordinance, at the Attorney General's Commission on Pornography, and documented her experiences and abuse in pornography in her autobiographies *Ordeal* and *Out of Bondage*.[44] As "Linda Lovelace," she was coerced into performing in *Deep Throat*, one of the most famous and lucrative pornographic films of all time, which also normalized the act of so-called deep-throating or fellatio to the bottom of one's throat. She had to be hypnotized to learn to relax the gag response so she did not choke.[45]

Forcing pornography on a person could also be understood as a form of sexual harassment. It defines the unwelcome thrusting of pornography on a person "in any place of employment, education, home or public place" as a civil rights violation, an act of sex discrimination.[46] Examples could include an employee routinely finding the break room at work plastered with naked women in full labial display;[47] showing children pornography as grooming for sexual abuse; adult women forced to view pornography by their boyfriends or husbands;[48] or a computer screen saver at an art school being constantly changed to pornography so that when women students want to use a shared computer, they are forced to view pornography to log in.[49]

The third cause of action provides: "It shall be sex discrimination to assault, physically attack, or injure any person . . . in a way that is directly caused by specific pornography."[50] This permits complaints to be made against the perpetrator of the attack, the makers, sellers, distributors, and/or exhibitors "of the specific pornography"[51] when it is proven to cause a specific assault or attack. The testimony of women (and men) at the public hearings held in Minneapolis documented the ways in which pornography was used as an instrument of their sexual assault.

The cause of action for defamation through pornography provides that the defamation of "any person through the unauthorized use in pornography of their proper name, image, or recognizable likeness" is a form of sex discrimination. It also requires that "public figures shall be treated as private persons,"[52] so there is no public figure exemption, such as exists under First Amendment jurisprudence for purposes of satire and criticism of public figures.[53] Examples that may fall under this cause of action include materials that turned public figures like Sarah Palin and Hillary Clinton into pornography. When Sarah Palin was running with John McCain as the vice-presidential candidate on the Republican ticket, a pornographic film was made entitled "Whose Nailin' Paylin?" in which a woman made to look like Palin engaged in explicit sex scenes.[54]

The cause of action for trafficking in pornography defines the production, sale, exhibition, or distribution of pornography (as previously defined) as a form of sex discrimination, a violation of civil rights.[55] In the Indianapolis statute, the final element of the definition ("women are presented as sexual objects for domination, conquest, violation, exploitation, possession, or use, or through postures or positions of servility or submission or display") is exempted from the trafficking provision, thus reserving the trafficking provision for the most violent materials.

This provision potentially allows any particular woman, or women as a class, to bring a suit against manufactures or distributors of pornography charging that the pornography in question harms women as such. To prove this claim, the plaintiff or plaintiffs would have to prove that the materials, in addition to being sexually explicit and graphic and containing the elements in the list of subparts, subordinated women. At such a trial, evidence that the pornography at issue harms women—or men or children or trans persons or all of them—would have to be presented and found credible. As MacKinnon and Dworkin write: "A trafficking complaint would provide the opportunity for women to attempt to prove to the satisfaction of a trier of fact that there is a direct connection between the pornography and harm to women as a class."[56] Only upon a successful suit, in which the evidentiary standard was met and a court ruled in favor of the complainants, would the pornography in question (the materials alleged to do the harms in the particular suit) be legally determined to be a form of sex discrimination.

7.5 SUBORDINATION

Philosophers have vexed themselves over what it means to say "pornography subordinates women." In an early philosophical engagement with the ordinance, William Parent argued that the claim that pornography is the subordination of women is "philosophically indefensible."[57] In reply to this criticism and those found in the decision ruling the Indianapolis ordinance unconstitutional, philosophers have defended the claim that pornography subordinates women. The claim may not need a philosophical defense, since it would have to be proven empirically in every suit under the law. However, reviewing these philosophical attempts helps clarify the claim.[58] Rae Langton, drawing on the work of J. L. Austin, who was footnoted in Catharine A. MacKinnon's work *Only Words*, carefully develops a philosophical defense of the argument that pornography subordinates women.[59] In his *How To Do Things With Words*, Austin develops a speech-act theory, which emphasizes that language does things in the world, it does not simply report or describe states of affairs. A classic example of a speech act is uttering the words "I do" in front of a recognized official (judge, minister, priest, etc.). The act of uttering those specific words in that specific context is the act of getting married. Thus, the speech, saying "I do," at the right time in the right context, constitutes the action of getting married. People perform actions through speech all the time.

These "performative functions" are important and distinct from other speech functions. Austin gives the following example to illustrate the different functions of speech: "One man says to another 'shoot her!' "[60] Considering this statement (after the fact, since if we witness it, we should immediately intervene), one can think about the meaning of what the speaker said, the effects of what the speaker said, or what saying "shoot her!" did—"the action constituted by the utterance itself."[61] Examining the meaning of the utterance "shoot her!" is concerned with what Austin calls the locutionary act of the speaker: What did the speaker *mean*? Considering the effects of the utterance "shoot her!" is concerned with what Austin calls the perlocutionary act of the speaker: the effects of what was said. Utterances might persuade, shock, convince, or have other effects on the hearer. To examine these is to examine the perlocutionary features of the utterance.[62] Finally, and most important to the present discussion, to ask "What did the man's utterance do?" is to inquire into the illocutionary force of the statement. When the man says, "shoot her!" he can be understood as urging or commanding another person to shoot a woman. In so doing, his utterance is itself a kind of action, and we can evaluate the kind of act it is in itself. When we look to understand the illocutionary act constituted by a specific utterance—what one is *doing* in uttering the words—we are aiming to understand the speech act itself: what it *did*.

To further illustrate the differences between locutionary, perlocutionary, and illocutionary speech acts, consider the following examples from MacKinnon's *Only Words*.[63] These examples are given in the context of a critique of the idea that since words are "expression," they are presumed to be speech in the sense that warrants First Amendment constitutional protection as expressing a viewpoint.

> . . . [S]ocial life is full of words that are legally treated as the acts they constitute without so much as a whimper from the First Amendment. What becomes interesting is when the First Amendment is invoked and when it is not. *Saying* "kill" to a trained attack dog is only words. Yet it is not seen as expressing the viewpoint "I want you dead"—which it usually does, in fact, express. It is seen as performing an act tantamount to someone's destruction, like saying "ready, aim, fire" to a firing squad. Under bribery statutes, saying the word, "aye" in a legislative vote triggers a crime that can consist entirely of what people say. So does price-fixing under the antitrust laws. "Raise your goddamn fares twenty percent, I'll raise mine the next morning" is not protected speech; it is an attempted joint monopolization, a "highly verbal crime."[64]

MacKinnon continues, "Along with other mere words like "not guilty" and "I do," such words are uniformly treated as the institutions and practices they constitute, rather than as expressions of the ideas they embody or further. They are not seen as saying anything (although they do) but as doing something."[65]

MacKinnon's aim in these passages is not the same as Langton's aim in developing a theory of speech acts that can explain the meaning of the claim that "pornography subordinates women." Rather, MacKinnon's more particular aim is to illustrate the ways in which laws, and the legal system more broadly, defines particular acts of speech or expressions as constituting crimes or actions that are subject to legal action. Her point isn't just that words do things in the world, though she does emphasize that claim. Her claim is that as a general matter, and as shown in these specific instances, we routinely regulate "only words" when those words are legally understood to constitute acts, when those acts are made into legal violations. Thus, her point is about how *the law* does things with words that do things in life, and that in many cases, such as shown in the examples above, legally regulating words that also constitute crimes or civil rights violations is not thought to raise First Amendment issues. This point will be important for evaluating Langton's philosophical "reconstruction" of MacKinnon's views and subsequent criticisms of Langton.

MacKinnon's examples do make the point that Langton is eager to demonstrate: words sometimes constitute actions, and words themselves can constitute the act of subordinating persons. Langton is concerned to defend this claim, and a second claim that pornography silences women, within her "philosophical reconstruction" of the claim of the ordinances that "pornography subordinates women."[66]

Central to Austin and Langton's account of how words *do things* is an account of "the felicity conditions" whereby words are able to function as acts in a particular context.[67] More plainly, this just means that utterances (words) do not always do the things we intend to do with them; social context matters for the ability of words to constitute particular actions. So, for example, prior to the recognition of same-sex marriage as a constitutional right of citizens in the United States, two persons of the same sex uttering the words "I do," in any context, could not function as the act of getting legally married. Whether saying "I do" constitutes the action of getting married depends on whether the felicity conditions—the socially and legally recognized conventions that confer the status of marriage—are in place.

Among the felicity conditions required for certain utterances to constitute particular actions is that the speaker is recognized to have a particular kind of authority as set by convention or law. Thus, in the case of marriage, for the speech act of declaring "I now pronounce you married" to constitute the act of "marrying" requires, among other things, that the speaker (the religious figure, judge, etc.) is recognized as having the requisite authority to marry people. My announcing to my friends "I now pronounce you married" fails to constitute the act of "marrying" because none of the requisite felicity conditions are in place, including my lacking the required authority as a legally recognized officiant.

In order to explain the claim that pornography subordinates women, then, Langton argues that pornography ranks women as inferior to men, as sex objects for use, and legitimates sexual violence against women. As Langton draws on Austin's explanation of how utterances get their illocutionary force, two important classes of illocutionary acts are relevant to the discussion of the illocutionary force of subordinating speech. Verdictives are speech acts with the illocutionary force of issuing a verdict. However, in order to have the illocutionary force that they do, someone invested with the authority to issue verdicts must utter them. A jury uttering the claim "we find you guilty" has such authority. Interestingly in the case of verdictives, recognized authorities have the power to make something true that was not previously so. They have creative power through their illocutions to bring about a new state of affairs, to make declarations as to *how things are*. An umpire's call authoritatively makes it the case that a ball is fair or foul, even when as a matter of fact, he gets the call wrong. There is no video review in baseball, and though a line umpire can overrule if he had a better view, it is still the case that some umpire's declaration makes a ball fair or foul.

Another form of authoritative speech Austin calls exercitives. Exercitives "are the exercising of powers, rights or influence. Examples are appointing, voting, ordering, advising, warning, &c."[68] Again, for a speech act such as "I appoint you Dean of the College" to have the illocutionary force of appointing, the utterer must possess the requisite authority for the utterance to have uptake— to be accepted as doing the thing the utterer aims to do, namely, appoint the next dean.

Langton characterizes both verdictives and exercitives as "authoritative illocutions."[69] She aims to explain how pornography gets its illocutionary force—its power to subordinate—in terms of its function to rank women as inferior, legitimate discriminatory behavior toward women, and to deprive women of important powers as it operates as authoritative (verdictive and exercitive) speech. Thus, on Langton's analysis, pornographic speech acts possess an authority that both constitutes the act of, and has the consequence of, subordinating women by pronouncing them as inferior.

It is important to be clear that in describing the illocutionary force of pornography, Langton is not saying that pornography causes persons to act in ways that harm women, through causing them to be sexually aggressive or violent. Of course, Langton (and MacKinnon) know that those causal effects are a consequence of pornography. But the causal effects of pornography are its perlocutionary effects, its effects on hearers/users, and those harmed by the users. The study of pornography's causal effects is an important part of the total evidence of pornography's harms, but illocutionary acts are not causal effects that flow from the utterance; they are the constitutive acts of the utterance—what the utterance *itself* does.

In order to fully defend the claim that "pornography subordinates women," Langton must explain how the utterances of pornographers in pornography has the requisite authority to constitute the act of subordination. To the question of authority, she says this: "Just as the speech of the umpire is authoritative within a certain domain—the game of tennis—so pornographic speech is authoritative within a certain domain—the game of sex. The authors of pornographic speech are not mere bystanders to the game; they are speakers whose verdict counts. Pornography tells its hearers what women are worth: it ranks women as things, as objects, as prey. Pornography tells its hearers which moves are appropriate and permissible: if it tells them that certain moves are appropriate because women want to be raped, it legitimizes violence."[70] These comments are to explain how pornographic speech *can* subordinate; as to whether *it does*, Langton remarks that such questions are not "to be settled from the philosopher's armchair."[71] While her work as a whole makes clear that she thinks that pornography does have the illocutionary force of subordinating women, here Langton is trying to show that the claim "pornography subordinates women" is conceptually clear, and as such, involves no "philosophical sleight of hand."[72]

Recently, the philosopher Nancy Bauer criticized Langton's use of Austin to defend the claim that "pornography subordinates women," and by extension criticized MacKinnon's claims that pornography is a form of sex discrimination, as well as the efforts embodied in the ordinances to address its harms.[73] Bauer argues that for pornographic speech to subordinate and silence women, it must have the requisite authority—the power to do so as recognized by convention or law.[74] She argues that Langton's attempt to defend the claim that pornography can, or likely does, have such authority fails.

According to Bauer, in order to vindicate the claim that pornography subordinates women, a "conception of authority on which pornographers can be seen to enjoy the power to fix the conventional signification of pornographic images and words—or, if you like, the rules in the language game of sex" is needed.[75] And the power to do that depends not simply "on what some authority ordains it to be but on what those who abide by the convention *recognize it and accept it* to be."[76] Thus, according to Bauer, pornography's authority (to subordinate, e.g.) must come from viewers' and users' acceptance and endorsement of "the pornographer's point of view."[77] But, if this is correct, then the power of pornography is contained in its effects on viewers (its perlocutionary force). Bauer further explains this by emphasizing that whatever authority pornography has is a *result* of such authority being granted by its audiences. And so, "this suggests that we should shift our attention from the speaker's illocutionary acts to whatever it is that motivates his auditor to vest his words with a certain power—or not? One might be tempted to think that pornography virtually inevitably makes people see the world in a certain way. But even that is simply to say that it has certain very strong perlocutionary effects."[78]

While this may seem like a purely academic debate, given all the technical jargon, it is not. What is at stake here is whether pornography is distinct in some way from other sexist materials that would warrant regulating pornography through the ordinance or some other law. If pornography merely has the effect of causing its viewers to hold and act on sexist beliefs, or even perpetrate sexual violence, then the grounds for singling it out for regulation are weakened, argue some. This is because a lot of our cultural practices, narratives, and images have the effect of causing sexist beliefs, behaviors, and even sexual violence. Critics who press this point argue that sexist advertisements, much historical literature, and even religious texts (such as the Bible or the Koran) have the *effect* of causing persons (especially men) to hold and act on sexist beliefs. They are granted authority by their readers. Thus, they continue, pornography is not special in this regard, and singling it out for regulation is unjustifiable. Cindy Stark makes a version of this argument, and indeed claims, "the more convincing their [feminists'] argument that pictures and words can, in themselves, harm the less convincing their claim that pornographic pictures and words should be singled out for regulation."[79]

Some even argue that these causal effects are evidence that pornography is a kind of speech that warrants legal protection and thus ought not to be regulated. Judge Easterbrook in his opinion in *American Booksellers v. Hudnut*, the case in which the Indianapolis ordinance was challenged, claimed that the fact that pornography has the power to subordinate women is evidence of its effectiveness as speech, hence evidence for its protection. Judge Easterbrook, writing of the view that pornography subordinates women, states: "There is much to this perspective. Beliefs are also facts. People often act in accordance with images and patterns they find around them. [. . .] Therefore we accept the premises of this legislation. Depictions of subordination tend to perpetuate subordination. The subordinate status of women in turn leads to affront and lower pay at work, insult and injury at home and rape on the streets. [. . .] Yet this simply demonstrates the power of pornography as speech."[80]

To reply to these various criticisms, it is crucial to situate the law in the context of civil rights laws.[81] Civil rights laws in the United States are responses to specific inequalities on the basis of group membership in social context. The Civil Rights Act of 1964 in the United States, for example, enumerated very specific actions deemed to violate the equality rights of persons, notably but not exclusively African Americans, because those actions were some of the primary social practices through which racial hierarchy was perpetuated and maintained in the US context. So, the act prohibits discrimination on the basis of race (color, religion, sex, or national origin) in public housing and accommodation, in voting registration, in access to public facilities, in employment, and other areas of social life in which persons were excluded or denied equality. The areas of social and political life included in the 1964 Civil Rights Act are not arbitrary or abstract. They were some of the primary social and political institutions and practices through which racial (and other) inequalities were enacted and maintained. They are a specific and concrete response to substantive inequalities that functioned to maintain and instantiate inequality on the basis of group membership.

So too are the ordinances. They are a response to a particular and specific form of inequality, in a particular and specific social and historical context. The definition of "pornography" is very, very specific. It is not aimed at all merely sexually explicit material. It is narrowly tailored to specific forms of graphic, sexually explicit presentations of gender inequality, objectifying and violent, that can be proven to subordinate women. Unlike other "speech," it functions sexually, not through any other rational or persuasive method. It circumvents those capacities.

As to how to show how pornography subordinates women in response to Bauer, the account of pornography's authority needs to be spelled out. For pornography does have authority. To respond to Stark and others, how pornography as such can constitute the act of subordination needs to be explained. Recall, Bauer argues that pornography itself does not have the requisite authority to fix linguistic meaning, because pornographers are not authorized in the way that judges are to issue authoritative rulings. So, she continues, any authority pornography has must come from viewers conferring such authority, but this account of authority would come through the effects of pornography on viewers and so relies on causal effects, not constitutive meanings. Stark, too, thinks that the effects of pornography on viewers is where to locate its power, but that this doesn't provide grounds for singling out pornography among other sexist material and practices for regulation.

The significance of separating illocutionary (constitutive) and perlocutionary (causal) effects of language, especially in the context of pornography, is overstated. Nothing about the reality of pornography or of subordination requires or even justifies such a distinction. Asking for a sharp divide between the two overlooks how effects are relied upon in determining meaning. The way words function—the effects they have—often determines their meaning. This is perhaps most obvious when words in certain contexts, come to mean something new or different from their original meaning. Prior to the *Obergelfell* (2015)[82] decision, saying the words "I now produced you married" in US states that did not recognize same-sex marriage could not have the effect, nor constitute the act of, marring two men or two women. The meaning of those words, legally, only constitutes and has the effect of marrying two persons of the same sex under the correct conditions. The meaning of the utterance "I now pronounce you married" is determined, in part, by the way it can be permissibly used.

Understanding that the effects of words are part of the evidence used in adducing the word's meaning illuminates the claims about pornography in the ordinances. So, legally calling pornography a practice of sex discrimination, an act of subordination on the basis of sex, identifies the way it functions (its effects in this historical context) as constituting its meaning as a social practice. Its function (the eroticization of inequality) determines its meaning. The fact it produces sexual arousal is both a cause and a consequence of existing within a rape culture in which the subordination of women to men is sexualized. The eroticization of inequality is at once a constitutive act and an effect; they are not separable.

Its sources of power—authority—are multiple. One key source of the authority that pornography enjoys to set social meanings—and to function in the way it does—is its social and legal status as "speech." The state, through its authoritative rulings, has determined that pornography, as such, is "speech" legally, and thus warrants protection (provided it is not obscene). The state thus creates the conditions under which pornography proliferates, virtually unregulated. Under such conditions, the authoritative ruling of the state functions to empower the proliferation of pornography and provide it with state-sanctioned protection. It authoritatively legitimates it, both the materials themselves and all the responses to them, including the sexual responses. Its power as "speech" is backed by the state. Given this state-sanctioned license to operate virtually unfettered, pornography is imbued with the social power to define and determine dominant meanings of sex. The consumers, mainly men, consume it as sex. They have sex with it. The eroticization of inequality is sex for them. Their authority to enforce this kind of sex on women is evidenced by the scope of sexual violence, including sexual harassment and rape. Women are, in fact, subordinated by the authority men enjoy, socially and legally, to force their vision of sex upon them.

"Sexy advertisements" do not do what pornography does. They are not used as a primer to rape. They are not used by rapists to select whom to rape and to get themselves aroused for the rapes they execute. Ads, admittedly part of a sexist culture, are not used to harm women in the way that pornography is used, as the empirical evidence shows. The concern that the ordinances of Dworkin and MacKinnon would sweep in such advertisements is based on distortion and misreading of the ordinances, both of the definition and the causes of action. Advertisements do not meet the definition: they are not graphic, but suggestive; they are not sexually explicit, meaning explicitly showing sex. So, any suggestive ad is a nonstarter from the definition. Beyond the definition, to use the ordinances someone must *prove* harm as specified by the causes of action.

At this point, the meaning and aims of the antipornography ordinances should be clear. To further make the case that the ordinances represent an effective and needed legal strategy to combat the harms of pornography, concrete knowledge of the industry and of the empirical evidence of the harms of both the production and consumption of pornography are required.

NOTES

1. Catharine A. MacKinnon, *Toward A Feminist Theory of the State* (Cambridge, MA: Harvard University Press, 1989), p. 138.
2. It might be said, then, that equality is an essentially contested concept. For a discussion of the idea of "essentially contested concepts" in political discourse, see William Connolly, *The Terms of Political Discourse* (Princeton, NJ: Princeton University Press, 1983).
3. The analysis of equality that follows is drawn from the work of Catharine A. MacKinnon as presented in *Sex Equality*, 3rd ed. (St. Paul, MN: Foundation Press, 2016) and many of her other writings published since 1979.
4. MacKinnon, *Sex Equality*, p. 3.
5. *Plessy v. Ferguson*, 163 U.S. 537 (1896).
6. MacKinnon, "Sex Equality: Difference and Dominance," in *Toward A Feminist Theory of the State* (Cambridge, MA: Harvard University Press, 1989), pp. 215–236.
7. *United States v. Virginia*, 518 U.S. 515 (1996).

8. *Loving v. Virginia*, 388 U.S. 1 (1967).
9. Ibid.
10. Ibid.
11. *Bradwell v. Illinois*, 83 U.S. 130 (1873).
12. *Reed v. Reed*, 404 U.S. 71 (1971).
13. See, for example, Christopher Vito, Amanda Admire, and Elizabeth Hughes (2017), "Masculinity, aggrieved entitlement, and violence: considering the Isla Vista mass shooting," *NORMA*, DOI: 10.1080/18902138.2017.1390658.
14. See Lindsay Parks Pieper, *Sex Testing: Gender Policing in Women's Sports* (Chicago: University of Illinois Press, 2016).
15. See *Price Waterhouse v. Hopkins*, 490 U.S. 228 (1989).
16. See Cordelia Fine's discussion in *Delusions of Gender: How Our Minds, Society, and Neurosexism Create Difference* (New York: Norton, 2010).
17. Patricia Hill Collins, *Black Sexual Politics* (New York: Routledge, 2004).
18. See Kimberlé Crenshaw, "Mapping the Margins: Intersectionality, Identity Politics, and Violence Against Women of Color," *Stanford Law Review*, Vol. 43 (1991), pp. 1241–1299.
19. Kimberlé Crenshaw, "Beyond Racism and Misogyny: Black Feminism and 2 Live Crew," in *Words That Wound: Critical Race Theory, Assaultive Speech, and the First Amendment*, eds. Mari J. Mastuda, Charles R. LawrenceIII, Richard Delgado, and Kimberlé Williams Crenshaw (Boulder, CO: Westview Press, 1993), pp. 111–132.
20. " 'Men-Ups' Photo Project Presents Men in Traditional Pin-Up Girl Poses," Jamie Peck, July 29, 2013, *The Gloss*, http://www.thegloss.com/culture/male-pin-up-photos-examine-gender-stereotypes/ (last accessed March 8, 2018). "Men-Ups!—Photographing Men as Pin Ups," *U Funk*, June 7, 2016, http://www.ufunk.net/en/photos/men-ups/ (last accessed March 8, 2018).
21. *Miller v. California*, 413 U.S. 15 (1973). Under the legal standard set in *Miller v. California*, in order to be found obscene, the material in question must meet three standards: "(a) the average person, applying contemporary community standards would find that the work, taken as a

whole, appeals to the prurient interest; (b) the work depicts, in a patently offensive way, sexual conduct; and (c) the work, taken as a whole, lacks serious literary, artistic, political, or scientific value."

22. Jennifer A. Johnson, "To Catch a Curious Clicker: A Social Analysis of the Online Pornography Industry," in *Everyday Pornography*, ed. Karen Boyle (New York: Routledge, 2010), pp. 147–163.

23. See *In Harm's Way: The Pornography Civil Rights Hearings*, edited by Catharine A. MacKinnon and Andrea Dworkin (Cambridge, MA: Harvard University Press, 1997), p. 427.

24. Bureau of Justice Statistics, Data Collection: National Crime Victimization Survey (*NCVS*, https://www.bjs.gov/index.cfm?ty=dcdetail&iid=245 (last accessed March 8, 2018).

25. In 2011, the NCVS changed the definition of rape. The numbers in this table refer to the legacy definition. The change is described here: "**Forcible Rape/Legacy Rape**—The carnal knowledge of a female forcibly and against her will. Rapes by force and attempts or assaults to rape, regardless of the age of the victim, are included. Statutory offenses (no force used—victim under age of consent) are excluded. **Legacy Rape**—See Forcible Rape **Revised Rape**—penetration, no matter how slight, of the vagina or anus with any body part or object, or oral penetration by a sex organ of another person, without the consent of the victim. Attempts or assaults to commit rape are also included; however, statutory rape and incest are excluded. In December 2011, the UCR program changed its definition of SRS rape to this revised definition. This change can be seen in the UCR data starting in 2013. Any data reported under the older definition of rape will be called "legacy rape." Note: In December 2011, the UCR Program changed its SRS definition of rape: "Penetration, no matter how slight, of the vagina or anus with any body part or object, or oral penetration by a sex organ of another person, without the consent of the victim." Starting in 2013, rape data may be reported under either the historical definition, known as "legacy rape" or the updated definition, referred to as "revised." See Uniform Crime Reporting Statistics, UCR

Offense Definitions, https://www.bjs.gov/ucrdata/offenses. cfm (last accessed March 8, 2018).

26. https://www.rainn.org
27. For discussion of the methodological limitations of such approaches, see Diana E. H. Russell and Rebecca M. Bolen, *The Epidemic of Rape and Childhood Sexual Abuse in the United States* (Thousand Oaks, CA: SAGE, 2000), especially "Introduction: From Revolution to Backlash," pp. 1–17.
28. Ibid., p. 4.
29. Ibid., p. 11.
30. Ibid.
31. Ibid., p. 39.
32. Ibid.
33. MacKinnon, *Sex Equality*, pp. 880–885.
34. Jon Krakauer, *Missoula: Rape and the Justice System in a College Town* (New York: Doubleday, 2015).
35. David Lisak, Lori Gardiner, Sarah C. Nicksa, and Ashely M. Cote, "False Allegation of Sexual Assault, An Analysis of Ten Years of Reported Cases," *Violence Against Women*, Vol. 16, No. 12 (2010), pp. 1318–1334.
36. https://www.rainn.org/statistics/criminal-justice-system
37. "The Judge in the infamous Brock Turner Case finally explains his decision—A Year Later," Cleve R. Wootson, Jr., *The Washington Post*, July, 2, 2017, https://www.washingtonpost. com/news/grade-point/wp/2017/07/02/the-judge-in-the-infamous-brock-turner-case-finally-explains-his-decision-a-year-later/?utm_term=.a80a729e524 (last accessed March 8, 2018).
38. "Here Is The Powerful Letter Stanford Rape Victim Read Aloud to Her Attacker," Katie J. M. Baker, June 3, 2016, *Buzzfeed.com*, https://www.buzzfeed.com/katiejmbaker/ heres-the-powerful-letter-the-stanford-victim-read-to-her-ra?utm_term=.ipwp60YaY#.on7RnjLoL (last accessed March 8, 2018).
39. MacKinnon and Dworkin, *In Harm's Way*, p. 444.
40. See Michael Rea for discussion of definition of pornography: M. C. Rea, "What is Pornography?" NOÛS, Vol. 35, No. 1 (2011), pp. 118–145.

41. *American Booksellers, Inc. v. Hudnut*, 771 F.2d 323 (1985), *aff'd mem.*, 475 U.S. 1001 (1986). A summary affirmation "allows the U.S. Supreme Court to uphold an appellate result without reading briefs, hearing oral argument, or expressing a view on the reasoning of the opinion below. A summary affirmance is a ruling on the merits, but the reasoning of the opinion so affirmed technically binds only the circuit in which it is issued." MacKinnon, *Sex Equality*, p. 1757.

42. See Catharine A. MacKinnon and Andrea Dworkin, *Pornography & Civil Rights: A New Day for Women's Equality* (© 1988 Catharine A. MacKinnon and Andrea Dworkin), pp. 41–52.

43. MacKinnon and Dworkin, *In Harm's Way*, p. 442.

44. Linda Lovelace (with Mike McGrady), *Ordeal: The Truth Behind Deep Throat* (New York: Citadel Press Books, 1980); and Linda Lovelace (with Mike McGrady), *Out of Bondage* (Mass Market Paperback, 1987). For her testimony in *In Harm's Way*, see pp. 60–68. For her testimony before the Attorney General's Commission on Pornography, see *Final Report of the Attorney General's Commission on Pornography* (Nashville, TN: Rutledge Hill Press, 1986), p. 205.

45. See her entire testimony in MacKinnon and Dworkin, *In Harm's Way*, pp. 60–68.

46. MacKinnon and Dworkin, *In Harm's Way*, p. 443; and *Pornography & Civil Rights*, pp. 49–50.

47. MacKinnon and Dworkin, *In Harm's Way*, p. 122.

48. MacKinnon and Dworkin, *In Harm's Way*, pp. 70–72.

49. This example is one of which I have personal knowledge. A friend in graduate school (not at the University of Illinois-Chicago, where I was a graduate student at the time) reported this to me in 1998.

50. MacKinnon and Dworkin, *In Harm's Way*, p. 443.

51. MacKinnon and Dworkin, *In Harm's Way*, p. 443.

52. MacKinnon and Dworkin, *In Harm's Way*, p. 430.

53. MacKinnon and Dworkin, *In Harm's Way*, p. 460. This cause of action was not a part of the Indianapolis statute, but a part of the model ordinance and the Massachusetts ordinance.

54. "'Nailin' Paylin'—Lights, Camera, Lots of Action," October

13, 2008, *TMZ.com*, http://www.tmz.com/2008/10/13/ porn-stars-give-nailin-paylin-a-dry-run/ (last accessed March 8, 2018).

55. MacKinnon and Dworkin, *In Harm's Way*, p. 442.
56. MacKinnon and Dworkin, *Pornography & Civil Rights: A New Day for Women's Equality*, p. 45.
57. William Parent, "A Second Look at Pornography and the Subordination of Women," *The Journal of Philosophy*, Vol. 87, No. 4 (April 1990), pp. 205–211.
58. Melinda Vadas was among the first, if not the first, philosopher to offer a philosophical defense of the claim, see her: "A First Look at the Pornography/Civil Rights Ordinance: Could Pornography be the Subordination of Women," *The Journal of Philosophy*, Vol. 84, No. 9 (September 1987), pp. 487–511. As Rae Langton's work is, in my view superior and more thorough, I focus on her account here.
59. In her footnote, MacKinnon carefully distinguishes her analysis from Austin's. She writes: "J.L. Austin's *How to Do Things with Words* (1962) is the original enunciation of the theory of performative speech, which examines language for which "the issuing of the utterance is the performing of an action— it is not normally thought of as just saying something," at 6– 7. While he does not confine himself to inequality, which is critical to my argument here, neither does he generalize the performative to all speech, as have many speech act theorists who came after him. Austin is less an authority for my particular development of "doing things with words" and more a foundational exploration of the view in language theory that some speech can be action." Catharine A. MacKinnon, *Only Words* (Cambridge, MA: Harvard University Press, 1993), p. 121.
60. J. L. Austin, *How to Do Things with Words* (Cambridge, MA: Harvard University Press, 1962), pp. 101–102.
61. Rae Langton, "Speech Acts and Unspeakable Acts," in *Sexual Solipsism* (New York: Oxford University Press, 2009), p. 27.
62. Austin, *How to Do Things with Words*, p. 102; and Langton, "Speech Acts and Unspeakable Acts," p. 27.

63. MacKinnon, *Only Words*.
64. MacKinnon, *Only Words*, p. 12.
65. Ibid., pp. 12–13.
66. Langton, "Speech Acts and Unspeakable Acts," p. 29.
67. Austin, *How to Do Things with Words*, p. 26; Langton, "Speech Acts and Unspeakable Acts," p. 33.
68. Austin, *How to Do Things with Words*, p. 151.
69. Langton, "Speech Acts and Unspeakable Acts," p. 27.
70. Langton, "Speech Acts and Unspeakable Acts," p. 45.
71. Ibid.
72. Langton, "Speech Acts and Unspeakable Acts," p. 46.
73. Nancy Bauer, *How to Do Things with Pornography* (Cambridge: MA: Harvard University Press, 2015).
74. Ibid., p. 76.
75. Ibid., p. 80.
76. Ibid.
77. Ibid.
78. Ibid.
79. Cynthia A. Stark, "Is Pornography an Action?: The Causal vs. Conceptual View of Pornography's Harm," *Social Theory and Practice*, Vol. 23, No. 2 (Summer 1997), pp. 277–306, 279.
80. *American Booksellers v. Hudnut*.
81. What follows is the argument I give in another article, and it is further elaborated there, see Watson, Lori, "Pornography," *Philosophy Compass*, Vol. 5, No. 7 (2010), pp. 535–550.
82. *Obergelfell et al. v. Hodges, Director, Ohio Department of Health, et al.* 576 U.S. ___ (2015).

8

Pornography

8.1 THE PORNOGRAPHY INDUSTRY

Pornography is an industry, a commercial industry that makes and sells pornography for profit. Often enough, thoughts about pornography evoke images of artists making sexual material as self-expression. Although some artists no doubt do create pornography, they are not part of the pornography industry. Nor are their materials the focus of the sex equality approach to pornography.

Pornography production and consumption is big business—very big. Estimates for the annual revenue generated by the pornography industry in the United States are somewhere between 13 and 14 billion dollars.[1] Globally, the pornography industry is estimated to generate 97 billion dollars annually. To put these numbers in perspective, in 2016 the National Football League (NFL) reported 13.3 billion in revenue.[2] The National Basketball Association (NBA) reported 8 billion.[3] The movie industry generated 11 billion domestically and 38 billion globally in 2016.[4] Starbucks, a single corporation, generated 21 billion in revenue in 2016, yielding 5.2 billion in profit.[5]

Porn sites don't just traffic in images and videos; they serve as a platform for advertisers of sex toys, sexual enhancement substances, penis size enhancing medical procedures, "escort services" and other forms of prostitution, and basically any good or service that falls into the "adult entertainment" category. The numbers cited above do not include these ancillary services and goods. For that reason, and because of the fact that the industry, as an industry of prostitution that trafficks in people for sexual use, is in some senses and at some points and in some places illegal and clandestine, the total size of the pornography industry as an economic engine is certainly larger than the reported numbers.

The pornography industry is organized much like other industries that want to protect their bottom line, given that it is money that is at stake.[6] The industry has its own trade magazines/websites (*Adult Video News* and *Xbiz*), tracks industry news, profiles "stars," holds an annual awards show (think Oscars for pornography), and tracks trends in the industry. *Xbiz* also provides detailed business advice to pornographers about marketing strategies, trends of users, and other data and reports deemed significant to industry insiders. The industry has its own lobbying and legal advocacy group, The Free Speech Coalition. Their mission statement reads: "As the national trade association to the adult entertainment and pleasure products industry, our mission is to lead, protect, and support the growth and well-being of businesses and workers in the adult industry, as well as the communities to which they belong."[7] The Free Speech Coalition has led industry efforts, including through lawsuits, to defeat laws requiring condom use in pornography, to challenge laws mandating age verification for those in pornography, to challenge laws limiting and regulating child pornography, and to challenge laws regulating access to pornography on the Internet.[8]

It is a common misconception to think of various aspects of the commercial sex industry as distinct and isolated. The major components of the industry—stripping, pornography, and prostitution—overlap and intertwine. Those who work in adult entertainment often flow back and forth between its various forms. So, for example, women who work in Nevada brothels, in those few counties where prostitution is legal in the United States, are often involved in pornography and stripping at various times.

Who are the "performers" in pornography and how do they become involved with it? Women involved in "the sex industry"—whether that be stripping, prostitution, or pornography—are there due to conditions of inequality. They are disproportionately young, in poverty, "members of socially disadvantaged racial groups or lower castes," and frequently have a history of abuse (including childhood sexual abuse).[9] Pornography defenders deny these facts. Sometimes they claim the presentation of such facts are part of a "feminist" agenda. Here is Dave Pounder, a pornography producer and male performer, with over ten years in the industry (answering this question from an interviewer: Could you offer a broad description of the typical personality profiles of male and female porn actors?):

> The female actresses, in my opinion, are all damaged (e.g., histories of sexual or emotional abuse). I know it sounds bad to say that, but that has been my experience after spending over a decade in the industry. I have yet to meet a non-damaged (i.e., no past history of sexual or emotional abuse or trauma) professional (e.g., attorney, doctor, professor) female who left her job to make adult videos.[10]

As a pornography performer and producer, Mr. "Pounder" is hardly a part of a feminist agenda to "misstate" the facts about women in pornography. And, his words say it all, the truth is there.

Another myth is that those in pornography are making a lot of money—that they are rich. Accurate numbers of the earnings of women and men in pornography are difficult to get, yet some reputable reporting provides a guide. CNBC ran a news story in 2016 reporting pay scales for women and men in pornography.[11] Their report states: "For a 'traditional' sex scene between a man and a woman, the average actress's compensation is typically between $800 and $1,000, depending on the studio's budget. Top-tier performers can earn as much as $1,500, occasionally $2,000, while newcomers with bad representation might earn as little as $300. More extreme acts, as you might expect, command higher rates. The most extreme—unsuitable for describing in polite conversation—can go for $1,800 to $2,500."[12] The acts that CNBC characterize as "unsuitable for describing..." include double penetration, multiple penetration, and what is known as "ATM" (ass to mouth). What this report did not describe is how much of this fee goes to pimps, also known as managers or agents. Typically, from reports of women who have fled the industry, it is the majority of the money. Male performers, in contrast, typically earn less. "With men, there's no pay differential depending on the sex act. Generally, male performers receive a fixed amount per scene or day, depending on how the shoot was booked. [. . .] In general, males average $500–$600 per scene or day. Better known male performers can earn $700–$900; superstars up to $1,500."[13] Adult men typically are not pimped.

To the extent that the numbers themselves may suggest a respectable annual income, the average length of time a woman in pornography stays in pornography is three months. Consumers demand fresh "meat." "Porn is an industry that regularly chews up and spits out performers. Many quit after just one scene or after a few months. Some stick around for a few years, but then disappear."[14] A very few are able to earn significant money in pornography, but these women are not representative of the thousands of women used in pornography.

With the evolution of the Internet, pornography has changed in ways that serve demand. In the days before videotape and the Internet, the majority of pornography was visual still images. Although so-called adult films did exist, pornography was primarily shown in so-called adult theaters. In order to circumvent obscenity laws, many of these films had plots of sorts, minimal as they were, as a means of claiming artistic value. Feature-length adult films are rare to nonexistent now, since they are expensive to make and not in demand. The average porn user spends twelve minutes on a porn site.[15] "Gonzo" pornography, as it is called by some,[16] is now the dominant form of pornography. It has no plot whatsoever. It is just recorded sex acts, sometimes followed by an interview with the woman scripted for the viewer, sometimes without such an interview. These interviews are a callback to the centerfold questionnaire of *Playboy*, where the women were asked questions like: What is your biggest turn on? What are your guilty pleasures? And what are your favorite movies? One suspects that in those twelve minutes, the viewer is not spending much time watching the after interview.

What is it that all the people who are providing these profits are watching? Pornhub.com, a popular pornography website, issues an annual report documenting trends in searches and demographics of users. According to their 2016 annual report, the top search terms, in order, for that year were: "lesbian," "stepmom," "MILF," "teen," and "stepsister." "Teen" was the top search term in 2015. "Teen" remained a top one or two search term in various other countries, including the United Kingdom and Canada. The top search terms in the United States were: "lesbian," "ebony," and "teen." Terms searched more frequently in the United States, compared to other countries, were: "big booty Latina," "big black dick," and "ebony." The relation of these selections to the powerlessness of age and the racism of white supremacy is obvious. Consider what the function and effect of the average consumer, a heterosexual man, selecting so-called lesbians (actually women doing what men want to see women doing when men are not around) or intrafamily sexual scenarios are.

Adult Video News is the "trade" magazine (online) in the porn industry in the United States. Among other things, this magazine provides information regarding the most popular videos, month to month. Here are some of the titles of top rentals for July 2017 (as reported in August 2017). In the category of "top 100 rentals," the top five, in order, were: *Interracial and Anal*, *Women Seeking Women 142*, *Women Seeking Women 143*, *Lesbian Seductions Older/Younger*, and *Cheer Squad Sleep Over 22*. In the category of "top 50 specialty rentals," the top five, in order, were: *Disciplined Teens*, *Hot Wife Bound*, *Nympho Nurses and Dirty Doctors*, *Bob's T Girls and Their Fucking Machines*, and *T Girls Porn 8* (featuring women made to look like teen girls). The category of gay porn features titles such as: *Straight Guys Try Cock* and *Virgin Bros Get Fucked*. Other titles worth emphasizing include *Breaking our Daughter*, number two on the "Top VOD Downloads"; and *Joanna Jett, the Trans MILF 6*, number six on the "top 50 specialty rentals" list.

There is a pattern here. Various forms of inequality that are not in themselves sexual, like age inequality, racial inequality, trans-identity-based inequality, the inequality between mother and child, nurses and doctors, and so on are erotized, turned into sex. The "sexiness" is in the inequalities, the hierarchy between the paired groups. The gay/straight divide is a sexual one, but it's presented in terms of the hierarchy between straight and gay or lesbian. Here too, inequality is eroticized.

The pornography industry, like other industries motivated by profit, is ever seeking methods of expansion. New forms of pornography emerge as technology advances, blurring the line (to the extent that one accepts there is any line[17]) between pornography and prostitution. Live webcams in which women (and some men) engage in live performances, directed by viewers, are an expanding part of the market in sex. Pages upon pages of women (and some men) sitting, waiting to "perform" on demand, are available via the Internet. These platforms categorize "the performers" along the lines of race, age, sex, the sexual acts they "specialize" in, and so on. They are lined up behind the web cams much like animals at the zoo, ready to be ordered up to perform "blow-jobs" on dildos; to "fuck" dildos; and in many cases to "perform" with another person, woman or man, on command of the buyer/viewer for sexual consumption on his computer screen.

8.2 EMPIRICAL EVIDENCE OF HARM

8.2.1 Production Harms

The legal theory out of which the ordinances of Dworkin and MacKinnon grew was originally designed to pursue legal action against those who coerced and harmed Linda Marchiano (Boreman) in the making of *Deep Throat*.[18] That legal strategy specifically aimed to provide grounds for redress in cases in which persons, such as Linda, were harmed in the making of pornography. The ultimate approach included addressing consumption harms, but was conceived, in the first instance, in light of production harms.[19] In the ordinance, these harms are actionable as coercion into pornography. To use this cause of action, the material in question must be pornography as defined. And, for each of the acts enumerated on the list of subparts—such as women being tied up, bound and gagged, etc.—the acts had to be done to the particular women who is suing for the purpose of making pornography. MacKinnon, in her testimony before the Attorney General's Commission on Pornography, calls "this the direct causal link between pornography and harm."[20] She says: "For every act you see in the visual materials, some of which I know you have seen, a woman had to be tied or cut or burned or gagged or whipped or chained, hung from a meat hook or from trees by ropes, urinated on or defecated on, forced to eat excrement, penetrated by eels and rats and knives and pistols, raped deep in the throat with penises, smeared with blood, mud, feces, and ejaculate."[21]

These acts are not simulations in the materials in question; they are done to women for the purpose of making pornography of them. The acts themselves are acts in which women are subordinated—placed in an inferior and degraded relation to those doing the acts, acting upon them—such that their inequality is sexualized. In addressing the production harms—the harms required to make the materials—the ordinance specifies that coercion into performing for pornography violates the civil rights of those so coerced, and is an act of sex discrimination.

Jenna Jameson, perhaps the most famous "porn star" in recent memory, writes in her *How to Make Love Like A Porn Star: A Cautionary Tale*: "Most girls get their first experience in gonzo films—in which they're taken to a crappy studio apartment in Mission Hills and penetrated in every hole possible by some abusive asshole who thinks her name is Bitch. And these girls, some of whom have the potential to become major stars in the industry, go home afterward and pledge to never do it again because it was such a terrible experience. But, unfortunately, they can't take the experience back, so they live the rest of their days in fear of what their relatives, their co-workers, or their children will find out, which they inevitably do."[22] She also describes having been raped as a youngster. Production harms are not "anecdotal" one-offs; they are constitutive of the industry. Women are the product, to be bought and sold, and consumer demand for whatever the consumer wants to see done drives the market and the industry.

In 2012 in Los Angles, a referendum called "Measure B" was placed on the ballot to require condom use in pornography for all vaginal and anal sex. The argument in favor of mandatory condom use in pornography was framed, in part, in terms of worker health and safety. A number of "performers" had contracted HIV in the years leading up to the proposal. The pornography industry presents itself as a legitimate business industry and the "workers" as "professional sex workers." Those supporting "Measure B" argued that on that premise, the industry should not be exempted from occupational health and safety standards applicable to all other work contexts. Activists documented the STIs and other injuries and their frequency in pornography production. These included: chlamydia of the eye (from ejaculate penetrating the eyes of women subject to "facials" meaning ejaculation on the face), gonorrhea of the throat, and fecal infections in the throat (from the common practice of what is known as "ATM" (ass to mouth) in which unprotected anal sex is followed immediately with unprotected oral sex), as well as HIV.[23]

The industry panicked, mounting a public campaign against "Measure B," spearheaded by its legal advocacy group, the Free Speech Coalition. They also threated to leave LA, preferring to shoot in other locations, notably Las Vegas, in which they were free to carry on as usual. "Measure B" passed. A huge decline in applications for permits to film in LA followed. The industry has largely relocated outside of LA, demonstrating that profit is its primary motive and any attempt to protect the rights and interests of those in such films is an existential threat. Apparently the industry cannot pay the actual cost of operating as it does.

This is demonstrably clear in industry efforts—through the Free Speech Coalition—to fight age-verification standards. Sections 2257 and 2257A of Title 18 of the United States Criminal Code require recordkeeping, labeling, and various forms of inspection for producers of sexually explicit material to document the age and participation of performers. The purpose of the law is to prevent underage persons, that is, children, from being used in pornography, which produces child pornography, which is actually illegal in the United States. The Free Speech Coalition filed suit in a federal court challenging the constitutionality of these regulations. They argued, inter alia, that the statutes violated the First and Fourth Amendments, by excessively burdening speech and permitting unreasonable searches (inspections).[24] They lost. In *Free Speech Coalition, Inc. v. Holder*, the appeals court rejected their claims.

Critics of restraints on pornography, enacted and proposed, object that there are already laws against rape or sexual assault, and the harms of coercion into pornography can be addressed through those laws. In fact, though, such laws do not address these particular harms. As documented above, rape is underreported, underprosecuted, and under-convicted. Women in pornography or prostitution face even greater hurdles to the just enforcement of such laws, as their "status" as a woman in pornography or prostitution is used as evidence that they could not have been raped.

Moreover, laws against rape or sexual assault, as now constructed, do not get at the scope of the injury either for those crimes or for the injury as captured by the ordinance of Dworkin and MacKinnon, since rape laws do not address inequality per se. Such laws, criminal or civil, do not capture rape is as a gender-based crime, an act of sex discrimination, as the ordinance of Dworkin and MacKinnon do. And no law addresses the pornography made through coercion: the profit incentive for the coercion as well as its immortality in the woman's life.

8.2.2 Consumption Harms

An enormous body of empirical literature examines the effects of pornography on users, dating back to the early 1970s. Early studies of the effects of pornography were actually studies aiming to investigate human aggression, and pornography was used in those studies, not to directly study pornography, but as a means to study the effect of media upon aggression.[25] In the course of this research, Zillman conducted numerous experiments and found that among men primed for aggression, exposure to "sexually arousing material" increased their level of aggression.[26] Additional laboratory studies by Zillman and others showed that sexual arousal to nonviolent pornography increased aggression, while sexually "pleasant" material (material that did not arouse subjects) lowered aggression.[27] A number of other studies in this early period demonstrated that repeated exposure to similar sexually explicit material desensitized viewers' sexual arousal and "foster[ed] an interest in uncommon sex displays" (e.g., BDSM and bestiality).[28]

Importantly, the studies just described are causal, not correlational, studies. This method involves empirically testing a hypothesis by a designed study with a control group (not exposed) and an experimental group (exposed). The purpose of the control group, like in other scientific investigation, is to isolate causal variables. If one group is exposed and the other is not, and there is a measurable difference between the two groups, then the researcher can infer a causal relationship between the variable in question (the one that the experimental group was exposed to).

Following this early research on aggression, which contained revelations about pornography's role in fomenting aggression, researchers began to study pornography directly. They began to investigate the effects of pornography across the following variables: whether it causes sexual aggression, desensitizes its viewers to sexual violence, increases sexist attitudes and beliefs, increases the viewers' interest and demand for more violent materials, is addictive, damages familial relationships, and causes erectile dysfunction, among other things.

Edward Donnerstein, Daniel Linz, and Steven Penrod, leading social scientists and media-effects researchers, published a book in the late 1980s summarizing and analyzing the body of research up to that point on the effects of pornography.[29] Concerning the effects of pornography showing acts considered to be violent (as covered in the definition in the ordinances authored by Dworkin and MacKinnon), these authors identify four questions that the empirical investigations aimed to answer: (1) "What are the effects of exposure to violent pornography on aggressive behavior?" (2) "How does violent pornography influence the viewers' attitudes and perceptions about sexual violence, particularly rape?" (3) "Do men who are exposed to violent pornography find it sexually arousing?" (4) "If there are effects from viewing violent pornography, is it due to the fact that the material is sexually explicit or that it is violent?"[30]

They describe the kind of pornography under investigation—so-called violent pornography—as material that contains women as being sexually coerced by a man using force "to obtain sexual gratification," and where the rape is presented as "pleasurable, sexually arousing, and beneficial to the female victim."[31] A more recent study conducted by Anna Bridges et al. published in 2008 found that 88.2% of scenes (of a sample of 304 scenes) contained physical aggression, while 48.7% contained verbal aggression, both primarily directed at women.[32] In a 2012 content analysis, Natalie Purcell found violent, abusive, and coercive behaviors in "nearly all" those analyzed, roughly half of the 250 "most popular, pornographic movies of the past 40 years."[33]

The studies that Donnerstein et al. conducted were laboratory studies in which participants were divided into experimental and control groups. The experimental groups, exposed to violent pornography, displayed increased negative attitudes toward women and increased aggression toward women. The studies also showed that "normal college-aged males become sexually aroused to violent pornography, especially if it contains the message that women enjoy rape."[34] What the pornography industry calls "positive outcome rape" scenarios were the most arousing, the most long lasting in their effects, and the most powerful in producing attitudinal and behavioral effects inimical to women's equality.

Further evidence for these effects is documented in Max Waltman's extensive literature review of the empirical findings over the last forty years on the casual impacts of pornography consumption.[35] Among the evidence Waltman reviews is a study of the effects of pornography on viewers in the context of a simulated rape trial. He reports of the study: "Male and female subjects in simulated rape trial juries who were exposed to common nonviolent pornography during five hours over six weeks recommended almost half the penalty recommended by control groups. The underlying mechanisms have been explained by psychologists and validated by survivor testimonies: nonviolent pornography that objectifies, degrades, or dehumanizes, which commercial pornography invariably does even without express violence, contributes to men categorizing women according to notions of 'whores' versus 'Madonnas' . . ."[36] Waltman further documents an enormous body of empirical research finding that the more pornography consumers consume, the more more sexual aggression and sexist attitudes they report, compared with low-consuming persons. Male pornography users are much more likely to "buy persons for sex," and battered women and women in prostitution are especially subjected to harms from pornography users.[37]

The evidence that pornography is both correlated and causally implicated in sex-based harms is overwhelming. In fact, a recent study of the effects of pornography viewing on "fraternity men" observes: "It is difficult to find a methodologically sound study that shows a lack of some kind of harm when men view pornography."[38] The authors continue their summary of findings: "The preponderance of research suggests significant negative impacts of pornography on men in the aggregate."[39] Such impacts include: increased acceptance of aggression and violence toward women, acceptance of rape myths, "stronger behavioral intent to rape," trivialization of rape, "decrease in empathy and compassion towards victims of sexual assault," "less bystander efficacy to intervene in a rape situation," and other misogynistic effects.

The more violent the pornography, the more negative the effects on the viewer. The authors of this study, evaluating the effects of pornography on bystander intervention, conclude: "This study showed that men who viewed pornography, particularly rape and sadomasochistic pornography, report a greater likelihood of raping, committing sexual assault, higher rape myth acceptance, lower willingness to intervene in a sexual assault situation, and lower efficacy to intervene in a sexual assault situation."[40]

Skeptics of the documented fact that pornography harms women often focus their challenge on the claim that pornography causes sexual aggression or violence. Some of these skeptics argue that pornography use reduces risk of violence perpetrated by users as it provides an outlet for users to release their sexual aggression, the so-called cathartic effect.[41] A recent meta-analysis (2016) analyzed twenty-two different studies from seven different countries investigating the question: "Is pornography consumption correlated with committing actual acts of sexual aggression?"[42] This meta-analysis adds to the body of research showing the harms of pornography consumption by analyzing data across these twenty-two studies correlating "direct measures of pornography consumption" with "direct measures of sexual aggression in general population studies."[43] Here, pornography is defined as "media featuring nudity and explicit sexual acts designed to arouse the consumer."[44] Thus, the definition is much broader than that of the ordinances of Dworkin and MacKinnon; it is not limited to only inegalitarian, objectifying, or violent forms of subordinating sexually explicit material.

This meta-analysis found: (1) "Pornography consumption was associated with an increased likelihood of sexually aggressive behavior for females as well as males."[45] (2) Age was not a factor in likelihood of sexual aggression among pornography users. Both teen and adult users were equally likely to engage in sexually aggressive acts. (3) "Violent and nonviolent pornography consumption were each associated with sexual aggression and the difference between the associations was not significant."[46] The authors advance three caveats concerning these findings. First, they emphasize that studies drawing on self-reports of users, who classify the material they use as either nonviolent or violent pornography, may not be fully reliable as to the distinction between the two, since "desensitized consumers" may not perceive extremely aggressive acts as violent (thus, misdescribing their consumption), and "content that is nonviolent is still objectifying and degrading."[47] Second, while the difference between violent and nonviolent users' likelihood of sexual aggression was not statically significant (both correlated with violence), "the violent pornography association was stronger."[48] Further, they note that statistical significance is affected by sample size, and only two of the studies in the meta-analysis measured nonviolent pornography consumption. Third, and finally, the authors of the nonviolent studies did not "clearly indicate whether each met all the criteria of nonviolence: fully consensual sex without any coercion or aggressive behavior."[49] (4) Pornography use "was associated with both verbal and physical aggression, but the association was stronger for verbal aggression" (which includes sexual harassment). They also note that verbal coercion to achieve sex is "still an act of sexual violence."[50] (5) "Pornography use was associated with an increased probability of the use or threat of force to obtain sex."[51]

An earlier meta-analysis by Hald et al. concluded, "the current results showed an overall significant positive association between pornography use and attitudes supporting violence against women in nonexperimental studies. In addition, such attitudes were found to correlate significantly higher with the use of sexually violent pornography than with the use of nonviolent pornography, although the latter relationship was also found to be significant."[52] This meta-analysis included nine studies with a total of 2,309 participants. The measures used to evaluate "attitudes supporting violence against women" were: the acceptance of interpersonal violence scale (a test rating individuals' attitudes regarding the acceptability of using force and violence in relationships), the adversarial sexual belief scale (measuring "the degree to which participants perceive male and female relations as 'fundamentally exploitative'"), the rape myth acceptance scale (measuring the degree to which people accept common rape myths, like the belief that women invite rape by what they are wearing or really mean "yes" although they are saying "no"), the attitudes toward rape scale (measuring their attitudes toward the acceptability of rape or forced sex), the likelihood of rape scale, the likelihood of sexual force scale, and the likelihood of sexual harassment scale (each measuring "the hypothetical potential of a man to rape or commit similar sexual aggressive acts given the assurance that he would face no punishment"), the perceptions of sexual harassment scale, and the sexual harassment proclivities scale (assessing "participants' proclivity to engage in sexual harassment").

These studies support the legislative findings in the ordinances as the basis for the laws, namely, that pornography is central in maintaining the civil inequality of the sexes and differentially harms women.[53] Consider as one example the claim that pornography "inhibits the just enforcement of laws" concerning rape and other forms of sexual violence that women experience. We know, as documented above, that rape is vastly underreported, under-investigated, under-prosecuted, and under-convicted as compared to all other violent crimes. Insofar as consumers of pornography occupy the positions of police investigator, judge, and jury member, and consumption of certain forms of pornography (as defined by the ordinances) is demonstrably shown to increase acceptance of rape myths and the acceptance of the use of interpersonal violence, then pornography is implicated in the systematic denial of women's equal civil rights to have a fair and impartial investigation and adjudication of crimes against them.

8.2.3 Population-Level Studies

Drawing on the work of A.W. Eaton, Altman suggests that the claim that pornography harms women should be understood not in the "but-for" causal sense, but as the claim that pornography is "a salient risk factor for a variety of harms to women."[54] Eaton advances her argument by drawing on an analogy with smoking and the evidence that eventually sufficed to prove the claim that smoking causes cancer, despite the lack of understanding of the actual causal mechanism. Smoking is neither necessary nor sufficient for any individual to get cancer, as we know. Some people who smoke may never get any smoking-related illness (including cancer). If fact, roughly one-third of smokers will never get a smoking-related illness. That means, of course, that two-thirds of smokers will get a smoking-related illness, and many of those will die from such illnesses. And, of course, some people get cancer (even lung cancer or other cancers that are more prevalent among smokers) despite never having smoked. Yet, it is commonly known that smoking "causes" cancer in the sense that it greatly increases one's risk of getting cancer, and not smoking or quitting smoking greatly reduces the risk of getting certain cancers. Actually, the findings are correlational.

Building on this analogy, and its reliance on a probabilistic model of causality, Eaton and Altman suggest that population-level studies are an important part of the total set of empirical evidence concerning the harms of pornography. As he develops his own analysis about the connection between pornography and its availability with the prevalence of sexual violence, Altman focuses narrowly on data concerning reported rapes. He notes a decline in reported rapes (relying on FBI Uniform Crime Reports) between the years 1994 and 2012. He also notes the increase in the availability of pornography through the Internet over the same period. Yet Altman's suggestive information here is problematic for a number of reasons.

First, the limited focus on rape is a problem. Sexual violence in the form of rape is only one of the harms that the ordinance of Dworkin and MacKinnon identifies among the ways in which women may be harmed by pornography. Sexual harassment, coercion into sex that may not track legal definitions of rape, and other forms of sexual battery and assault and discrimination are significant harms not captured by a limited focus on legal definitions of rape.

Second, Altman focuses on "reported" rapes during the period. This is a fatal flaw. A more accurate, though still vastly incomplete as noted previously, source of information is the National Crime Victims Survey (NCVS). The NCVS, as described earlier, is a survey conducted by the Bureau of Justice Statistics, in order to collect social scientific data on the kinds and number of crimes committed in the United States each year.[55]

The numbers this survey reports under the category of rape and sexual assault are as follows: 268,574 in 2010; 244,188 in 2011; 346,830 in 2012; 300,165 in 2013;

284,345 in 2014; and 431,837 in 2015.[56] The numbers in the early to mid-1990s are significantly higher: 898,239 in 1993; 674,291 in 1994; 563,249 in 1995; 437,198 in 1996; and 553,523 in 1997.[57] However, the raw data itself doesn't explain the drop. Without a qualified social scientific investigation, it would be simply guessing to suggest an explanation. Two factors, though, are relevant and worth mentioning when considering this data: the overall level of violent crimes dropped dramatically during the same period, and the rate of incarceration grew dramatically. Thus, it is very likely that some of the offenders in the early 1990s were in jail subsequently, and unable to reoffend, at least concerning the public at large. As Altman notes, his data does not amount to a serious statistical analysis and does not control for a range of variables.

Exact figures of incidences of rape, sexual violence that doesn't fall under the legal definitions of rape, other forms of sexual assault and battery, and sexual harassment are not fully captured in NCVS data, due to underreporting as well as the cultural silence and shame that keeps victims hidden. However, the recent social media campaign "#metoo" gives some insight into how deep and pervasive sexual violence and harassment actually are. Following the revelations of Harvey Weinstein's pattern of sexual harassment, sexual abuse, and rape of women over whom he had power, a large number of women, including very famous Hollywood actresses, publicly revealed that they too had been sexually harassed, some physically violated, by Weinstein. The public revelations by powerful figures such as Ashley Judd, Angelina Jolie, and Gwyneth Paltrow seemed to buoy the confidence of many women to speak out about their own experiences with sexual harassment and sexual violence.

Actress Alyssa Milano sparked the ensuing social media firestorm of "#metoo" by posting on Twitter: "Suggested by a friend: If all the women who have been sexually harassed or assaulted wrote "Me too" as a status, we might give people a sense of the magnitude of the problem."[58] Milano's tweet ignited the subsequent flood of social media posts, half a million tweets in the first twenty-four hours.[59] "Other social media platforms saw a huge #MeToo trend; Facebook revealed to *CBS News* that in the twenty-four hours after Milano posted her tweet, 12 million posts and comments went up, and 45% of all US users had friends who'd posted #metoo."[60] Though all this activity immediately following Milano's tweet seemed to spark a movement, the "#metoo" campaign was originally started by Tarana Burke in 2006.[61] #Metoo has brought attention to the depth and severity of sexual harassment and sexual violence so that the reality may be being acknowledged. The consciousness raising and solidarity captured by the "#MeToo" movement gives some reason for optimism that, finally, sexual harassers and perpetrators of sexual violence cannot count on the shield of shame and silence that has allowed them to operate with impunity for millennia. But, this much is clear: the focus of Altman and others on reported rapes as anything approaching an accurate measure of sexual violence and sexual harassment in the culture is woefully, even outrageously, inadequate.

The key disagreement between liberals like Altman and those supporting the sex equality approach to pornography is whether the body of evidence documented here is sufficient to warrant legal intervention in some form. This, despite the fact that the ordinances themselves draw no conclusions on this question at all; they only allow access to court to use the evidence to show harm in each instance. Liberals like Altman claim that it is not adequate for this purpose, while sex equality advocates claim that it is. Thus, the debate is primarily over the appropriate standard of social understanding for permitting legal intervention that allows proof to be presented.

Objections to the claim that the body of literature surveyed above provides sufficient evidence of the harms of pornography to warrant a civil legal claim, in which harms would have to be proven, that are, repeated by Altman, include: even if aggression is a result of exposure in laboratory settings, this doesn't suffice to establish a "real-world" connection between pornography and violence against women; men do not masturbate to climax in the studies, and so the studies can't rule out the "safety-valve hypothesis" suggesting that ejaculation relieves aggression; some of the studies focus on men in the 18–24 age group and so are not sufficiently random, and as such don't consider the potential "pacifying effects" of marriage and children on older men; and even if the studies provide evidence that some men are more likely to show aggression toward women, this isn't sufficient to undermine the argument from sexual autonomy.

Taking each objection in turn, the "real-world" evidence that Altman claims is absent is there. The testimony of victims, as documented in the Minneapolis hearings for the ordinance of Dworkin and MacKinnon, is real-world evidence. So too is subsequent testimony by women and girls, especially, of the ways in which pornography was used to harm them. Critics often dismiss such testimony as "anecdotal," suggesting that it is unreliable or doesn't constitute evidence. Such testimony is evidence of a particular harm that a particular person (woman) experienced. Alone such testimony doesn't provide evidence of the scope of the problem—that is, how widespread such harms are—but it is still evidence, precisely the kind of evidence used in court cases every day to show damage.

As to the "safety-valve hypothesis," Altman's claim seems to be that because men don't ejaculate in the laboratory studies, we can't know whether, when they do ejaculate in their homes while viewing pornography, this act relieves or removes any of the aggression resulting from viewing the pornography. Yet, there are long-term longitudinal studies of pornography users. And they consistently find that more individual pornography use predicts sexist attitudes and behaviors. Many such studies are "naturalistic studies" and not laboratory studies, and so it is probably safe to assume that the men in question are, indeed, ejaculating.[62] Also, a focused look at pornography makes clear that its primary aim is arousal; it is erection. Assuming that ejaculation relieves this effect or merely primes the pump is an assumption for which there is no evidence whatever.

Finally, does "settling down" in a marriage with children have a "pacifying effect" on men? Given the rates of domestic abuse and battery, as well as the common reports that rapists as well as users of prostituted women are married men, makes one less optimistic that marriage has a general pacifying effect. Here, too, there is no evidence for Altman's claims. But, even if Altman is correct that more harms are committed by men in the 18–24 category— though statistics show the age range for significant pornography consumption is broader, up to age 34—this "fact," if it is a fact, doesn't undermine the case for addressing pornography in accordance with the ordinances of Dworkin and MacKinnon, which only permit proven harmful instances to be addressed. Youth is a predictor of crimes across many categories, especially violent crimes, but just because younger people are overrepresented in the perpetrator category does not mean that laws against such acts are considered unnecessary.

Many people express skepticism over the claim that pornography use shapes the beliefs, attitudes, and behaviors of users. Sometimes when expressing such skepticism, it is claimed that pornography is just fantasy, a form of escape, and totally different and distinguishable from "real life." An underlying assumption in this kind of skepticism has to be the claim that pornography is simply different than other forms of media, in some way not typically expressed. The thought has to be something like this because even those who express this skepticism will readily admit the ways in which other forms of media influence behavior.

The entire advertising industry is built on the verifiable assumption that exposure to positive images of products, activities, and behaviors, etc., directly influences people's buying beliefs, attitudes, and most importantly purchasing behaviors. In other words, all the activities of "marketing" are premised on the assumption that exposure to messages associated with whatever someone is selling is an effective method for getting people to buy it. Indeed, the goal of marketing is to impact people's behavior (and in so doing make a profit). That Apple has been so successful in getting people to buy its products (and continually upgrade them, spending more money, even when the old version is perfectly functional) is largely due to its very effective marketing strategies. Apple sells not only phones and computers; it sells a way of life, a way of presenting oneself to others, and a way of being "cool." Their ability to sell the latter through marketing is part of why Apple products are so popular and in demand.

Moreover, there is an entire business industry devoted to collecting and then reselling data concerning the buying habits, patterns, and preferences of various groups. Often called "big data," these firms cull information about groups—men aged 18–34 and single, men aged 35–45 and married, women aged 35–45 and married with children, and so on—and sell this demographic information to other companies, who then use it to develop specific marketing strategies for specific demographics. And to further underscore the point that media—both through images and words—has powerful effects on behavior: just consider the recent presidential election or, really, any political campaign. The effort of candidates to "get their message out," to craft and hone that message on the basis of political polls and focus groups, is a basic function of campaign management in modern elections. The behavior they are targeting is voting, and the method is media campaigns (and perhaps other more nefarious methods, such as voter suppression and gerrymandering, but the main point remains).

Thus, the strangeness of claiming that somehow pornography, as distinct from all these other media forms, does not directly affect the beliefs, attitudes, and behaviors of consumers is apparent. How is it that somehow pornography, almost alone, is an exception to the general knowledge about how images and words impact behavior? This question is even more confounding when we emphasize that pornography is used as sex, through sexual arousal and ejaculation. Sexual arousal, as Altman notes, is a powerful motivator and interest of most people. The claim that pornography has little to no effect on people's behaviors is thus hard to reconcile with common sense. However, we don't have to rely on common sense to settle the question as to the effect of pornography consumption on human behavior.

NOTES

1. See Jennifer Johnson, "To Catch a Curious Clicker: A Social Network Analysis of the Online Pornography Industry," *Everyday Pornography*, ed. Karen Boyle (London: Routledge, 2010), pp. 147–163; and Gail Dines, *Pornland* (New York: Beacon Press, 2010).
2. "Thanks to Roger Goodell, NFL Revenues to Surpass 13 Billion in 2016," Jason Belzer, February 29, 2016, *Forbes.com*, https://www.forbes.com/sites/jasonbelzer/2016/02/29/thanks-to-roger-goodell-nfl-revenues-projected-to-surpass-13-billion-in-2016/#466062d91cb7 (last accessed March 8, 2018).
3. "NBA Begins New Season Flush with Cash as Revenue Expected to Hit 8 Billion," John Lombardo, October 24, 2016, *Street & Smiths SportsBusiness Journal*, http://www.sportsbusinessdaily.com/Journal/Issues/2016/10/24/In-Depth/Lead.aspx
4. Statista: The Statistics Portal, https://www.statista.com/topics/964/film/
5. MarketWatch.com, http://www.marketwatch.com/investing/stock/sbux/financials
6. See Gail Dines, *Pornland*, for an analysis of the business of pornography.
7. https://www.freespeechcoalition.com
8. *Free Speech Coalition v. Holder*, available online at http://www2.ca3.uscourts.gov/opinarch/133681p1.pdf
9. Catharine A. MacKinnon, "Trafficking, Prostitution, and Inequality," *Harvard Civil Rights-Civil Liberties Law Review* Vol. 46 (2011), pp. 271–309, pp. 276–281 at 271.

10. "A Chat with Author and Former Pornographer Dave Pounder," Gad Saad, July 16, 2013, *Psychology Today*, https://www. psychologytoday.com/blog/homo-consumericus/201307/ chat-author-and-former-pornographer-dave-pounder
11. "Porn's dirtiest secret: What everyone gets paid," Chris Morris, Wednesday, January 20, 2016, https://www.cnbc. com/2016/01/20/porns-dirtiest-secret-what-everyone-gets-paid.html
12. Ibid.
13. Ibid.
14. Ibid.
15. This data is from Alexa.com, a site that provides statistics about Internet usage and traffic. I originally did research on this site in 2011, and this number is from that research. At that time, the information was free from Alexa.com. Now, you have to pay. Thus, I did not update the information. My original research is drawn from a variety of top porn websites, including xhamster.com, and this is what the Alexa data showed at that time (2011): "There are 57 sites with a better three-month global Alexa traffic rank than Xhamster. com. While we estimate that 20% of the site's visitors are in the US, where it is ranked #58, it is also popular in Turkey, where it is ranked #25. The site has a bounce rate of about 19% (i.e., 19% of visits consist of only one page view). Compared with internet averages, Xhamster.com appeals more to men; its visitors also tend to consist of childless, low-income users browsing from home and school who are not college graduates. Visitors to the site spend about 50 seconds on each page view and a total of twelve minutes on the site during each visit."
16. See Gail Dines, *Pornland*.
17. Many states in the United States treat pornography as a form of prostitution. California is one big exception. A 1988 California Supreme Court case, *People v. Freeman* (250 Cal. Rptr. 598 (1988)), distinguished between prostitution and pornography on the grounds that paying someone to be filmed having sex is different than paying someone to have sex. The court's reasoning here is arguably incoherent, for it

depends on a distinction between pornography and prostitution lying in whose sexual gratification is aimed at by the
sex acts. Since, according to the court, the pornographer is
not paying for "actors" to engage in sex for *his* sexual gratification, it is distinct from prostitution. As any woman who
has escaped this kind of filming may tell you, even this distinction is a dubious one.

18. Catharine A. MacKinnon, *Butterfly Politics* (Cambridge, M.:
    Harvard University Press, 2017); "Testimony on Pornography,
    Minneapolis," p. 96.
19. Ibid.
20. MacKinnon, *Butterfly Politics*, p. 102.
21. Ibid., p. 101.
22. Jenna Jameson, *How to Make Love Like a Porn Star: A
    Cautionary Tale* (New York: Harper Collins, 2004), p. 132.
23. I have seen this data, but it is not publicly available, and I am
    not at liberty to share it.
24. *Free Speech Coalition, Inc. v. Holder*, 957 F. Supp.2d 564
    (2013).
25. Daniel Linz and Neil Malamuth, *Communication Concepts
    5: Pornography* (London: SAGE, 1993), p. 17.
26. Ibid., p. 18.
27. Ibid., pp. 18–20.
28. Ibid., pp. 20–21.
29. Edward Donnerstein, Daniel Linz, and Steven Penrod,
    *The Question of Pornography: Research Findings and Policy
    Implications* (New York: The Free Press, 1987).
30. Donnerstein et al., *The Question of Pornography*, p. 87.
31. Ibid., p. 88.
32. Ana J. Bridges et al., Aggression and Sexual Behavior in Best-
    Selling Pornography Videos: A Content Analysis, *Violence
    Against Women*, Vol. 16 (2008), pp. 1065–1085.
33. Natalie Purcell, *Violence and the Pornographic Imaginary: The
    Politics of Sex, Gender and Aggression in Hardcore Pornography*
    (London: Routledge, 2012), pp. 179–181.
34. Donnerstein et. al., *The Question of Pornography*, p. 107
35. Max Waltman, "Appraising the Impact of Toward a Feminist
    Theory of the State: Consciousness-Raising, Hierarchy

Theory, and Substantive Equality Laws," *Law & Inequality: A Journal of Theory and Practice*, Vol 35 (2017), pp. 353–391.

36. Waltman, "Appraising the Impact of Toward a Feminist Theory of the State," p. 369.
37. Waltman, "Appraising the Impact of Toward a Feminist Theory of the State," pp. 365–372.
38. John D. Foubert, Matthew W. Brosi, and R. Sean Bannon, "Pornography Viewing Among Fraternity Men: Effects on Bystander Intervention, Rape Myth Acceptance and Behaviorial Intent to Commit Sexual Assault," *Sexual Addition & Compulsivity*, Vol 18 (2011), pp. 212–231, p. 212.
39. Foubert et al., "Pornography Viewing Among Fraternity Men," pp. 213–215.
40. Foubert et al., "Pornography Viewing Among Fraternity Men," p. 227.
41. Paul J. Wright et al., "A Meta-Analysis of Pornography Consumption and Actual Sexual Aggression in General Population Studies," *Journal of Communication*, Vol. 66 (2016), pp. 183–205.
42. Ibid., p.183 (quoting abstract).
43. Ibid., p. 184.
44. Ibid., p. 184.
45. Ibid., p. 197.
46. Ibid., p. 198.
47. Ibid., p. 198.
48. Ibid., p.198.
49. Ibid., p.198.
50. Ibid., p. 199.
51. Ibid., p. 199.
52. Gert Martin Hald, Neil M. Malamuth, and Carlin Yuen, "Pornography and Attitudes Supporting Violence Against Women: Revisiting the Relationship in Nonexperimental Studies," *Aggressive Behavior*, Vol. 36 (2010), pp. 14–20.
53. In *In Harm's Way: The Pornography Civil Rights Hearings*, edited by Catharine A. MacKinnon and Andrea Dworkin (Cambridge, MA: Harvard University Press, 1997), pp. 426–427, and p. 439.
54. See Altman's contribution in this book and A. W. Eaton, "A

Sensible Antiporn Feminism," *Ethics*, Vol 117, No. 4 (2007), pp. 674–715.

55. The NCVS webpage describes its purpose and methods as follows: "The Bureau of Justice Statistics' (BJS) National Crime Victimization Survey (NCVS) is the nation's primary source of information on criminal victimization. Each year, data are obtained from a nationally representative sample of about 90,000 households, comprising nearly 160,000 persons, on the frequency, characteristics, and consequences of criminal victimization in the United States. The NCVS collects information on nonfatal personal crimes (rape or sexual assault, robbery, aggravated and simple assault, and personal larceny) and household property crimes (burglary, motor vehicle theft, and other theft) both reported and not reported to police. Survey respondents provide information about themselves (e.g., age, sex, race and Hispanic origin, marital status, education level, and income) and whether they experienced a victimization. For each victimization incident, the NCVS collects information about the offender (e.g., age, race and Hispanic origin, sex, and victim-offender relationship), characteristics of the crime (including time and place of occurrence, use of weapons, nature of injury, and economic consequences), whether the crime was reported to police, reasons the crime was or was not reported, and victim experiences with the criminal justice system." https://www.bjs.gov/index.cfm?ty=dcdetail&iid=245

56. Bureau of Justice Statistics, NCVS Victimization Analysis Tool (NVAT), https://www.bjs.gov/index.cfm?ty=nvat

57. Bureau of Justice Statistics, NCVS Victimization Analysis Tool (NVAT), https://www.bjs.gov/index.cfm?ty=nvat

58. "#MeToo: Social media flooded with personal stories of assault," Lisa Respers France, Mon. October 16, 2017, http://www.cnn.com/2017/10/15/entertainment/me-too-twitter-alyssa-milano/index.html

59. https://www.bustle.com/p/this-is-how-many-people-have-posted-me-too-since-october-according-to-new-data-6753697

60. Ibid.

61. " "The Woman Who Created #MeToo Long Before Hashtags,"
Sandra E. Garcia, *New York Times*, Oct. 20, 2017, https://
www.nytimes.com/2017/10/20/us/me-too-movement-
tarana-burke.html
"An activist, a little girl and the heartbreaking origin of 'Me Too,'"
Cassandra Santiago and Doug Criss, Tue. October 17, 2017,
http://www.cnn.com/2017/10/17/us/me-too-tarana-burke-
origin-trnd/index.html
62. See Waltman, "Appraising the Impacts of TFTS."

9

Defenses of Pornography

DEFENSES OF A "RIGHT" TO pornography typically rest on
one of three types of claims: the right to free speech entails
a right to pornography; the right to sexual autonomy entails
a right to pornography; or, on some interpretation of what
the equal treatment of persons requires of the state, a right
to pornography follows.

9.1 FREE SPEECH DEFENSE
OF PORNOGRAPHY

Given that many continue to see any restrictions on pornography as implicating freedom of speech, a discussion
of defenses of pornography grounded in free speech rights
is warranted. Some maintain in particular that the sex
equality approach to pornography amounts to a ban or censorship. It will be shown that that criticism misreads and
misconceives the ordinances. Beyond this, a key conceptual
claim underlying various principles of First Amendment jurisprudence is a supposed sharp distinction between "ideas
and conduct." As the Court states this point: "To preserve
these freedoms, and to protect speech for its own sake, the
Court's First Amendment cases draw vital distinctions between words and deeds, between ideas and conduct."[1] This

supposed distinction functions in Court decisions to protect pornography, and so pornographers, as well as socially
dominant groups more broadly. Understanding this is essential for appreciating the sex equality approach to pornography. The Court's approach, by contrast, here protects
pornography, including virtual child pornography, allowing
a thriving market of such material to operate effectively
unfettered. The First Amendment doctrinal commitment
to "viewpoint neutrality" is also examined and exposed as a
non-neutral doctrine, one that in practice serves to reinforce
and cement existing social hierarchies. This becomes especially clear in examining the *American Booksellers v. Hudnut*
decision, in which the anti-pornography ordinances were
ruled unconstitutional by a court of appeals panel.[2]

Some critics have called the trafficking provision of the
ordinances a form of "censorship,"[3] a term that typically
refers to criminal prohibitions by government, not human
rights violations of abused people. Historically, censorship
by law, or de jure censorship, relies on a state censor—a
person or agency—responsible for vetting material in advance of publication or exacting criminal sanctions upon
those found to be guilty of publishing, writing, or circu-
lating forbidden materials. The ordinances do not do any
of this. They are not criminal laws; they are civil rights
laws. The government has no authority under them to vet
materials prior to publication nor is it empowered to sue.
Police and jail are not involved. The ordinances place in the
hands of women or other violated people the power to defend their own human rights. Insofar as any critics of the
ordinance allege censorship in this sense, they simply fail
to understand the law and how civil law, specifically civil
rights law, works.

De facto censorship is censorship "in effect," due to unavailability or other factors rather than government control. So, for example, if all booksellers in a particular region were to refuse to carry certain books, their refusal would have the same effect as censorship, even though there was no law directing them to act as such. A widespread refusal to publish feminist work could be considered political censorship, although it is typically regarded as a speech right of publishers rather than a denial of speech rights to writers. De facto censorship in the not strictly legal sense might also manifest itself if booksellers feared reprisal for selling or distributing particular materials. This concern is typically termed the "chilling effect," where manufacturers or distributors of pornography are imagined to restrain from producing or selling materials that they fear may open them to legal liability. Some critics voice this concern of the ordinances' trafficking provision.

One claim of de facto censorship rests upon the belief that suits that are successful under the trafficking provision will result in specific material being removed from circulation. Legally speaking, this would be termed relief and would have to be predicated on a showing of harm, harm that would end when the materials were no longer trafficked in the jurisdiction. Another version of the claim of de facto censorship asserts that the threat of civil action will "chill" producers, sellers, and distributors of pornography, because they know their products meet the definition stipulated in the ordinance. If this is a result of the materials they refrain from publishing or distributing that violate human rights, their actions would be termed "voluntary compliance" with the law—the usual way equality laws function.

To think the first claim of de facto censorship has merit requires denying that pornography causes harms or simply not caring that it does, including not valuing the people it harms. The language of "censorship" generally carries with it an accusation that whatever is being "censored" is unjustly unavailable. But if specific material is removed from circulation because it is proven to cause real concrete harm, it is not unjust to stop it. Although product liability laws are quite different from civil rights laws, the effect they have in removing harmful products from sale and distribution is similar. Supposing that after a civil suit, claimants successfully demonstrate, in accordance with relevant legal standards, that the product in question is dangerous and harmful to consumers, and as such the product is removed from circulation, and those injured are provided economic relief. It is typically understood that such legal victories embody justice—not unjust governmental interference or violation of the rights of sellers or distributors of the product. Note also that obscenity law permits the removal of material from circulation with no showing of material harm at all.

As for the concern about a "chilling effect," compare laws against sexual harassment. Sexual harassment laws have no doubt "chilled" sexual harassment in work and education, a vast amount of which is effectuated through words and expressive actions. The degree to which sexual harassment laws have been an effective tool for combating the sex discrimination experienced by women, men, and gender-non-conforming people in education and the workplace is cause for celebration, not regret or charges of censorship. It is thought that sexual harassment laws rightly chill harassers, because the harms of sexual harassment are seen as real. The concern that the pornography industry would be chilled by the ordinance, like the concern over unjust availability of pornography, simply rests on denying its harms or valuing inflicting those harms over the people harmed by their infliction.

Nadine Strossen provides a stark example of what can only be a willful misreading of the ordinances, presumably intended to trigger habitual fears and hysteria about censorship, protecting pornographers. She includes in *Defending Pornography* a reproduction of an image by artist Saelon Renkes of a pregnant woman's nude torso, including her visible breasts; her hand is placed on her stomach with a child's hand grasping hers. The hand-painted photograph is called "Second Child Coming."[4] Strossen claims that the image falls within the purview of the definition, which she characterizes as "dangerously vague." Part of the problem with the ordinance, she charges, is that it "does not take account of the artist's—or model's—intent. It holds all depictions of women's bodies hostage to the (mis) perceptions of particular viewers."[5]

Strossen is a lawyer, former president of the ACLU, and a member of the law faculty at New York Law School; she is Harvard educated. It is hard to believe she believes what she has written here. Not only would such an image not fall within the scope of the definition, but also the mere existence of any image is not sufficient to ground the causes of action within the ordinance. This image is neither graphic nor sexually explicit; it does not graphically depict sex at all. Strossen selectively quotes one of the ordinance's further enumerated conditions as if that alone constitutes the definition. She makes no mention of the causes of action or of the requirement that any specific piece of material meeting the definition must be shown to harm someone in one of the four ways specified (coercion, force, assault, or trafficking in subordination). Instead she raises the specter of "radical feminist" censorship through her blatantly inaccurate and unfounded "interpretation" of the law.

She then immediately discusses *ACLU v. Reno*, a case in which the constitutionality of the Communication Decency Act (1996) was adjudicated. The Communication Decency Act, in the tradition of obscenity-based approaches, aimed to regulate material that is "patently offensive" or "indecent." These concepts play no role in the ordinances; the entire legal framework upon which the ordinances are grounded repudiates the obscenity-based approach. Strossen writes that material can be "banished" because "under the model antipornography law promoted by procensorship feminists like Andrea Dworkin and Catharine MacKinnon, all it takes is one person who considers the work to be "subordinating" or "degrading" to women."[6] This is legally utterly false. Her critique, in short, entirely misses its target.

Under current US constitutional law, material with sexual content is protected as speech unless it is child pornography or obscene under the standards set forth in *Miller*. Altman and I agree that an obscenity-based approach is misguided; my rejection of obscenity as a standard overlaps with his at some points. However, my analysis extends beyond his by showing they ways in which the obscenity-based approach has functioned to create the conditions for the proliferation of pornography, including virtual child pornography.

Obscenity-based approaches aim to regulate material with sexual content that is deemed obscene. It does not necessarily aim to restrict pornography. Though pornography and material that have sexual content are often conflated in common usage, they are not identical. The sex equality approach defended here is not concerned with sexual content per se. Nor is it concerned with whether some materials may appeal to "the prurient interest in sex." Compared with obscenity, which can potentially encompass all material with sexual content deemed to be sexually arousing and be unacceptable to community standards at the time and place, the sex equality approach to pornography is limited in scope. Compared with the ordinances, what counts as obscene can be very broad and can vary widely.

Further, obscenity-based approaches do not aim at the harm of pornography. The so-called harm of such material— appealing to the prurient interest—is its offensiveness, as measured by contemporary community standards. The concept of offense is not itself well defined in the legal cases culminating in *Miller*. Philosopher Joel Feinberg offers a helpful catalogue of the mental states generally thought characteristic of "being offended." These include: "unpleasant sensations, disgust, shocked sensibilities, irritation, frustration, anxiety, embarrassment, shame, guilt, boredom, and certain kinds of responsive anger and fear."[7] Effectively, "offense" is a subjective state in which the offended party *feels* aggrieved by the "offending" material, remark, or suggestion. The most apt states on Feinberg's list regarding reactions to pornography are likely disgust; shocked sensibilities; anxiety; embarrassment; shame; guilt; anger; or fear; and for many, after repeated exposure, boredom. Aside from the fact that none of these asserted harms form any part of the sex equality approach to pornography, they are a troubling basis for legal restriction of expressive material.

The reactive attitudes reflected in being offended are highly subjective and variable. Typically, the topics likely to cause such offense challenge or threaten dominant cultural values. In the context of sex, that has included, and does include for many, any representation of same-sex sexuality, for example. In this sense, the claim of being offended amounts to "I don't approve of that." It essentially amounts to a negative moral judgment. Whether one wants to work out a view in which being exposed, confronted, or having knowledge of the mere existence of groups, persons, or sex acts or forms of sexuality one doesn't like constitutes an injury of some kind, it should be clear that relying on such a basis for state action through law is anathema to liberal, democratic values, including importantly equality. Liberal democratic values include a commitment to guaranteeing protection of minority groups against the whims and power of majorities. An obscenity-based approach to pornography potentially allows for majorities to impose their values regarding representations of kinds of sex and sexualities (and so potentially categories of persons) deemed offensive to dominant sensibilities. This is another kind of threat to equality.

Appeals to "offense" as a basis for condemnation of racism, sexism, homophobia, or other institutionalized forms of inequality, as well as pornography, are similarly misguided. When those who want to condemn statements of others that embody racism, sexism, or homophobia challenge the speaker by asserting they are "offended," they aren't fully capturing the harm or the wrongness of such statements in a substantive equality theory. While it may be true that hearers of such claims are offended, in the sense that they are disgusted or outraged, the equality claim they want to make to the speaker is not merely that they are disgusted or outraged. Rather, they want to make a claim about a substantive harm not just to them as individuals, but also to the group that the bigot, sexist, or homophobe targets, on behalf of whom they are protesting. That someone was offended by what another said doesn't alone capture the further claim about the ways in which racist, sexist, or homophobic speech acts can substantively harm members of those groups. The harm of such speech acts is in its power to subordinate, to further the social reality in which persons of color, women, gays and lesbians, non-normatively gendered persons, trans persons, persons with disabilities, and so on, are regarded and treated as less than other people, as unequal. These harms are concrete and real, not subjective or dependent on attitude or viewpoint as such.

Altman well describes the historical evolution of obscenity culminating in *Miller*, the case setting forth present controlling constitutional doctrine on obscenity. In the obscenity approach, obscenity was originally deemed non-speech, thus without First Amendment protection. Obscenity could be criminalized consistent with the First Amendment because it was not speech.[8] The Court has also ruled that child pornography can be constitutionally prohibited as a form of child abuse. Pornography that uses actual children in its production is thus not protected speech. The rationale for banning child pornography accepted by the Court in the *Ferber* case was that the materials were a form of sexual abuse, a harm that obscenity law was insufficient to address.[9] The Court recognized that the sex acts required to make such material, and the state interest in the protection of children, were sufficient to justify its being banned, consistent with First Amendment principles.

Yet the Court has held virtual child pornography protected speech unless obscene. "Virtual pornography" describes three kinds of images. In the context of child pornography, "virtual pornography" often refers either to an image of an adult body with a child's head imposed upon it, known as "morphing"; or the use of youthful-looking adults in place of children (referred to as "barely legal" pornography).[10] These "virtual" images are often used in place of actual children in to skirt child pornography laws, which actually prohibit the materials, compared with such material of adults.

"Virtual pornography" can also mean wholly computer-generated material, sometimes referred to as animated pornography or anime porn. It is often extremely life-like. Animated technology is so sophisticated now that there is nothing really cartoonish or caricature-like about these images. These computer-generated images can be manipulated by consumers to allow direct control over the sexual acts being performed by the subjects in the pornography. Animated pornography also potentially allows for even more violence than found in pornography that uses actual persons. Tahl Price, cofounder of Priceless films, a company specializing in animated pornography, is reported emphasizing this point in a recent interview: "Tahl waxes enthusiastic about his ideas for combining sex and violence in ways you can't pull off in live action . . . He shows me an unreleased scene in which a woman is stabbing a man to death during coitus—a comic-book interpretation of the praying mantis mate-then-eat-your-male concept of sex."[11]

Such virtual images, specifically of children, were the subject of *Ashcroft v. The Free Speech Coalition*,[12] which considered whether certain provisions of the 1996 Child

Pornography Prevention Act (CPPA) ran afoul of First Amendment guarantees. The Court ruled that these provisions of the CPPA were overbroad and inconsistent with First Amendment protections, thus unconstitutional. In ruling the provisions of the CPPA overbroad, the Court found that those provisions impermissibly restricted protected speech. The CPPA expanded "the federal prohibition on child pornography to include not only pornographic images made using actual children but also 'any visual depiction, including any photography, film, video, picture or computer or computer generated image or picture'" that "is or appears to be" or "conveys the impression" of a "minor engaging in sexually explicit conduct."[13] Thus, the CPPA aimed to make illegal all three types of virtual child pornography: images of actual adults adulterated to look like children, the use of youthful-looking adults meant to appear as children, and wholly animated images of children engaged in sex acts. But the respondents did not challenge, and the Court did not rule on, the section of the CPPA that prohibited the practice of morphing, in effect, allowing the provision to stand. However, the Court comments on that provision that "although morphed images may fall within the definition of virtual child pornography, they implicate the interests of real children and are in that sense closer to the images in *Ferber*."[14]

Although the Court has held that child pornography does not command the same First Amendment protection enjoyed by non-obscene material involving adults, in *Ashcroft* it held that virtual child pornography can be regulated only if it is obscene. Thus, virtual child pornography is afforded constitutional protection, whereas child pornography that uses actual children is not. In *Ferber v. New York*, the precedent-setting case regarding child pornography, the Supreme Court held that "material which depicts . . . sexual performances by children under 16" need not be obscene to be legally proscribable. The separate opinion of Justice Sandra Day O'Connor made clear that the concerns of obscenity were irrelevant to whether children were harmed by pornography.[15] The *Ferber* decision departed from *Miller* by centering its concern on harm—harm to children in that case. Criminalizing child pornography was found consistent with the protection of the freedom of expression even where not obscene because of the harm it does to those used in making it. *Ashcroft* finds that virtual pornography of children is ontologically distinct from pornography that uses actual, living children, making it an altogether distinct *kind* of thing. Virtual child pornography is not "intrinsically related" to the sexual abuse of children because it does not require the actual sexual abuse of children to make it:[16] "the CPPA prohibits speech that records no crime and creates no victims by its production."[17]

Addressing the government's claim that virtual child pornography is linked to the sexual abuse of actual children, the Court simply declares "the causal link is contingent and indirect," thus insufficient to warrant overriding the speech interests at stake. In addressing the specific issue of morphing, the Court writes: "Rather than creating original images, pornographers can alter innocent pictures of real children so that the children appear to be engaged in sexual activity. Although morphed images may fall within the definition of virtual child pornography, they implicate the interests of real children and are in that sense closer to the images in Ferber."[18] Apparently there can be harms to a child being used to make child pornography even if the child is not sexually used to make it. Despite this potential broadening of the interests at stake, the Court denies that the proliferation of virtual child pornography is a discrete and concrete harm to children—something of an unresolved tension within the opinion.

So, in *Ashcroft*, the Court dismisses the economic-deterrence rationale for the permissibility of regulating child pornography accepted in *Ferber*—namely, that "the advertising and selling of child pornography provide an economic motive for and are thus an integral part of the production of such materials."[19] The Court dismisses a similar rationale for the ban on virtual pornography claiming: "The argument that eliminating the market for pornography produced using real children necessitates a prohibition on virtual images as well is somewhat implausible because few pornographers would risk prosecution for abusing real children if fictional, computerized images would suffice."[20] In other words, what the Court is suggesting is that if computerized images of children engaged in sexually explicit acts would suffice—read: satisfy the consumers' desires to use children sexually in pornography—then there would be no need for child pornography made through the use of actual children. This is an unsupported conjecture inconsistent with the dynamics of the child pornography trade, in which particular identified children often become sold, traded, and collected at a premium.

The suggestion that computer-animated child pornography may help eliminate the market for pornography using actual children is unsupported by evidence. In the pornography market, the claim is constantly made that the material shows actual people. Presumably, the pornographers know their audience's requirements. The Court also ignores the well-documented fact that users of child pornography are typically child sexual abusers. They form Internet groups on the dark web and share their child pornography between one another, often of children they are abusing. The photos of actual sexual abuse of children is the child pornography the buyers want. It circulates among such abusers as "trophies." The idea that animated child pornography could have a substitution effect on this market of users lacks credibility.

The Court also entirely misses the fact that the pornography is not simply used to gratify a desire for children engaged in sexual acts, but as a tool for grooming children to accept and perform sexual acts. Given that child pornography that contains actual children is widely used as an "instruction manual" by predators, animated child pornography, insofar as it does resemble cartoons or video games, is likely to be a child sex abuser's "dream" tool in breaking down children to accept their sexual violation. The fact that the Court does not acknowledge such harm or its potential is consistent with its failure to recognize the harms of pornography, child or adult, inflicted through its consumers. Nowhere in its analysis is a concern with equality. The inequality of children to adults is singularly obvious, but the Court doesn't see virtual child pornography as raising equality interests at all.

In the wake of *Ashcroft*, the "barely legal" genre of pornography exploded. "Barely legal" is a pornography industry term for pornography that purportedly uses performers over the age of 18 but presents them as teens or children. For example, youthful appearing girls are placed in setting with teddy bears surrounding them in a child's bedroom, or with child-oriented posters and bedding, and/or they may have on braces, and/or have their hair styled in pigtails, and/or be wearing a school uniform, and/or children's pajamas, and various other props used to infantilize them. All pubic hair is removed, a now common practice. The Internet became saturated with pornography depicting sex between adults and youthful-looking adults made to look like children, including incestuous sex and the forced sex of "virgins" by their "fathers" or stand-in "daddys," as reflected in dramatic age differences between the men and the girls used in it.

As noted previously, "teen porn" was for several years the number one pornography search term on the Internet and consistently ranks in the top five, not only in the United States, but also globally. Through its decision in *Ashcroft*, the US Supreme Court secured the material conditions for this material to proliferate and fuel demand, virtually unregulated. The Free Speech Coalition, the legal lobbying arm of the pornography industry, has subsequently challenged the age-verification standards, which require pornography producers to verify that the performers they use are 18 or older. Appeals courts have rejected their arguments. However, the "barely legal" genre continues to thrive, and it is almost certain that within it some actual child pornography, meaning sexual abuse and exploitation of minors, occurs. Consumers who are conditioned to eroticize the sexuality and inequality of children, as depicted in this genre, depend on the persons being used, mainly small women, being indistinguishable from actual children.

In response to the *Ashcroft* decision, pornography researchers Neil Malamuth and Mark Huppin critiqued the Court's dismissal of the harms of virtual child pornography and the lack of evidence provided by the government in defending the CPPA. They argue that both failed to draw on the body of "peer-reviewed, empirically validated research science" documenting the harms of child pornography and virtual child pornography.[21] They highlight that studies "suggest that sexual interest or arousal in children is not confined to a "sick few."[22] The evidence for this conclusion is drawn from research that measures "penile arousal" (i.e., erections) in response to "images of children,"[23] so not subject to the potential biases and limitations of self-reports. In one particular study they summarize, in a "sample of non-pedophilic men, reactions to pictures of pubescent and pre-pubescent girls averaged 70% and 50%, respectively, as strong as their responses to adult females."[24]

Further, they document the evidence of the use of child pornography in the sexual abuse of children, including as a grooming tool and in preparation for an assault. They conclude, "the fact that a substantial percentage of child molesters report that pornography use increased their likelihood of offending, and the fact that those who offend repeatedly against children are more likely to be pedophilic, suggest that the wider availability of any form of child pornography to such offenders (including virtual child pornographic images indistinguishable from that using actual children) is likely to add fuel to the fire."[25] In the absence of any substantive equality analysis of this pornography, the Court creates the conditions for it to exponentially multiply, leaving unaddressed, denying relief or redress, to the countless victims harmed in and by it.

The ordinances, in contrast, provide the legal grounds for such relief. Where material meets the definition of pornography, the causes of action, forcing pornography on a person, assault or physical attack due to specific pornography, or the trafficking provision, each provide an avenue for legal remedy to those harmed by virtual child pornography, when they can prove that harm was caused by the pornography in question.

9.2 EQUALITY WITHIN THE FIRST AMENDMENT

Missing within the Court's approach to virtual child pornography, or pornography generally, is an analysis of substantive equality. First Amendment jurisprudence, much like the dominant strand of 14th Amendment jurisprudence discussed in the first section here, incorporates within its doctrine a formal model of equality.[26] This understanding of equality, again, which says that equality concerns are concerns over treating like cases (or persons) alike, does not contain within itself the resources for identifying inequalities that are the result of social hierarchies. This limitation, combined with the absence of a theory of power, has produced a First Amendment doctrine that serves to benefit the socially powerful, and secure their interests, and the expense of socially dominated groups.[27]

Formal equality, within the First Amendment requires "viewpoint neutrality."[28] This requirement doctrinally requires that regulations of speech/expression must be "viewpoint neutral." Thus, when the Court decides that a law regulates expression on the basis of viewpoint, even in cases of racist speech or other hate speech, First Amendment jurisprudence protects it, and perhaps surprisingly, deems attempts at suppressing it discriminatory. This is illustrated in the case of R.A.V. v. City of St. Paul (1990).

In *R.A.V.*, a group of white teenagers who burned a cross on the front lawn of a black family who lived in their neighborhood were charged with a crime under an ordinance that criminalized a variety of acts, including cross burning and displaying swastikas, as bias-motivated crimes, a misdemeanor. Justice Scalia, writing for the majority, found the ordinance was unconstitutional viewpoint discrimination. The essence of the majority decision was that because the ordinance only targeted speech/expressive conduct that concerned "specified disfavored topics," such as words "on the basis of race, color, creed, religion or gender," the law discriminated based on viewpoint.[29] Put simply, the Court declared that the ordinance aiming to prohibit speech/expressive conduct, including burning crosses on black people's front yards, that targeted historically subordinated groups was discrimination against those engaged in such speech/expressive conduct—those expressing the racist, sexist, or other prejudiced views through this conduct. Thus, perhaps shockingly, rather than seeing the acts of cross burning and the display of swastikas as discriminatory acts that the ordinance in question aimed to criminalize, the Court declared the government's attempt to stop the burning of crosses and the displaying of swastikas as discriminatory because, according to them, burning crosses expresses a viewpoint. Never mind that the viewpoint also constitutes an act of racial hatred and racial terrorism.

This ruling demonstrates the way the Court's reliance on purported neutrality serves to guarantee the status quo conditions under which unequal power distributions—between black and white people in this particular case—are left to function as social hierarchies, and attempts to remedy such inequality through legislation are prohibited by the First Amendment.[30] As MacKinnon artfully puts the point about the doctrine of viewpoint neutrality: "In the law of freedom of speech, it also converts practices of inequality into expression of the idea of inequality, transforming actionable discrimination into speech protectable from viewpoint discrimination."[31] The normative commitment to "neutrality" in contexts of inequality serves to protect existing social hierarchies. Just as a commitment to racial neutrality—so-called "color blindness"—in contexts of racial inequality serves to benefit those who are at the top of the social hierarchy (whites in the United States), a commitment to "viewpoint neutrality" serves to protect those with the social power of speech, while robbing those at the bottom of various social hierarchies of the power to use the state as a vehicle for equality.

The lesson to be drawn here is that in its embrace of "neutrality" as a guiding principle within First Amendment jurisprudence, the Court, and so the state, protects the powerful, a decidedly non-neutral stance.[32] As such, discriminatory practices—practices of inequality—insofar as they are deemed to express a viewpoint, which they are whenever they are identified as having a discriminatory basis like race or sex, are protected as speech. The practices themselves; the hierarchies that underwrite them, considered "discussions"; and the grounds considered "disfavored topics" are left in place, in the name of freedom of speech, the groups subordinated through such practices effectively left without legal redress.

The case in which the civil rights ordinance against pornography, authored by MacKinnon and Dworkin at the request of localities, was ruled unconstitutional similarly rejected the substantive equality analysis supporting the ordinance, ruling that the definition of pornography amounted to viewpoint discrimination and thus violated the First Amendment. That case, *American Booksellers v. Hudnut*, authored by Judge Easterbrook in the 7th Circuit, claimed:

> The ordinance discriminates on the ground of the content of the speech. Speech treating women in the approved way—in sexual encounters "premised on equality" (MacKinnon, *supra*, at 22)—is lawful no matter how sexually explicit. Speech treating women in the disapproved way—as submissive in matters sexual or as enjoying humiliation—is unlawful no matter how significant the literary, artistic, or political qualities of the work taken as a whole. The state may not ordain preferred viewpoints in this way. The Constitution forbids the state to declare one perspective right and silence opponents.[33]

However, as noted above, Easterbrook goes on to agree that pornography does indeed subordinate women in the ways the ordinance claims. Again, he writes: "Therefore we accept the premises of this legislation. Depictions of subordination tend to perpetuate subordination. The subordinate status of women in turn leads to affront and lower pay at work, insult and injury at home, battery and rape on the streets. In the language of the legislature, 'pornography is central in creating and maintaining sex as a basis of discrimination. Pornography is a systematic practice of exploitation and subordination based on sex which differentially harms women. The bigotry and contempt it produces, with the acts of aggression it fosters, harm women's opportunities for equality and rights [of all kinds].' Yet this simply demonstrates the power of pornography as speech.

All of these unhappy effects depend on mental intermediation."[34] So, according to Easterbrook, the fact that pornography, or other subordinating "speech," has the power to subordinate, because it allegedly works through someone's head at some point, is just evidence that it is speech of exactly the sort that warrants First Amendment protection.

In contrast, a First Amendment jurisprudence that adopted a substantive approach to equality would not abstract away from the material context and effects of certain categories of speech. It would not ask whether a viewpoint was expressed. It would examine whether, through the expression, hierarchy, practices of subordination, were enacted. Civil rights laws, prohibiting as they do actions which constitute discrimination against protected classes (for instance, race, sex, age, nationality, disability), certainly restrict in some sense the "expression" of the viewpoint that African Americans, women, disabled persons are inferior, as it simultaneously prohibits discrimination that treats them as inferior, keeping them inferior on the basis of a protected class status. This doesn't trouble the First Amendment because "expression" of such a viewpoint, through material acts, such as a "whites only" sign on a public accommodation, is understood to constitute the act of discrimination on the basis of race. That is, the expression is understood to constitute an act of discrimination because of the way it functions to secure white supremacy, a racial hierarchy.

This same approach to providing civil redress when civil rights to equality are violated is embodied in the civil rights ordinances against pornography. Contrary to Judge Easterbrook's analysis, which vacillates between understanding that pornography performs subordination and denying that fact, the Indianapolis ordinance aims not to regulate merely "the expression of the viewpoint" that women are inferior. Rather, it aims to provide civil rights remedies for persons harmed through pornography—that is, through actions that though they may also express a viewpoint, as say rape does, are not simply the expression of a viewpoint. Rather, they would have to be documented instances of subordination, of material not merely ideational inequality.

9.3 "FEMINIST" CRITIQUES OF THE SEX EQUALITY APPROACH TO PORNOGRAPHY

The anti-pornography movement represented by the introduction of the Minneapolis and Indiana civil rights ordinances on behalf of people harmed through pornography produced the conditions for a backlash: a "feminist pro-pornography movement." The ensuing debates are often referred as "the sex wars" or "the porn wars." The self-styled "pro-sex feminists" argued against the ordinances of Dworkin and MacKinnon that had been advanced in Minneapolis, Indianapolis, Bellingham, Washington, Cambridge, Los Angeles, and Boston and advocated for unfettered markets in pornography. A subset of the pro-pornography women, who used their purported "feminism" as a credentialing device, engaged in legal advocacy as well.

Some of those engaged in legal advocacy against the civil rights ordinances called themselves F.A.C.T.—Feminist Anti-Censorship Task Force. Under this banner, they filed an amici curiae brief in the *American Booksellers Association v. Hudnut* case.[35] There they attacked the ordinances claiming: (1) the laws represented a protectionist approach to women's sexuality; (2) women's liberation required greater sexual freedom for women and that pornography, as defined by the ordinance, exemplified sexual freedom for women; (3) the Indianapolis statute was "promoted and defended" by an alliance between those who supported it and conservatives ("The New Right"); (4) the Indianapolis ordinance is censorship, "suppressing" speech; (5) pornography is fantasy, and the empirical evidence is insufficient to establish that pornography, as defined by the ordinance, causes harms to women; (6) whether some material is "subordination" is subjective and not meaningful; (7) other forms of sexist "speech," such as common advertisements, do at least as much harm as pornography; (8) sexist speech like pornography is political speech and thus at the core of First Amendment concerns; (9) the pornography covered by the definition of the ordinance can be erotically pleasurable to women and, as such, be sexually liberating; and (10) the ordinance reinforces sexist stereotypes.[36]

Apart from those criticisms that have already been addressed, two require direct response. First among these is the false claim that the advocates of the civil rights ordinances, including MacKinnon and Dworkin, were in some alliance with conservatives, "the New Right," as it was called. As a factual matter, this is simply false. Neither MacKinnon nor Dworkin allied themselves with, worked with, or sought the support of the so-called "New Right." This allegation was simply an attempt to smear MacKinnon and Dworkin and the ordinances. It was created by a PR firm that advised the Media Coalition, a group that contained pornographers and others who sued Indianapolis for passing the ordinance, in a strategy document leaked to the civil rights advocates.[37]

Moreover, as should be crystal clear, the ordinances do not share any of the premises that a conservative, or moralistic, critique of pornography advances. A conservative critique of pornography typically rests on traditional moral views about the value of sex, including an endorsement of heterosexuality as the only permissible form of sex, and of sex roles which support inequality between men and women. Indeed, a conservative view of sex underlies the obscenity-based approach to pornography insofar as that approach embodies a form of protectionism for traditional values concerning sex and sexuality, and the view that sex is dirty and women's bodies are inherently seductive and filthy. As made clear in the presentation of the ordinances themselves and their conceptual grounding, sex equality, and so the dismantling of sex-based hierarchy, is the basis for the ordinances. The fact that there is nothing conservative about that was clear in the failure of conservatives to back and pass the ordinances.

An enduring aspect of the F.A.C.T. position is the claim that pornography—even pornography that presents women as being raped—can be a source of liberation for women. Carole Vance and Gayle Rubin have defended this position in their scholarly work and were central to F.A.C.T.'s legal advocacy. Both Rubin and Vance claim that much sexual pleasure is centrally about power and danger.[38] And women taking the "power" position or dominant role in sexuality, or enjoying subordination, is a radical form of freedom for women. The F.A.C.T. brief emphasizes that even when women enjoy "rape fantasies," they are "rebels," apparently because having such a fantasy insists "on an aspect of her sexuality that has been defined as a male preserve."[39]

Rubin situates her particular critique in the context of concerns about marginalized sexualities, gays and lesbians, practitioners of BDSM (bondage, domination, sadism, and masochism), persons into various other forms of "kink," incestuous relationships, and even those into "child-adult sex" (who most people would call child rapists).[40] She argues that "society" overemphasizes the value of sex, and this leads to an overinvestment of meaning in sex. Central to her argument is the claim that most legal regulations of sex, sex acts, or sexuality have historically served to marginalize "alternative sexualities." According to Rubin, these regulations, in combination with dominant social beliefs about sex, reinforce a view of sexuality in which "normal" and "good" (or morally permissible) sex and sexualities are straight (meaning heterosexual, i.e., between women and men), monogamous, occur in marriages, are aimed at reproduction, and the like. These dominant and powerful views about sexuality are repressive toward women and sexual minorities; they manifest a pervasive attempt to control women's sexuality and deny them "agency" over their own sexual desires and pleasure, claims Rubin.

Further, she claims that the anti-pornography feminist arguments and the ordinances of Dworkin and MacKinnon and the cities that wanted their laws for their citizens represent another version of a regressive sexuality, an "anti-sex attitude," and furtherance of categories of "deviant" and "normal" sexuality that repress and shame sexual minorities. A further part of these critiques has been to simply assert that pleasure in domination is part of what makes sex "sexy," and when combined with the view that "all sex is good sex," any critique of sexual practices, including ones that are harmful to people by their own testimony, is "regressive" in their view. F.A.C.T. and its defenders consistently ignore and deny the testimony of women harmed by pornography, preferring to defend an abstract vision of "good sex" to confronting the factual evidence of harm and inequality that women report. Denying the testimony of women, reducing their experience to exaggerated hysteria, in the name of "feminism" is a form of misogyny.

A similar critique emerges from those who defend or make or produce what they call "feminist pornography." In 2013, a group of self-proclaimed feminist pornographers and scholars produced an edited volume called *The Feminist Porn Book: The Politics of Producing Pleasure*.[41] They define "feminist porn" as material "that uses sexually explicit imagery to contest and complicate dominant representations of gender, sexuality, race, ethnicity, class, ability, age, body type, and other identity markers. It explores concepts of desire, agency, power, beauty, and pleasure at their most confounding and difficult, including pleasure within and across inequality, in the face of injustice, and against the limits of gender hierarchy and both heteronormativity and homonormativity."[42] They explicitly frame themselves in opposition to the sex equality approach to pornography and repeat the false claim that the movement was "in collusion" with the conservative Right.[43] They claim that the sex equality approach to pornography is repressive and anti-sex. Apparently, a sexuality of equality is inconceivable to them, or at least equality is not sexy to them.

The underlying theme of both sets of critique is that the only basis for criticizing any sexual act is that it was non-consensual. All consensual sex—and according to the F.A.C.T. brief, even some non-consensual sex such as rape—is good sex. However, even this is somewhat unclear in Rubin's work, since she defends sex with children, albeit with the claim that children are capable of consent in some sense she thinks relevant, though she doesn't define what consent means. Additionally, the claim that "all consensual sex is good sex" does not extend to the kinds of images of sex represented in pornography. In other words, in the "feminist porn" view, representing rape or non-consensual sex through pornography is perfectly defensible, despite non-consensual acts being presented as such in it. After all, many women who have rape fantasies, they claim, get off on domination and submission, or other forms of violence in sex, and critiquing such desires in their view is analogous to "patriarchal" attempts to control women's sexuality.

One disagreement between these advocates and those who advocate for a sex equality model for regulating pornography is over whether the ability of some women to take up, or enact, a dominant role in sexuality amounts to a vision of liberation for women. Sex equality advocates argue that relationships of domination and subordination, including sexually scripted roles in which someone is the dominator and another the subordinate, do not constitute liberation for anyone, especially the people at the bottom of the hierarchy. They remain hierarchical, hence unequal, including if people are orgasming to the inequality. The so-called pro-porn feminist movement, as it were, retains the categories of inequality and lack of freedom that have served to subordinate women in particular, and also children of both sexes, for thousands of years. That some natal females might be able to move into the role of dominator doesn't provide a class-based liberation project for women, who are subordinated by gender, not sex. Some women will still be at the bottom of that hierarchy, as any hierarchy necessitates subordinates. And whoever enacts a masculine role is in the male position, hierarchically speaking, without regard to biology. It is simply sexist to act as if only men in this position are oppressors.

Consider an analogy with some of the policies advocated by liberal feminists in the late 1960s and early 1970s. At that time in the United States, many feminists advocated for more open competition and equal opportunity for women in access to education and professions. Over time many of their arguments were successful in shaping public policy, and women's participation in the labor force grew dramatically over the next several decades. But whom did these policies benefit? Primarily they benefited white and already economically privileged women. This group of women made significant gains in education and employment. But, given that gender norms were untouched by such policies— norms that held women responsible for being the primary caregivers of children and for the household labor necessary to sustain the family, for instance—many of these women were able to pursue new opportunities only by employing other women, who had fewer opportunities to begin with and none of these new ones, to perform those duties. That is, white and economically privileged women hired other women, women of color and less economically privileged women, to care for their children and clean their houses, prepare meals, do laundry, etc. Thus, "women's liberation" in this sense was largely effective only for some women, those already most privileged in society, hence able to take advantage of it. Women at the bottom of other social hierarchies, due to race and class, for example, did not enjoy equality much less a newfound freedom, and their continued subordination was necessary for the advances of the women who were in a position to take advantage of new opportunities. It turns out that "equal opportunity for all" was hardly "equal" or "for all." This is what some women moving into positions of privilege formerly occupied almost entirely by men often looks like.

By the same token, the idea that liberation for women as a class can come from some women being in the dominant position is a false proposition. It may be hard to envision what true sexual liberation for women as a group amounts to, given that sexuality has operated under the yoke of male dominance for so long. But re-inscribing the norms of dominant male sexuality in the context of women's sexuality or LGBT sexuality—essentially what these pro-pornography feminists advocate—does not have emancipatory potential for all, nor does it advance women's social and legal equality at all.

9.4 CANADIAN LAW AND THE GAY AND LESBIAN ARGUMENT

Some object to the sex equality approach to pornography on the grounds that any legal approach as such is likely to be applied in a discriminatory manner, where sexually explicit material featuring gay, lesbian, or other "non-traditional sexualities" will suffer greater and more damaging legal surveillance than heterosexual pornography. Moreover, thinking that "the law"—as in the state—is the institution empowered by the ordinances, and its human rights approach, rests on a misreading or misunderstanding or misrepresentation, or all three. As stated, the ordinances are civil rights law, in which particular persons harmed by pornography are empowered to bring claims for damages they have to prove against those who harmed them in order to seek relief. The state, as such, is not the "prosecutor" in such cases and has no role other than providing a venue for claims to be litigated.

Another objection pressed by those focused on the potential impacts of any law on gay and lesbian or other non-normative sexualities is that the availability of sexually explicit material for gays and lesbians, and others similarly non-normative in their sexual identities and practices, is a crucial outlet for positive representation of such sexualities in a cultural context in which few such positive representations exist. These issues arose in the Canadian context. The Canadian law against pornography differs from the sex equality approach defended here, beginning with the fact that it is a criminal law. It also retains a notion of obscenity relying on community standards, prohibiting "any publication a dominant characteristic of which is the undue exploitation of sex, or of sex and any one of . . . crime, horror, cruelty, and violence," in violation of a community standard of violence,"[44]—all concepts far from obscenity as implemented in US law.

Heightening the contrast with the United States, the legal interpretation of this prohibition is expressed in sex equality terms in two important cases in Canada, *Butler* and *Little Sisters*. In *Butler*, police seized all the pornography for sale in an "adult" video store in Winnipeg in 1987. The owner, Donald Victor Butler, was charged with possession and sale of obscene materials under the above definition and convicted.[45] He challenged the constitutionality of the law under the new Canadian Charter of Rights and Freedoms provision protecting freedom of expression. The Supreme Court of Canada held in *Butler v. Regina* that the law in question was constitutionally permissible despite contravening freedom of expression, because of Parliament's interest in guaranteeing equality, importantly between women and men. The Canadian Charter of Rights and Freedoms "permits the rights guaranteed in its Constitution to be expressly overridden if the challenged law is found to be justified under section 1" of the Charter which provides for "a free and democratic society."[46] Thus in Canada, freedom of expression (and any other right) can be constitutionally limited when such limitations are necessary to secure equality.

In a landmark decision prior to *Butler, Andrews v. Law Society of British Colombia* (1989), the first case "brought under the equality provision of the new Canadian Charter of Rights and Freedoms," the Canadian Supreme Court adopted a substantive model of equality, simultaneously rejecting formal equality—understood as identical or same treatment for those similarly situated—as promoting inequality under unequal conditions. Thus, the Court emphasized that equality, recognized as a condition that does not yet exist socially, will sometimes require differential treatment to fulfill the "purpose of the guarantee and securing for individuals the full benefit of the *Charter's* protection."[47] The Canadian Court emphasized that bringing about equality for historically disadvantaged groups will in some contexts require specific substantive policies aimed at promoting their equality.[48]

This is the background for the *Butler* decision, where the Court found that pornography that is degrading and dehumanizing could have been regarded as harmful, including to sex equality, by Parliament. Rejected was grounding the tests for illegality in concerns over public morality or "moral disapprobation."[49] Although it embraces a sex equality rationale for its constitutionality and cognizes the reality of its harm as something Parliament could legislate to stop, the Canadian law against pornography is a criminal law and relies on community standards, both features of anti-pornography laws strongly criticized by MacKinnon and Dworkin. Thus, those who claim that Canada adopted the approach of Dworkin and MacKinnon to pornography are only partly right.

In *Little Sisters*, a gay and lesbian bookstore in Vancouver, called Little Sisters Book and Art Emporium, filed suit against the Canadian Department of Justice claiming discrimination in the administration of the laws (i.e., claiming they were singled out for unjust enforcement) and violation of their rights of freedom of expression.[50] The central aspects of the bookstore's legal argument were the claims that gay and lesbian pornography is substantively different than heterosexual pornography, insofar as, they claimed, "homosexual erotica plays an important role in providing a positive self-image to gays and lesbians, who may feel isolated or rejected in the heterosexual mainstream," that sado-masochism "performs an emancipatory role in gay and lesbian culture" and should not be judged by the same standards as heterosexual pornography that is BDSM, and that same-sex relationships are constitutionally different such that gender discrimination is "not an issue."[51]

The Supreme Court of Canada ruled in *Little Sisters* that gay and lesbian pornography, merely because it is gay or lesbian, is not thereby necessarily immune from the

Butler standard, nor qua being gay or lesbian, does it attract Butler's inequality attention. In other words, they held that gay and lesbian pornography can harm, just as heterosexual pornography can, but the fact it is gay or lesbian does not do that harm. Specifically, the Court acknowledged that gay and lesbian pornography can violate constitutional protections of sex equality. However, this is not simply because the pornography is gay or lesbian in content or because gay and lesbian audiences buy this pornography. Rather, the Court recognized that when harms are found in pornography that violate sex equality principles, it doesn't matter if the material is "gay" or "lesbian" or "straight."

Christopher Kendall has written a groundbreaking book in which he argues, contrary to this often repeated claim that gay male pornography is a vehicle for gay male liberation, "that gay male pornography will only achieve that which the homophobe has strived to do all along: the silencing of gay men by encouraging masculine mimicry and the public expression of the polar opposite of equality."[52] Kendall thus argues that same-sex pornography, and specifically gay male pornography, can and often does subordinate on the basis of sex, and gay men (as well as lesbians and all women) are its victims.

In the course of this argument, Kendall vividly describes and analyzes the materials for which *Little Sisters* sought protection. They included graphic sexually explicit subordination, much like common heterosexual pornography. The same sexist, gendered, misogynist sex role stereotypes were present, just attached to men. They divided the men into dominant and subordinate—hierarchy of top and bottom—in the sexual acts. The "bottoms" were invariably characterized as "like women," their sexuality defined in terms of the pleasure and power of "the top." Rape scenarios were presented in which younger men are dominated by older men, sexualizing the inequality of age as well as sex role. Threats and homophobic slurs were commonly directed at the guy in the subordinate, bottom role. Inequality was eroticized through military-themed pornography depicting the rape of "prisoners of war," prison rape, radicalized inequality, and the use of racial slurs especially against black and Asian men, sex with children, and incest.[53] Looking back to the descriptions of the eroticization of inequality in mainstream heterosexual pornography above, you will see the main point of distinction between heterosexual and gay pornography is simply the use of men rather than women to sexualize and eroticize the inequality.

Further, Kendall argues that gay male pornography, in its dominant forms, is homophobic. He writes of gay male pornography: "Much, if not all of it presents an image of male sexuality and power that shows and reinforces attitudes and behaviors about what it takes to be a "real man." Its message, that gay men should reject any expression of male-male sexuality that is equal and non-hierarchical, has implications that reach far beyond the gay male community. For women, the acceptance of a sexuality premised on male-female purity is but one more tool with which to preserve that gender hierarchy necessary for social inequality. As such, gay male pornography also amounts to a practice of sex discrimination."[54] Kendall's analysis reveals that just because something is gay or lesbian, that does not insulate it from sex equality critique. Gender hierarchy, not biology, is the relevant factor for the production and reproduction of inequality.

9.5 DO WE HAVE A "RIGHT" TO PORNOGRAPHY?

Ronald Dworkin was among the first set of legal academics to criticize the sex equality approach to pornography as embodied in the ordinances and to attack MacKinnon's writings in particular. His review of *Only Words*, published in *The New York Review of Books*, argues that a sex equality approach to pornography undermines rather than promotes equality.[55] To him, the First Amendment protects equality interests, as well as speech interests. He claimed that the equality interest at stake in some matters of speech is the equal right to the opportunity to shape the moral (and political) environment of the society in which one lives. This view rests on a narrow formal reading of equality, missing the substance of inequality that women, in particular, experience, including unequal access to speech and silencing through hierarchically abusive speech.

Consumers of pornography, as well as its manufacturers, are by Dworkin's lights expressing their opinions, tastes, and preferences. Those might be "disgusting" or "offensive" to others—especially women—but, according to Dworkin, "no one may be prevented from influencing the shared moral environment, through his own private choices, tastes, opinions, and example, just because these tastes or opinions disgust those who have the power to shut him up or lock him up."[56] Dworkin grounds a "right to pornography" in an equality right within the First Amendment: the right to an equal opportunity to shape the cultural and so, "moral," environment of society.

Ronald Dworkin dismisses the claim that women's equality in particular, an equal right for women to shape the "moral" environment or to exercise freedom of expression, is undermined by pornography. He further argues that even if it is so undermined, that doesn't justify restriction of pornography. He argues that the way for women, or others who are targeted by the tastes and preferences of pornography users, to respond is to simply combat their degrading messages by equally seeking to shape the "moral" environment by exercising their own speech rights. Dworkin writes:

> But we cannot count, among the kinds of interests that may be protected in this way, a right not to be insulted or damaged just by the fact that others have hostile or uncongenial tastes, or that they are free to express or indulge them in private. Recognizing that right would mean denying that some people—those whose tastes these are—have any right to participate in forming the moral environment at all. In a genuinely egalitarian society, however, those views cannot be locked out, in advance, by criminal or civil law; they must instead be discredited by the disgust, outrage, and ridicule of other people.[57]

Rae Langton criticizes Ronald Dworkin's argument, claiming that he fails to draw the proper conclusions concerning pornography even from within his own theoretical framework.[58] As Langton carefully reconstructs his argument, in the context of his larger defense of liberal egalitarianism, it amounts to this: arguments in favor of addressing the harms of pornography (and its consumption) inevitability rest on some form of moralism. That is, Dworkin understands all arguments in favor of some form of restriction of pornography (excepting child pornography) as rooted in a belief that pornography is "ignoble or wrong."[59] He doesn't distinguish between the sex equality approach to pornography and the obscenity-based argument. On his view, in this critique, both arguments ultimately rest on a moral condemnation of pornography and what he calls "the external preferences" of those who argue in favor of restriction to condemn consumption of pornography. Liberal rights, significantly the foundational right to equal treatment, on Ronald Dworkin's view, are "trumps" against policies grounded in the preferences of the majority. In short, he says that even if the majority of persons hold the view that pornography consumption or distribution is "base and lacking in value," those preferences do not warrant a policy of restriction within a liberal framework because, as noted above, he thinks that all citizens have an equal moral right to shape the "moral" (and cultural) environment of a political society.

As Langton rightly points out, Ronald Dworkin has mischaracterized the sex equality argument concerning pornography. The sex equality argument, as we have seen, is not similar or analogous to obscenity-based arguments that appeal to shared moral values of the community; rather, it is grounded in a substantive equality argument that is premised on a critique of hierarchical power as discrimination. Ronald Dworkin simply misses this point, and as such fails to consider that pornography undermines women's equal rights to "influence the shared moral environment," in his terms—though it does much more than this. In other words, and as Langton also emphasizes, a permissive policy on pornography undermines the "equal respect and concern" that women have as a matter of legal right to be free from discrimination, and so, even within Ronald Dworkin's own view, a powerful argument in favor of restriction of pornography follows.[60]

Langton's conclusion may be surprising insofar as it advances the claim that liberal political philosophy has the internal resources to advance an equality argument in favor of the MacKinnon-Dworkin approach to pornography, where pornography is understood as undermining the civil rights of women. MacKinnon and Andrea Dworkin are both deeply skeptical of liberal political philosophy and see it as a historically and conceptually limited framework from which to argue for substantive equality. MacKinnon, in articulating her critique of formal equality, as discussed in the first section, "Free Speech Defense of Pornography," identifies liberal jurisprudence and liberal political philosophy as structurally flawed such that liberal principles often become a vehicle for reproducing social inequalities.

There is much to agree with in MacKinnon's critique of liberalism, especially as it concerns the way that neutrality, or purported neutral principles in constitutional law, are invoked as justifications to maintain the status quo in contexts of inequality. However, I don't think that liberal political philosophy is conceptually bereft in the way that MacKinnon does. Elsewhere, Christie Hartley and I have defended a reconstruction of liberal political philosophy in which a deep commitment to substantive equality is central to its vision of a fully just society.[61] The core argument emphasizes a particular rendering of liberalism in which relational equality among citizens is central to the legitimacy of the state and any political principles that flow from it. Such equality demands, among other things, that citizens stand in relation to one another as free and equal persons, and not as "dominated, or manipulated, or under the pressure of an inferior social position,"[62] when matters of their basic rights and justice are at stake. From this core commitment to relational equality among citizens, we argue that the state has an obligation to eradicate social hierarchies that threaten, undermine, or thwart citizens' substantive equality.[63] With regard to pornography, this view entails that if pornography undermines women's enjoyment of the rights and status of free and equal citizens on a basis of equality, then the liberal state has good reason to adopt a sex equality approach to pornography and to eliminate pornography and the related practices that produce and reproduce such inequality.[64]

Altman is also a liberal, but contrary to the view just expressed, he argues that citizens (men as an overwhelming matter of practice) have a "moral right" to pornography. Altman's approach is squarely a liberal argument, appealing as it does to individual rights in the context of liberal democracies. He locates the right to pornography within a broader right to sexual autonomy, departing from many traditional liberal arguments. He also sensibly recognizes that the sex equality argument against pornography is powerful. His argument and its conclusions are conditional to the extent that he thinks that if sufficient evidence were available (and convincing) that pornography produced the harms that the sex equality argument identifies, then it appears that Altman would concede that pornography must be restricted. However, he doesn't find the empirical evidence convincing or sufficient. This evidence, previously examined, despite Altman's denials, exists.

The plausibility of Altman's approach to defending a moral right to pornography as grounded in the right to sexual autonomy crucially depends on denying the plausibility of the findings of the empirical research concerning the harms of pornography for women. For if Altman were convinced of the evidence and the harms, on his view he would have to concede that women's right to sexual autonomy—and, importantly, their equal right to sexual autonomy—supports some form of restriction. In other words, given the framework of Altman's argument, women have an equal right to sexual autonomy, and if pornography undermines that right, then men's right to consume pornography is justly restricted. Altman doesn't directly make this point, as he is committed to denying the empirical evidence's veracity.

Additionally, to the extent that Altman addresses the potential concern regarding women's right to sexual autonomy, he limits his discussion to whether pornography causes sexual violence, acknowledging that if so, sexual violence certainly robs women of their sexual autonomy. Yet, even in Altman's own account of sexual autonomy, sexual violence should be understood as only one of many potential threats to sexual autonomy. Sexual autonomy is a much broader concept of control over one's sexuality than simply avoiding sexual violence. Moreover, Altman doesn't consider the extent to which pornography may undermine the sexual autonomy of boys and men—the primary users of pornography. Nor does he consider the many forms of restriction on freedom promoted by the sexualized inequality pornography demonstrably promotes in society, not all of which is sexual but all of which is unequal to the systematic detriment of women.

Altman argues that "the right to sexual autonomy is an especially weighty or important personal liberty," and "pornography is an aspect of the right to sexual autonomy."[65] As a matter of fact this translates to: men who use pornography for sexual arousal and satisfaction have a right to have a whole class of women who are systemically disadvantaged in multiple intersecting ways kept available and used to make it, so they can have their masturbatory sex lives the way they want them. In defense of the claim that the right to sexual autonomy has a significant and central place in the set of personal liberties (against which persons have a right of noninterference by others or the state), Altman emphasizes a pessimistic view of human life in which humans are inevitably subject to an intense struggle against suffering and misery. The main problem here is that the suffering and misery of women used to make pornography, and violated by those who use it, do not figure in this struggle. Sexual pleasure is one especially significant palliative, giving respite and relief in the context of such a struggle, on Altman's view. In this view, left out are those who never receive such relief but continue to be violated in the name of the respite of those who have more power than they do.

In addition to this aspect of the significance of sexual pleasure, Altman argues that control over one's sexuality and sexual activities is central to the social meaning of personhood—understood as "part of the recognition of an adult as a free and equal member of society."[66] In the course of emphasizing the significance of sexual self-determination for one's status as a free and equal person, Altman correctly notes the ways in which the denial of sexual autonomy—control over one's sexuality—has been an instrument of degradation for women, and women in slavery especially. To be denied sexual autonomy is to be placed in a slave-like condition—marked with a "badge" of inferiority. However, he fails to interrogate the way in which protection of men's "right" to sexual autonomy has, as a matter of practice in the real world, the world in which pornography is made and used, meant the denial of women's equality, including an equality right to sexual autonomy.

Altman's own idiosyncratic explanation of why a lack of sexual autonomy is connected to having a degraded social status is that "it means that others have social permission to spill their disgusting sticky substances onto or into you without your consent."[67] It may be that such disgust forms a part of the basis for revulsion people express toward victims of rape or women in prostitution; however, this particular account of the value of sexual autonomy as a guard against degradation, and low social status, is far from essential to the claim that we have a right to sexual autonomy. It is, actually, backwards, suggesting that there is something biologically, not socially, degrading or disgusting about sexual interactions in which bodily fluids are exchanged. By distinction, others emphasize the centrality of bodily integrity and control over one's body to personhood, both as a status and as an empirical matter. Persons who experience loss of control over the boundaries of their bodies—sexual and otherwise—not only experience a degraded social status but also frequently post-traumatic stress disorder, anxiety, depression, dissociation, suicidal ideation, and other psychological injuries that undermine their sense of self, unity of self, and abilities to function as integrated persons.[68] Women in prostitution, including even more severely when they are prostituted in pornography, are documented with sky-high amounts of these injuries.[69] This is because they are being serially raped.

Whatever the precise sources of the importance of sexual autonomy, control over one's body, and sufficient social status to exercise such control, is clearly a right central to one's recognition as an equal person. Altman and I do not disagree about the conclusion that sexual autonomy is a right of persons and essential to their status as free and equal citizens. We disagree about whether this right to sexual autonomy entails a right to pornography. Altman argues that it does insofar as people (especially men) use pornography as sex, as a masturbation tool.

Does a right to sexual autonomy entail a right to pornography? The answer depends an account of rights and as well as an account of what it means to exercise one's sexual autonomy. Philosophers distinguish between negative and positive rights to capture the difference between rights that entail freedom from interference by others (negative rights) and rights that entail obligations by others to secure the right in question (positive rights). Altman's argument suggests that he conceives of the right to sexual autonomy as a negative right, for he emphasizes that persons have rights against governmental interference with respect to their use of pornography as an exercise of their sexual autonomy.

Negative rights are rights to noninterference, imposing duties on others to refrain from placing obstacles to the pursuit, enjoyment, or exercise of rights. In contrast, claiming a positive right entails that some identifiable other—maybe an individual or maybe the government—has a positive duty to do something to guarantee the right in question.

Philosophers sometimes use the language of liberty versus autonomy to capture the negative/positive right distinction. Calling something a basic liberty means that one has a negative right that others refrain from interfering with one's exercising one's freedom in this respect. Whereas appeals to autonomy often aim to capture the sense in which one has a positive right to assistance, in some way, such that it is recognized that one's ability to act autonomously—in a self-governing fashion—often requires minimal levels of education, various kinds of resources, and so on. Autonomy rights also include negative or liberty rights to noninterference, but the point is that they often require more than just this. If persons as citizens have a right to autonomy, broadly construed, it implies a right to sufficient education, for example, in one's youth and formative years so that one's autonomy may be realized in adulthood. Those who hold such a view advocate for some minimum state-supported education necessary for the state to fulfill its positive duty, and thus guarantee the positive right to autonomy.

Is a right to sexual autonomy a negative or positive right? Is it better to describe any such right as a right to sexual liberty, rather than a right to sexual autonomy? Consider the following contrast. A right to sexual liberty (understood as a negative right) entails a right to be left alone, as it were, in acting upon one's sexual desires (with the caveat that such a liberty is justifiably restricted when one's so acting interferes with another's sexual liberty). A right to sexual autonomy, in contrast, can be broadly defined as the ability to direct one's sexual life authentically. This includes, at least, the ability to reflectively endorse one's sexual desires and preferences and the ability to act on those desires and preferences. From this it follows that not being able to act on one's reflectively endorsed sexual desires and preferences is an autonomy limitation. This is just a conceptual point: one has more or less autonomy depending on one's ability to act on one's reflectively endorsed desires. But, additionally, emphasizing a right to sexual autonomy suggests that the way one has formed one's sexual preferences and desires matters for one's freedom with respect to them.

Defenders of negative freedom (liberty) are not concerned, from the point of view of evaluating the freedom of the individual, with the way in which one's preferences, desires, and beliefs are formed. What matters from the point of view of evaluating the individual's freedom (liberty) is whether one can do what one wants. Or more apt for the discussion of access to pornography, what matters is whether a man can do what he wants. How the man stands in relation to his beliefs, preferences, and desires is not of concern. He may reflectively reject them, he may not reflect at all, or he may wholeheartedly endorse them. Each of these ways of relating to his desires is consistent with his being free (at liberty) with respect to them so long as he is not interfered with by outside forces.

Again, defenders of negative liberty do not advocate for unlimited and unfettered ability to act on one's beliefs, desires, and preferences. They recognize that liberty rights are limited by equality insofar as other individuals also possess such rights. Thus, as is commonly said, "my liberty to swing my right fist about ends where your nose begins." Nonetheless, the concept of "sexual autonomy" invokes something more robust than what defenders of sexual liberty have in mind. Philosophical analyses of autonomy generally point to the way in which an individual stands in relation to their beliefs, desires, and preferences as salient for assessing their freedom/autonomy. Although accounts of autonomy differ precisely on what that way is, they all recognize that an individual can hold beliefs, desires, and preferences, which, upon reflection, they reject. Such an individual would be described as non-autonomous with respect to that particular belief, desire, or preference. "Brainwashing" is a classic example in which persons can be said to be non-autonomous. So, for example, if someone is placed under hypnosis and told that the Earth is flat, and afterwards believes that the Earth is flat, it is fair to describe their belief as alien in some sense. The individual does not hold this belief autonomously. This is an extravagant example, but it makes the point that autonomy is a distinct concept from liberty.

Philosophers who work on the concept of autonomy, aiming to specify its meaning and the conditions for its realization, generally agree that cultural conditions, and processes of enculturation, can interfere with autonomy. Beauty norms are an obvious example of the way in which cultural norms and conditions shape a person's beliefs and desires, both about themselves and others, in ways that the person may not reflectively or authentically endorse despite adhering rigidly to them. An overwhelming desire to be thin, or to have larger breasts, or fuller lips, or fewer wrinkles, leads many to undergo costly and potentially dangerous cosmetic surgeries or engage in extreme dieting that they would reject given sufficient reflection or, importantly, alternative cultural conditions.

Altman doesn't directly address these distinctions and the issues that arise from them for his account, although he expresses skepticism that pornography or its use can alter a person's preferences, sexual or otherwise. In support of this skepticism, he draws on his own experience as a pornography user, noting that he only found pornography arousing that cohered with his antecedent sexual desires. By way of making this claim, he likens his sexual preferences to those of gays and lesbians, who by Altman's judgment "discover" their sexuality as consisting of same-sex sexual attraction, and "nothing subsequently budges them from that initial mode of sexuality."[70] Yet, contrary to Altman's report of his personal experience, voluminous empirical research demonstrates that pornography use, in fact, powerfully shapes users beliefs, attitudes, and sexual desires, including of "unpredisposed normals." A 2016 study investigating men's online pornography usage patterns found that "49% reported sometimes searching for sexual materials or being involved in online sexual activities they previously thought uninteresting or disgusting."[71]

Altman's analogy to same-sex sexual attraction is not persuasive; neither is the underlying claim about same-sex sexual attraction being such a rigid "given" an accurate description of lesbian sexuality (and, perhaps, too, some forms of gay male sexuality). I am a lesbian. My own experience of coming to live as a lesbian is not describable in Altman's terms of discovering some antecedent "given" truth about my sexuality or sexual preferences. At the point in my life at which I came to think I wanted to be sexually intimate with women, I had no idea what my particular and specific sexual preferences with women were. This isn't because I was sexually naïve, but rather because the experience of coming to find women as potential sexual partners was utterly transformative. I had no prior experience with women, though

I did with men. I had no idea, in concrete terms, about what sex with women was like. Coming to develop (not uncover) my particular sexual desires and how to express them with women was not the experience of unearthing some set of antecedent, fixed set of preferences, but rather a process of creating and cultivating those desires in light of experience with specific others. I am not suggesting that my particular historical narrative is the same for all lesbians or gay men or bisexuals or even heterosexuals; however, my experience does reveal that the claim that sexual desires are antecedent and fixed in some way, prior to experience, may be as particular to Altman as my experience is to me. I was genuinely heterosexual from puberty until my early twenties, and the experiences of developing and defining my sexuality in that context were no different than my later experiences of developing and defining my sexuality as a lesbian. (I do not believe I was "born gay" and am skeptical of any such claims or purported science establishing any form of "innate" sexuality, including heterosexuality.)

In any case, Altman's claim that his own sexuality and preferences have remained stable and unaltered by viewing pornography may well be very particular to him. There is, as we have seen, a substantial body of empirical literature that suggests that Altman is not like most men in this regard. There is also considerable evidence to suggest that men who use pornography may think this, but it may not be true. Given his assumptions about the relative fixed nature of sexual preferences and his defense of the right to pornography as a right to be left to act on those preferences (at least as concerns oneself), Altman's defense of a right to pornography is better understood as grounded in a defense of sexual liberty rather than a defense of sexual autonomy. Were it a defense of sexual autonomy, he might have considered the ways in which pornography interferes with this right, both for men and for women.

The ways in which the ubiquity of pornography undermines sexual autonomy is the subject of a new wave of anti-pornography activism, education, and scholarship. Those working in these areas document the ways in which pornography limits, undermines, and restricts the development of authentic sexuality, for both women and men, and interferes with interpersonal intimacy. One critical focus of such research and advocacy concerns pre-teen and teen boys. The average age of exposure to pornography for boys is 12.[72] That number has been decreasing over the last thirty to forty years. The average age of exposure to pornography for girls is about 14,[73] though, of course, given other facts about culture and gender, the role pornography comes to play in the life of girls is very different than in the life of boys.

For many boys, pornography is their first sexual encounter. For an overwhelming numbers of boys, it becomes a routine companion to masturbation. Despite claims to the contrary, pornography is monotonous in its representation of heterosexual sex. Typically, it goes like this: oral sex, vaginal sex, anal sex, maybe some return to oral or vaginal sex, cum shot, over. "The narrative arc," so to speak, is fairly tightly scripted and written by formula. Foreplay, in all its variations and complexity, is nonexistent. Discussion, imagination, and interaction between the woman and man in heterosexual sex, the kind that occurs in mutually wanted sex (What do you want to do? How to you want to do it? Want to try this or that?) aren't in pornography. It's typically thrust in this or that orifice, flip her over, come. Or force something on her, come, she is ecstatic. To the extent that this functions as sex education for many youths, especially, boys, it can hardly be said to be autonomy enhancing. For girls, and in turn women, pornography also undermines sexual autonomy understood as the ability to authentically determine one's sexual beliefs, desires, and preferences.[74] Pornography presents women as sexual objects in which male sexual desires control and define the sexual interaction. Any pleasure she shows is typically faked.

Thus, the sexual autonomy argument as a ground to a right to pornography raises difficult issues to which Altman fails to pay sufficient attention. First, the pervasiveness of pornography, and its role as a tool of "sex education," meaning sexual conditioning without any critical distance, may undermine the sexual autonomy of boys and men; it certainly acts as a significant obstacle to the sexual autonomy of girls and women insofar as an objectified subordinated sexuality is imposed on them by its consumers. So, pornography may well be best understood as a threat to sexual autonomy rather than an exercise of it. But, even if, as Altman says, pornography does not construct the desires of boys and men, despite vast empirical evidence to the contrary experimental, social, and experiential alike, its capacity to limit the sexual autonomy of women includes, but is not limited to, the threat or actualization of sexual violence. Altman focuses narrowly on sexual violence as the manner in which pornography may undermine the sexual autonomy of women; this is because he thinks it is the strongest case in favor of restriction, and failing to find credence in the empirical literature, he fails to see a threat to women's sexual autonomy. However, not only is the empirical evidence far stronger than he credits, the ways in which pornography may undermine or thwart women's sexual autonomy also extend far beyond acts of sexual violence. Thus, on this view, the sexual autonomy of men may undermine the sexual autonomy of women, and given Altman's commitment to equal sexual autonomy, this suggests that he should come down in favor of some form of legal response to protect and guarantee, on an equal basis, the sexual autonomy of women.

Even more, why should we think that a right to sexual autonomy entails something so specific as a particular right to buy pornography on the open market? Consider an analogy to the right of self-defense. We all have a right to self-defense, which, at the very least, entails a negative right to not be interfered with in specific and direct instances where self-defense is required. But, we may reasonably ask how far even the negative right extends. Does it entail a right to construct a perimeter around one's house with "booby-traps" to ward off or engage potential threats? Maybe it does, but surely we can limit the kinds of such traps allowed—land mines, for example, may reasonably be forbidden. Does the right to self-defense entail a right to acquire any manner and number of weapons for self-protection? Does it entail a right to machine guns, automatic weapons, or semi-automatic weapons, or even guns at all? Does it entail a right to bombs, grenades, or other weapons? I suspect most people will think the state has reasonable grounds for restricting, limiting, or even forbidding various instruments of self-protection, even while recognizing a general right to self-defense.

Now apply this analogy to a right to sexual autonomy. Even if we grant such a right, it does not follow that such a right entails a right to specific materials one might use to exercise that right. Nor does it entail a right to a market in anything, in particular something that inflicts damage on others in its making and use.

If the Second Amendment enumerated a right to self-defense, rather than a right to bear arms specifically, the debate concerning gun control would look very different from a legal standpoint. In interpreting the scope of the right to self-defense, we would rightly ask whether access to weapons was necessary to secure that right, and if so, which kinds of weapons. Considerations for protecting the rights to self-defense would be weighed against the evidence of harms when we have full and open access to virtually any kind of gun and the impacts of that policy on society as a whole, as well as, obviously, the thousands of people who die each year as a result of gun violence in the United States in particular.

As this analogy shows, Altman's defense of a right to pornography as flowing from a right to sexual autonomy is only successful to the extent that it denies the harms of pornography, both in general and in particular. However, Altman resists this analysis, arguing that even if pornography harms, there is still no case to be made for restricting access to or markets in it in any way. Here he makes his own analogy with alcohol. He argues that alcohol is known to cause various harms (to self and others, insofar as it may contribute to violence or drinking and driving that results in harms to others). But, says Altman, no one can reasonably think that we should ban alcohol. Of course, and again, the ordinances of Dworkin and MacKinnon do not ban pornography, and so the analogy is not directly parallel. Nonetheless, to the point that alcohol harms in many ways and those harms are analogous to the harms of pornography, it is simply not the case that the harms are relevantly similar. The fact that the harms of pornography are borne largely by women, or other persons in positions of social inequality, means that pornography's harms are directed at persons on the basis of their group membership. They are discriminatory and cumulatively connected to all the other harms of second-class status, including intersectional ones. The harms of alcohol are not like this; on the whole, its harms are more diffuse and not part of a set of systematic practices that subordinate persons on the basis of their protected group membership. The argument for regulating alcohol is not analogous to or parallel with the sex equality argument against pornography.

NOTES

1. *Ashcroft v. Free Speech Coalition*, 535 U.S. 234 (1996), p. 253.
2. The analysis provided here is drawn from Catharine A. MacKinnon, "The First Amendment: An Equality Reading," 2017 manuscript, on file with the author.
3. Nadine Strossen, *Defending Pornography: Free Speech and the Fight for Women's Rights* (New York: New York University Press, 2000).
4. Strossen, *Defending Pornography*, printed in forward of the book, no page number.
5. Strossen, *Defending Pornography*, p. xx.
6. Strossen, *Defending Pornography*, p. xxii.
7. Joel Feinberg, *Harm to Others: The Moral Limits of the Criminal Law* (New York: Oxford University Press, 1984), p. 46.
8. Kathleen M. Sullivan and Gerald Gunther, *Constitutional Law*, 6th ed. (Foundation Press, 2007), p. 842.
9. 1. "the use of children as subjects of pornographic materials is harmful to the physiological, emotional, and mental health of the child"; 2. the Miller standard "for determining

what is legally obscene is not a satisfactory solution to the child pornography problem . . ." *Ferber v. New York*, 458 U.S. 747 (1982).

10. Byrant Paul and Daniel G. Linz, "The Effects of Exposure to Virtual Child Pornography on Viewer Cognitions and Attitudes Toward Deviant Sexual Behavior," *Communication Research* Vol. 15, No. 1 (February 2008), pp. 3–38.

11. Regina Lynn, "Animated Porn Makes Movies," *Wired*, http://www.wired.com/print/culture/lifestyle/commentary/sexdrive/2006/12/72205 (last accessed August 29, 2008).

12. *Ashcroft v. The Free Speech Coalition.*

13. *Ashcroft v. The Free Speech Coalition.*

14. *Ashcroft v. The Free Speech Coalition.*

15. *Ashcroft v. The Free Speech Coalition.*

16. Ibid.

17. Ibid.

18. Ibid., p. 242.

19. *Ferber v. New York.*

20. *Ashcroft v. The Free Speech Coalition.*

21. Neil Malamuth and Mark Huppin, "Drawing the Line on Virtual Child Pornography: Bringing the Law in Line with the Research Evidence," *NYU Review of Law & Social Change*, Vol. 31 (2007), pp. 773–827.

22. Ibid., p. 792.

23. Ibid.

24. Ibid.

25. Ibid., p. 800.

26. MacKinnon, "The First Amendment: An Equality Reading," p. 2.

27. MacKinnon, "The First Amendment: An Equality Reading," pp. 2–3.

28. Ibid.

29. *R.A.V. v. City of St. Paul*, 505 U.S. 377 (1992).

30. MacKinnon, "The First Amendment: An Equality Reading," p. 24.

31. MacKinnon, "The First Amendment: An Equality Reading," p. 4.

32. MacKinnon, "The First Amendment: An Equality Reading,"

pp. 52–53.

33. *American Booksellers v. Hudnut.*
34. *American Booksellers v. Hudnut.*
35. Nan D. Hunter and Sylvia A. Law, "Brief Amici Curiae of Feminist Anti-Censorship Task Force, et al., in American Booksellers Association v. Hudnut, *University of Michigan Journal of Law Reform*, Vol. 21 (1988), pp. 69–136. (Hereinafter, "F.A.C.T. Brief").
36. F.A.C.T. Brief, pp. 69–136.
37. See Catharine A. MacKinnon, "The Roar on the Other Side of Silence," in *In Harm's Way*, p. 21.
38. Gayle Ruben, "Thinking Sex: Notes for a Radical Theory of the Politics of Sexuality," in *Pleasure and Danger: Exploring Female Sexuality*, ed. Carol Vance (Boston: Routledge & Kegan Paul, 1984), pp. 267–319; see, also: Carol Vance "Pleasure and Danger: Toward a Politics of Sexuality, also in *Pleasure and Danger: Exploring Female Sexuality*, pp. 1–28.
39. F.A.C.T. Brief, p. 121.
40. Ruben, "Thinking Sex: Notes for a Radical Theory of the Politics of Sexuality."
41. Tristan Taormino, Constance Penley, Celine Perranos Shimizu, and Mereille-Miller Young, *The Feminist Porn Book: The Politics of Producing Pleasure* (New York: The Feminist Press, 2013).
42. Ibid., p. 9.
43. Ibid., p. 10.
44. MacKinnon, *Sex Equality*, p. 1791.
45. *Butler* and Christopher Kendall, *Gay Male Pornography: An Issue of Sex Discrimination* (Vancouver: University of British Columbia Press, 2004), p. 5.
46. MacKinnon, *Sex Equality*, p. 29.
47. *Andrews v. Law Society of British Columbia* (1989) 1. S.C.R. 143 (Can.).
48. MacKinnon, *Sex Equality*, p. 36.
49. *Butler v. Regina* (1992) 1 S.C.R. 452 (Can.).
50. *Little Sisters Book & Art Emporium v. Canada* (Minister of Justice) (2000) SCC 69 (Can.).
51. Ibid.

52. Kendall, *Gay Male Pornography*, p. xiii.
53. Kendall, *Gay Male Pornography*, p. 129.
54. Kendall, *Gay Male Pornography*, p. 129.
55. Dworkin, "Women and Pornography," *New York Review of Books*, October 21, 1993.
56. Ibid.
57. Dworkin, "Women and Pornography," p. 9.
58. Langton, "Whose Right? Ronald Dworkin, Women, and Pornographers," in *Sexual Solipism*, pp. 117–164.
59. Ibid., p. 136.
60. Ibid., p. 151.
61. "Is A Feminist Political Liberalism Possible?" coauthored with Christie Hartley, *Journal of Ethics and Social Philosophy*, Vol. 5, No. 1 (Fall 2010); and *Equal Citizenship and Public Reason: A Feminist Political Liberalism* coauthored with Christie Hartley, (New York: Oxford University Press, 2018).
62. John Rawls. "The Idea of Public Reason Revisited," in *John Rawls: Collected Papers*, ed. Samuel Freeman (Cambridge, MA: Harvard University Press, 1999), pp. 573–615.
63. *Equal Citizenship and Public Reason: A Feminist Political Liberalism* coauthored with Christie Hartley.
64. I argue that the civil rights approach to pornography, as defended here, is a public reason argument that Rawlsian liberals should endorse in "Pornography and Public Reason," *Social Theory and Practice*, Vol. 33, No. 3 (July 2007), pp. 467–488.
65. Altman, p. 33.
66. Altman, p. 44.
67. Altman, p. 45.
68. See Judith Herman, *Trauma and Recovery: The Aftermath of Violence from Domestic Abuse to Political Terror* (New York: Basic Books, 1997); and Susan J. Brison, *Aftermath: Violence and the Remaking of the Self* (Princeton, NJ: Princeton University Press, 2002).
69. See Melissa Farley, ed., *Prostitution, Trafficking, and Traumatic Stress* (New York: Routledge, 2003).
70. Altman, p. 70.

71. From Waltman's "Appraising the Impacts of TFTS," p. 366, fn. 54. There he is summarizing the research findings from Aline Weary & J. Billieux, "Online Sexual Activities: An Exploratory Study of Problematic and Nonproblematic Usage Patterns in a Sample of Men," *Computers in Human Behavior*, Vol. 56 (2016), 257, 259–260.
72. *Big Porn Inc: Exposing the Harms of the Global Pornography Industry*, eds. Melinda Takard Resit and Abigail Bray (North Melborne, Victoria: Spinifex, 2011), pp. xvi–xvii.
73. Ibid.
74. Drucilla Cornell has advanced an argument that pornography undermines the sexual autonomy of women by limiting what she calls our "imaginary domain" to cultivate and define our own "sexuate being" (roughly, this means our sexual orientation, but broadly defined, in the sense of how we understand and define our own sexual selves). However, she rejects the MacKinnon and (Andrea) Dworkin approach to pornography, and argues that state regulation of pornography to protect women's imaginary domain should involve zoning laws and the like so as to prevent pornography from being "forced" on women. See Drucilla Cornell, *The Imaginary Domain: Abortion, Pornography & Sexual Harassment* (New York: Routledge, 1995).

10

Conclusion

THE ARGUMENTS PRESENTED THUS FAR aim to make the case that the legal approach to pornography, in the form of the civil rights ordinances authored by Catharine MacKinnon and Andrea Dworkin and requested, considered, and passed by a number of local jurisdictions in the United States, is both legally and philosophically defensible. The arguments presented aim to address social and legal policy; they don't, as such, provide guidance as to what any individual should do concerning pornography consumption. While the legal and policy question may be of interest, the greater question of many readers may be "What should I do?" "Is it wrong for *me* to use pornography?"

Answering these questions would require another book, but one important consideration can inform reflection. Many of my male friends have openly discussed their pornography use with me, knowing as they do that I am a philosopher who writes on the subject. Invariably, in these conversations, they aim to defend the "kind" of pornography they use or have used as not subordinating women. And their own behavior as not subordinating to women. In some cases, they have claimed, in light of reading feminist critiques of pornography, that they are "very, very careful" as to what they choose to masturbate to. I always ask: "How do you know?" How do they know the particular and individual history of any woman in the pornography they are masturbating to? How do they know she is there willingly or without the force of economic destitution? How do you know she hasn't been coerced, including by racism or sexism? How do they know how old she really is? How do they know whether she has a history of sexual abuse in childhood, which may have been her entry into the pornography industry? How do you know she is not being trafficked?

The answer is: they don't. Reflective as they are, as men who claim to value sex equality, my friends are typically deeply troubled by this line of questioning. Admitting that they don't know any of these facts about the women they are masturbating to—and this isn't even about what masturbating to their use does to these men themselves—leads them to question whether using pornography is consistent with the other beliefs they hold, especially their belief that they, as individuals, should not participate in institutions of inequality. It can also make the pornography unsexy, that is, interfere with the narrative they tell themselves sexually, to promote their arousal to the materials, that the women who appear to be there willingly or to be enjoying themselves are neither. Once many men know what it takes to make pornography, and face what it does to them as a user, they realize they have to stop. The real question is, what are you participating in and promoting, when you buy and use pornography? A vicious industry is what you are participating in. Unconscious acculturation and conditioning to denigrating sexual stereotypes is what you are doing to yourself. Now you know.

REFERENCES

Austin, J. L. *How to Do Things with Words* (Cambridge, MA: Harvard University Press, 1962).

Bauer, Nancy. *How to Do Things with Pornography* (Cambridge: MA: Harvard University Press, 2015).

Bridges, Ana J., Robert Wosnitzer, Erica Scharver, Chyng Sun, and Rachel Liberman. "Aggression and Sexual Behavior in Best-Selling Pornography Videos: A Content Analysis Update," *Violence Against Women*, Vol. 16, No. 10 (2010), pp. 1065–1085.

Brison, Susan J. *Aftermath: Violence and the Remaking of the Self* (Princeton, NJ: Princeton University Press, 2002).

Connolly, William. *The Terms of Political Discourse* (Princeton, NJ: Princeton University Press, 1983).

Cornell, Drucilla. *The Imaginary Domain: Abortion, Pornography & Sexual Harassment* (New York: Routledge, 1995).

Crenshaw, Kimberlé. "Mapping the Margins: Intersectionality, Identity Politics, and Violence Against Women of Color," *Stanford Law Review*, Vol. 43 (1991), pp. 1241–1299.

Donnerstein, Edward, Daniel Linz, and Steven D. Penrod. *The Question of Pornography: Research Findings and Policy Implications* (New York: The Free Press, 1987).

Dines, Gail. *Pornland* (Boston: Beacon Press, 2010).

Dworkin, Ronald. "Women and Pornography," *New York Review of Books*, October 21, 1993.

Eaton, A. W. "A Sensible Antiporn Feminism." *Ethics*, Vol. 117, No. 4 (2007), pp. 674–715.

Feinberg, Joel. *Harm to Others: The Moral Limits of the Criminal Law* (New York: Oxford University Press, 1984).

Fine, Cordelia. *Delusions of Gender: How Our Minds, Society, and Neurosexism Create Difference* (New York: Norton, 2010).

Final Report of the Attorney General's Commission on Pornography (Nashville, TN: Rutledge Hill Press, 1986).

Foubert, John D., Matthew W. Brosi, and R. Sean Bannon. "Pornography Viewing Among Fraternity Men: Effects on Bystander Intervention, Rape Myth Acceptance and Behaviorial Intent to Commit Sexual Assault," *Sexual Addition & Compulsivity*, Vol. 18 (2011), pp. 212–231.

Hald, Gert Martin, Neil M. Malamuth, and Carlin Yuen. "Pornography And Attitudes Supporting Violence Against Women: Revisiting the Relationship in Nonexperimental Studies," *Aggressive Behavior*, Vol. 36 (2010), pp. 14–20.

Hartley, Christie, and Lori Watson. "Is A Feminist Political Liberalism Possible?," *Journal of Ethics and Social Philosophy*, Vol. 5, No. 1 (Fall 2010), pp. 1–21.

Herman, Judith. *Trauma and Recovery: The Aftermath of Violence from Domestic Abuse to Political Terror* (New York: Basic Books, 1997).

Hill Collins, Patricia. *Black Sexual Politics* (New York: Routledge, 2004).

Hunterin, Nan D., and Sylvia A. Law. "Brief Amici Curiae of Feminist Anti-Censorship Task Force, et al., in American Booksellers Association v. Hudnut," *University of Michigan Journal of Law Reform*, Vol. 21 (1988), pp. 69–136. ("F.A.C.T. Brief")

Jameson, Jenna. *How to Make Love Like a Porn Star: A Cautionary Tale* (New York: Harper Collins, 2004).

Johnson, Jennifer A. "To Catch a Curious Clicker: A Social Analysis of the Online Pornography Industry," in *Everyday Pornography*, ed. Karen Boyle (New York: Routledge), pp. 147–163.

Kendall, Christopher. *Gay Male Pornography: An Issue of Sex Discrimination* (Vancouver: University of British Columbia Press, 2004).

Krakauer, Jon. *Missoula: Rape and the Justice System in a College Town* (New York: Doubleday, 2015).

Langton, Rae. "Speech Acts and Unspeakable Acts," in *Sexual Solipsism* (New York: Oxford University Press, 2009), pp. 25–63.

———. "Whose Right? Ronald Dworkin, Women, and Pornographers," in *Sexual Solipism*, pp. 117–164.

Lisak, David, Lori Gardiner, Sarah C. Nicksa, and Ashely M. Cote. "False Allegation of Sexual Assualt, An Analysis of Ten Years of Reported Cases," *Violence Against Women*, Vol. 16, No. 12 (2010), pp. 1318–1334.

Linz, Daniel, and Neil Malamuth. *Communication Concepts 5: Pornography* (London: SAGE, 1993).

Lovelace, Linda (with Mike McGrady). *Ordeal: The Truth Behind Deep Throat* (New York: Citadel Press Books, 1980).

———. (with Mike McGrady). *Out of Bondage* (Mass Market Paperback, 1987).

MacKinnon, Catharine. *Butterfly Politics* (Cambridge, MA: Harvard University Press, 2017).

———. "The First Amendment: An Equality Reading," 2017 manuscript, on file with the author.

———. *Sex Equality*, 3rd ed. (St. Paul, MN: Foundation Press, 2016).

———. "Trafficking, Prostitution, and Inequality," *Harvard Civil Rights-Civil Liberties Law Review*, 46 (2011), pp. 271–309.

———. *Women's Lives, Men's Laws* (Cambridge, MA: Harvard University Press, 2005).

———. *Only Words* (Cambridge, MA: Harvard University Press, 1993).

———. *Toward a Feminist Theory of the State* (Cambridge MA: Harvard University Press, 1989).

MacKinnon, Catharine A., and Andrea Dworkin (eds.), *In Harm's Way: The Pornography Civil Rights Hearings* (Cambridge, MA: Harvard University Press, 1997), p. 427.

MacKinnon, Catharine A., and Andrea Dworkin. *Pornography & Civil Rights: A New Day for Women's Equality* (© Catharine A. MacKinnon and Andrea Dworkin, 1988), pp. 41–52.

Malamuth, Neil, and Mark Huppin. "Drawing the Line on Virtual Child Pornography: Bringing the Law in Line with the Research Evidence," *NYU Review of Law & Social Change*, Vol. 31 (2007), pp. 773–827.

Parent, William. "A Second Look at Pornography and the Subordination of Women," *The Journal of Philosophy*, Vol. 87, No. 4 (April 1990), pp. 205–211.

Parks Pieper, Lindsay. *Sex Testing: Gender Policing in Women's Sports* (Chicago: University of Illinois Press, 2016).

Paul, Bryant, and Daniel G. Linz. "The Effects of Exposure to Virtual Child Pornography on Viewer Cognitions and Attitudes Toward Deviant Sexual Behavior," *Communication Research*, Vol. 15, No. 1 (February 2008), pp. 3–38.

Purcell, Natalie. *Violence and the Pornographic Imaginary: The Politics of Sex, Gender and Aggression in Hardcore Pornography* (New York: Routledge, 2012).

Rawls, John. "The Idea of Public Reason Revisited," in *John Rawls: Collected Papers*, ed. Samuel Freeman (Cambridge, MA: Harvard University Press, 1999), pp. 573–615.

Rea, M. C. "What Is Pornography?" *NOÛS*, Vol. 35, No. 1 (2001), pp. 118–145.

Resit, Melinda Takard, and Abigail Bray, eds. *Big Porn Inc: Exposing the Harms of the Global Pornography Industry* (North Melborne, Victoria: Spinifex, 2011).

Ruben, Gayle. "Thinking Sex: Notes for a Radical Theory of the Politics of Sexuality," in *Pleasure and Danger: Exploring Female Sexuality*, ed. Carol Vance (Boston: Routledge & Kegan Paul, 1984), pp. 265–319.

Russell, Diana, E. H., and Rebecca M. Bolen. *The Epidemic of Rape and Childhood Sexual Abuse in the United States* (Thousand Oaks, CA: SAGE, 2000).

Stark, Cynthia A. "Is Pornography an Action?: The Causal vs. Conceptual View of Pornography's Harm," *Social Theory and Practice*, Vol. 23, No. 2 (Summer 1997), pp. 277–306.

Strossen, Nadine. *Defending Pornography: Free Speech and the Fight for Women's Rights* (New York: New York University Press, 2000).

Sullivan, Kathleen M., and Gerald Gunther. *Constitutional Law*, 6th ed. (Foundation Press, 2007).

Taormino, Tristian, Celine Parreñas Shimizu, Constance Penley, and Mireille Miller-Young. *The Feminist Porn Book: The Politics of Producing Pleasure* (New York: The Feminist Press, 2013).

Vadas, Melinda. "A First Look at the Pornography/Civil Rights Ordinance: Could Pornography Be the Subordination of Women," *The Journal of Philosophy*, Vol. 84, No. 9 (September 1987), pp. 487–511.

Vance, Carol. "Pleasure and Danger: Toward a Politics of Sexuality," in *Pleasure and Danger: Exploring Female Sexuality*, ed. Carol Vance (Boston: Routledge & Kegan Paul, 1984), pp. 1–27.

Vito, Christopher, Amanda Admire, and Elizabeth Hughes. "Masculinity, Aggrieved Entitlement, and Violence: Considering the Isla Vista Mass Shooting," *NORMA* (2017), DOI: 10.1080/18902138.2017.1390658.

Waltman, Max. "Appraising the Impact of Toward a Feminist Theory of the State: Consciousness-Raising, Hierarchy Theory, and Substantive Equality Laws," *Law & Inequality: A Journal of Theory and Practice*, Vol. 35 (2017), pp. 353–391.

Watson, Lori. "Pornography," *Philosophy Compass*, Vol. 5, No. 7 (2010), pp. 535–550.

Watson, Lori, and Christie Hartley. *Equal Citizenship and Public Reason: A Feminist Political Liberalism* (Oxford: Oxford University Press, 2018).

Weary, Aline, and J. Billieux. "Online Sexual Activities: An Exploratory Study of Problematic and Nonproblematic Usage Patterns in a Sample of Men," *Computers in Human Behavior*, Vol. 56 (2016), pp. 257, 259–26.

Wright, Paul J., Robert S. Tokunaga, and Ashley Kraus. "A Meta-Analysis of Pornography Consumption and Actual Sexual Aggression in General Population Studies," *Journal of Communication*, Vol. 66 (2016), pp. 183–205.

Legal Cases

US Law

American Booksellers, Inc. v. Hudnut, 771 F.2d 323 (1985), *aff'd mem.*, 475 U.S. 1001 (1986).

Ashcroft v. The Free Speech Coalition, 535 U.S. 234 (1996).

Bradwell v. Illinois, 83 U.S. 130 (1873).

Ferber v. New York, 458 U.S. 747 (1982).
Free Speech Coalition, Inc. v. Holder, 957 F. Supp.2d 564 (2013).
Loving v. Virginia, 388 U.S. 1 (1967).
Miller v. California, 413 U.S. 15 (1973).
Obergelfell et al. v. Hodges, Director, Ohio Department of Health, et al., 576 U.S. ___ (2015).
People v. Freeman, 250 Cal.Rptr. 598 (1988).
Plessy v. Ferguson, 163 U.S. 537 (1896).
Price Waterhouse v. Hopkins, 490 U.S. 228 (1989).
R.A.V. v. City of St. Paul, 505 U.S. 377 (1992).
Reed v. Reed, 404 U.S. 71 (1971).
United States v. Virginia, 518 U.S. 515 (1996).

Canada Law
Andrews v. Law Society of British Columbia (1989), 1. S.C.R. 143 (Can.). *Butler v Regina* (1992) 1 S.C.R. 452 (Can.).
Little Sisters Book & Art Emporium v. Canada (Minister of Justice) (2000), SCC 69 (Can.).

Other Sources

"A Chat with Author and Former Pornographer Dave Pounder," Gad Saad, July 16, 2013, *Psychology Today*, https://www.psychologytoday.com/blog/homo-consumericus/201307/chat-author-and-former-pornographer-dave-pounder (last accessed March 8, 2018).
Alexa.com, https://www.alexa.com
"An Activist, a Little Girl and the Heartbreaking Origin of 'Me Too.'" Cassandra Santiago and Doug Criss, Tue. October 17, 2017, http://www.cnn.com/2017/10/17/us/me-too-tarana-burke-origin-trnd/index.html (last accessed March 8, 2018).
Bureau of Justice Statistics, NCVS Victimization Analysis Tool (NVAT), https://www.bjs.gov/index.cfm?ty=nvat (last accessed March 8, 2018).
Bureau of Justice Statistics, Data Collection: National Crime Victimization Survey (NCVS, https://www.bjs.gov/index.cfm?ty=dcdetail&iid=245 (last accessed March 8, 2018).
The Free Speech Coalition, https://www.freespeechcoalition.com (last accessed March 8, 2018).

"Here Is The Powerful Letter Stanford Rape Victim Read Aloud to Her Attacker," Katie J. M. Baker, June 3, 2016, *Buzzfeed. com*, https://www.buzzfeed.com/katiejmbaker/heres-the-powerful-letter-the-stanford-victim-read-to-her-ra?utm_term=. ipwp60YaY#.on7RnjLoL (last accessed March 8, 2018).

"The Judge in the Infamous Brock Turner Case Finally Explains His Decision—A Year Later," Cleve R. Wootson, Jr., *The Washington Post*, July 2, 2017, https://www.washingtonpost. com/news/grade-point/wp/2017/07/02/the-judge-in-the-infamous-brock-turner-case-finally-explains-his-decision-a-year-later/?utm_term=.a80a729e524 (last accessed March 8, 2018).

MarketWatch.com, http://www.marketwatch.com/investing/stock/sbux/financials (last accessed March 8, 2018).

"'Men-Ups' Photo Project Presents Men in Traditional Pin-Up Girl Poses," Jamie Peck, Jul. 29, 2013, *The Gloss*, http://www. thegloss.com/culture/male-pin-up-photos-examine-gender-stereotypes/ (last accessed March 8, 2018).

"Men-Ups!—Photographing Men as Pin Ups," *U Funk*, June 7, 2016, http://www.ufunk.net/en/photos/men-ups/ (last accessed March 8, 2018).

"#MeToo: Social Media Flooded with Personal Stories of Assault," Lisa Respers France, Mon. October 16, 2017, http://www. cnn.com/2017/10/15/entertainment/me-too-twitter-alyssa-milano/index.html (last accessed March 8, 2018).

"'Nailin' Paylin'—Lights, Camera, Lots of Action," October 13, 2008, *TMZ.com*, http://www.tmz.com/2008/10/13/porn-stars-give-nailin-paylin-a-dry-run/ (last accessed March 8, 2018).

"NBA Begins New Season Flush with Cash as Revenue Expected to Hit 8 Billion," John Lombardo, Oct. 24, 2016, *Street & Smiths SportsBusiness Journal*, http://www.sportsbusinessdaily. com/Journal/Issues/2016/10/24/In-Depth/Lead.aspx (last accessed, March 8 2018).

"Porn's Dirtiest Secret: What Everyone Gets Paid," Chris Morris, Wed, Jan. 20, 2016, https://www.cnbc.com/2016/01/20/porns-dirtiest-secret-what-everyone-gets-paid.html (last accessed March 8, 2018).

RAINN (Rape, Abuse & Incest National Network), https://www.rainn.org

Regina Lynn, "Animated Porn Makes Movies," *Wired*, http://www.wired.com/print/culture/lifestyle/commentary/sexdrive/2006/12/72205 (last accessed August 28, 2008).

Statista: The Statistics Portal, https://www.statista.com/topics/964/film/ (last accessed March 8, 2018).

"Thanks to Roger Goodell, NFL Revenues to Surpass 13 Billion in 2016," Jason Belzer, Feb. 29, 2016, *Forbes.com*, https://www.forbes.com/sites/jasonbelzer/2016/02/29/thanks-to-roger-goodell-nfl-revenues-projected-to-surpass-13-billion-in-2016/#466062d91cb7 (last accessed March 8, 2018).

Uniform Crime Reporting Statistics, UCR Offense Definitions, https://www.bjs.gov/ucrdata/offenses.cfm (last accessed March 8, 2018).

"The Woman Who Created #MeToo Long Before Hashtags," Sandra E. Garcia, *The New York Times,* Oct. 20, 2017, https://www.nytimes.com/2017/10/20/us/me-too-movement-tarana-burke.html (last accessed March 8, 2018).

INDEX

Page numbers followed by n indicate notes.

Missoula, Montana, 177–78
modernization, 137
Mohr, Richard, 36
monogamy, 49
Montana, 180
moral disapprobation, 270
moral rights, 26–33, 277–78.
    See also Rights
moralism, 274–75
morality
    Christian, 136
    sexual, 134
Morgan, Robin, 87
morphing, 248

Nagel, Thomas, 36, 43
National Basketball Association
    (NBA), 207
National Crime Victimization
    Survey (NCVS), 175–76,
    202–3n25, 226–28,
    237n55, 304
National Football League
    (NFL), 207
Native Alaskan women, 177
nature, 169
Nazi/Jew pornography, 170
negative rights, 281–82
neutrality, 257
    racial, 257
    viewpoint, 239–40,
    255–57, 259
New Right, 261–62
The New York Review of Books, 273
New York Society for the
    Suppression of Vice,
    115, 137–38
norms, 125–26
    beauty, 284
    gender, 165–66
    of pornography, 126
Nussbaum Martha, 44

*Obergefell et al. v. Hodges, Director,
    Ohio Department of Health,
    et al.*, 198, 304
obesity, 170
objectification: of women, 119–20,
    220–21, 288
obscene libel, 51–52
obscenity
    in ancient times, 136–37
    anti-obscenity laws, 51–59,
    115, 138–39
    approaches to pornography
    based on, 5–6, 51–79, 172–73,
    244–46, 275
    Cabinet of Obscene
    Objects, 136–37
    criminalization of, 247
    definition of, 121
    and harms of child
    pornography, 250
    legal tests of, 51–52,
    57–58, 121
    sexually explicit materials, 20,
    23, 52–53, 139–40
O'Connor, Sandra Day, 250
offense, 246–47
older women, 169–70
Only Words (MacKinnon),
    187–90, 273
opportunity, equal, 266–67, 273
oral sex, 168
*Ordeal: The Truth Behind
    Deep Throat* (Lovelace),
    184, 204n44
Out of Bondage (Lovelace),
    184, 204n44

pagan culture, 132–35
Palin, Sarah, 186
Paltrow, Gwyneth, 227–28
Parent, William, 187
patent offenses, 172–73

Made in the USA
Las Vegas, NV
25 November 2022